IMAGES
*of America*

# FAMOUS PEOPLE OF QUEENS

**On the Cover:** Immigrants from more than 60 countries united at the Unisphere in Flushing Meadows Corona Park for Jonathan Kane's "A Great Day In Queens" photograph in 2018. The Jackson Heights artist was paying homage to his home, the world's most diverse borough, and his father, Art Kane, whose "A Great Day In Harlem" image immortalized 57 jazz musicians at a brownstone on 126th Street in Manhattan for the cover of *Esquire* magazine in 1958. (Jonathan Kane.)

IMAGES
*of America*

# FAMOUS PEOPLE OF QUEENS

Rob MacKay

ARCADIA
PUBLISHING

ISBN 978-1-4671-0949-9

Published by Arcadia Publishing
Charleston, South Carolina

Printed in the United States of America

Library of Congress Control Number: 2022951511

For all general information, please contact Arcadia Publishing:
Telephone 843-853-2070
Fax 843-853-0044
E-mail sales@arcadiapublishing.com
For customer service and orders:
Toll-Free 1-888-313-2665

Visit us on the Internet at www.arcadiapublishing.com

*This book is dedicated to the borough's two most outstanding native daughters: Asha and Sarika MacKay.*

# CONTENTS

# Acknowledgments

Thanks to so many people. If I failed to include you in this list, please forgive me. Here goes: Alex Florez, Antonin Scalia Papers (Harvard Law School), Archbishop Molloy High School (AMHS), Bowne House Archives, Bruce Sussman, Caltech Archives, Central Intelligence Agency, Charles Casillo, Charlotte Jackson, Cincinnati & Hamilton County Public Library, Congressional Medal of Honor Society (CMHS), Congresswoman Sheila Jackson, Cornell University Library, David Cortes, Dominick Totino, Emil Cohen, Georgia Institute of Technology, Greater Allen AME Cathedral of New York, Greater Astoria Historical Society (GAHS), Harvard University, Heather Hazzan/The Licensing Project, Janette Beckman, Jeff Gotlieb, Jeff Simmons, Jonathan Kane, John Harrington, King Manor Museum, LaGuardia and Wagner Archives, LaGuardia Community College Institutional Archives, Lewis Latimer House Museum (LLHM), Library of Congress (LOC), Luba Mason, Michael Perlman, Museum of the City of New York, Nancy Brown, National Aeronautics and Space Administration (NASA), National Archives, National Baseball Hall of Fame Museum (NBHFM), National Council of Churches, New York City Council, New York City Municipal Archives, New York Public Library (NYPL), New York University, Oberlin College, Oberlin Conservatory Library, Peter Vecsey, Prime Minister Fumio Kishida of Japan and his cabinet, Queens College Special Collections and Archives, Queens Museum, Queens Public Library (QPL), Queens Tourism Council (QTC), Richard Shpuntoff, Rock & Roll Hall of Fame, Rockefeller University, Ruth Horowitz, *Scribner's Monthly*, Sean Chen, Smithsonian Institute, Sri Chinmoy Center, Stanford News Service/Linda A. Cicero, Stanford University Libraries, St. John's University Archives and Special Collections (SJU), St. John's University Athletics, The Andrew Goodman Foundation, The Andy Warhol Museum, The Hindu Temple Society of North America, The Neustadt Collection of Tiffany Glass, Travis Chantar, US Department of Defense, US Navy, US Olympic and Paralympic Committee, University of Virginia School of Law, White House, and Women's Basketball Hall of Fame (WBHF).

# INTRODUCTION

On the one hand, a time-honored, anonymous phrase proclaims that "home is the starting place of love, hope, and dreams." But on the other hand, the phrase "Nobody is a prophet in his/her own land" rings true, and it comes from the Bible.

So how do a birthplace and a home influence us? Better yet, what is the story behind the many outstanding people from Queens? You know, the fearless risk takers, confident world leaders, freak of nature geniuses, eternally creative musicians, disciplined and determined athletes, and selfless heroes that appear in this book?

Is there something in the water? Were they lucky or did they cheat? Did they have tiger moms or superior genes?

The correct answer might include a bit of all these suggestions. Then again, there might not be a correct answer.

Maybe their outstanding lives were influenced by the fact that the borough is located across a river from Manhattan, where the world's best doctors, lawyers, businesspeople, public relations gurus, and artists go to shine. Maybe it is because Queens is a heavily populated borough, and it is simply the law of large numbers in action. Or maybe it is because it has been the world's most diverse county for decades and thus a first stop for immigrants hungering to obtain the American Dream.

These are simply theories. But the fact remains that some of the most incredible humans grew up in Queens. They created entire industries, developed lifesaving vaccines, and helped define popular culture. And many of them overcame poverty and other disadvantages along the way.

Their stories relay triumph, but they also relate Queens history.

John Bowne was an English immigrant who arrived in the 1600s, before the borough had its current name. By confronting the Dutch rulers at the time, he helped establish freedom of religion in the land. He was exiled for his cause, but he returned as a celebrated hero. Of course, he did not stop there, spending the rest of his life helping the Flushing community and fighting slavery.

Fast forward to the 1800s, and German immigrant Conrad Poppenhusen is building his rubber factory in College Point. He is creating hundreds of jobs and helping the economy boom, but he is also extremely generous. Using his own money, he drains marshes, paves roads, plants trees, constructs a railroad station, installs sewers, and lays water and gas lines. He also creates the Poppenhusen Institute, a community center that housed the first free kindergarten in the United States (established in 1870) as well as a vocational high school, courthouse, jail, bank, library, and grand ballroom. He is long gone, but take a walk around the neighborhood these days, and his last name is everywhere.

Enter the modern world, and John Wang is operating the Queens Night Market behind the New York Hall of Science in Corona. The open-air bazaar averages more than 15,000 weekly visitors who fill their bellies and flavor their palates with everything from Peruvian ceviche to Jamaican jerk chicken to Cambodian fish amok. He got the idea while spending summers with family members in Taiwan, where night markets are common due to the midday heat.

Only in Queens.

Looking forward, it appears the borough will continue to be a beacon for foreigners looking to improve their lives. As this book goes to print, a community of immigrants from Bangladesh is growing in northwestern Queens. At the same time, Nigerians are moving to southeastern Queens. In the center of the borough, Jews from Samarkand in the former Soviet Union are remaking their lives.

Expect many of the next generation's native sons and daughters to realize tremendous accomplishments in various industries. Heck, some will probably create new industries. Best of luck to all of them. Maybe they will cause the need to write a second edition of this book in a few centuries.

# *One*

# Music Royalty

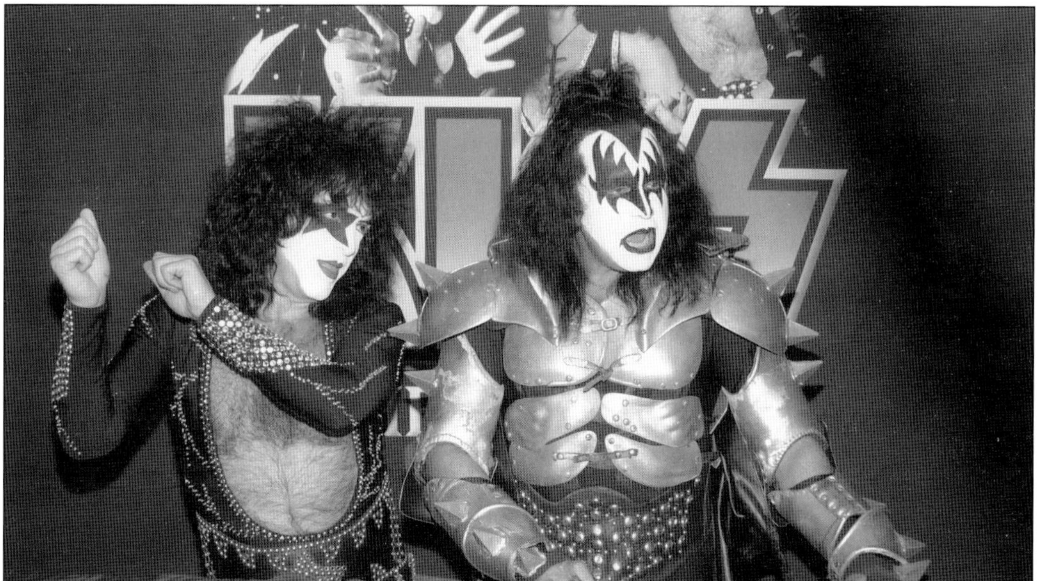

Born in Israel in 1949, Chaim Witz Jr. moved to Flushing at the age of eight. After graduating from Newtown High School in 1967, he joined forces with Kew Garden Hills rocker Stanley Bert Eisen, drummer Peter Criss, and guitarist Paul "Ace" Frehley to form KISS. He became known as Gene Simmons (right), while Eisen became Paul Stanley (left). The high-heeled, make-up-heavy band broke records and norms on the way to multiple Grammys and Rock & Roll Hall of Fame membership. (Depositphotos.)

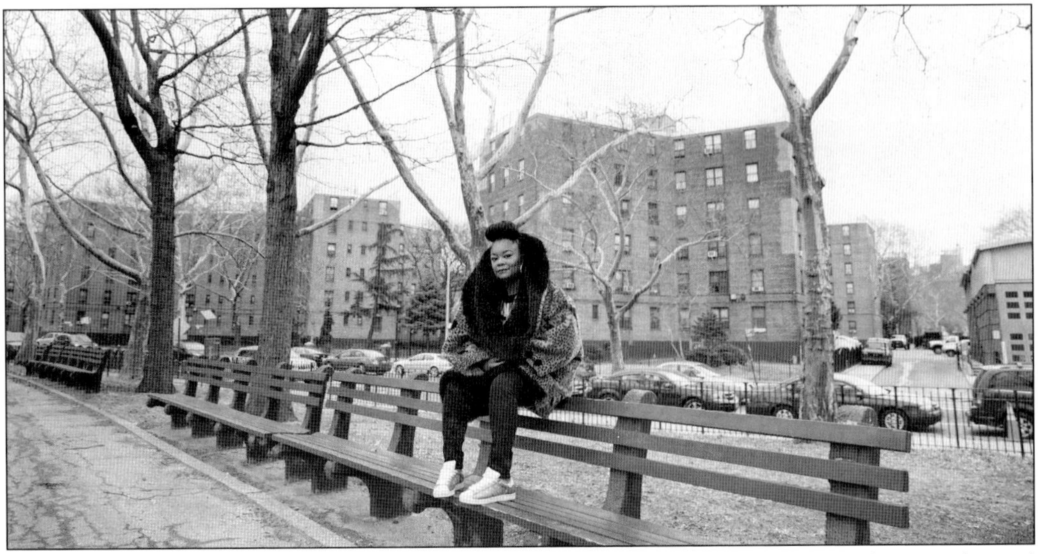

In the 1980s, Queensbridge was the epicenter of battle rap with participants trading insults and boasts in rhyme. Lolita Shanté Gooden beat all comers—even at the age of 10 with ponytails and braces. In 1985, the 14-year-old, with the stage name Roxanne Shanté, hit it big with "Roxanne's Revenge." The song led to so much success that she retired at the age of 25. Since then, she has appeared in commercials and films, moved to New Jersey, and founded a nonprofit. (Heather Hazzan/The Licensing Project.)

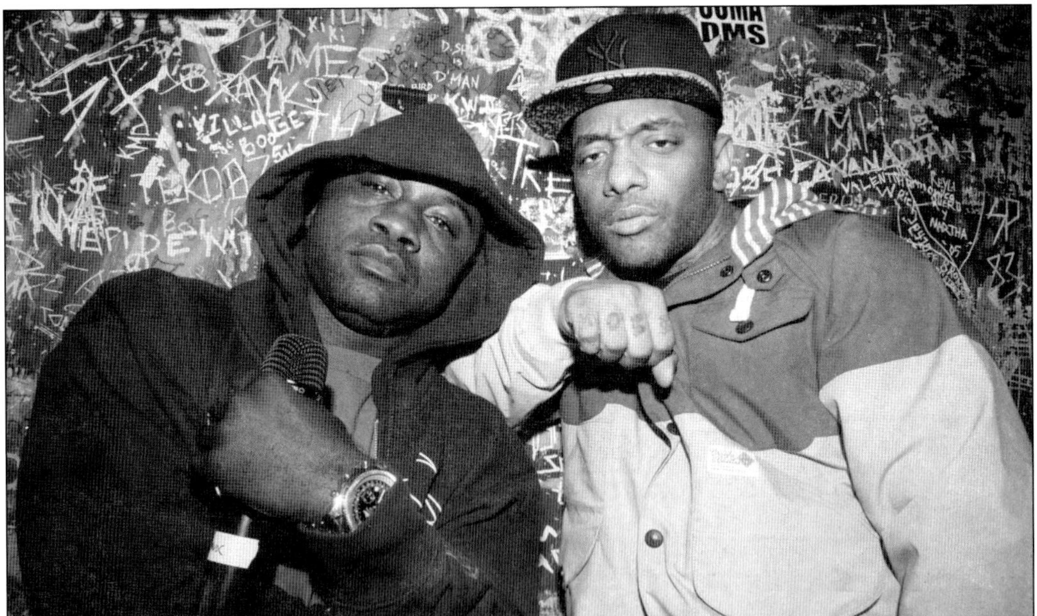

The New York City Council plans to add Prodigy Way to the intersection of Twelfth Street and Forty-First Road in Queensbridge in 2022. Born Albert Johnson in 1974, Prodigy (right) grew up there with Kejuan Waliek Muchita (also known as Havoc, left). As the duo Mobb Deep, they churned out East Coast hip hop on the way to selling more than three million records in the 1990s and popularizing a dialect called the "dunn language." In 2006, they became the first rap duo to perform in India. (Alamy.)

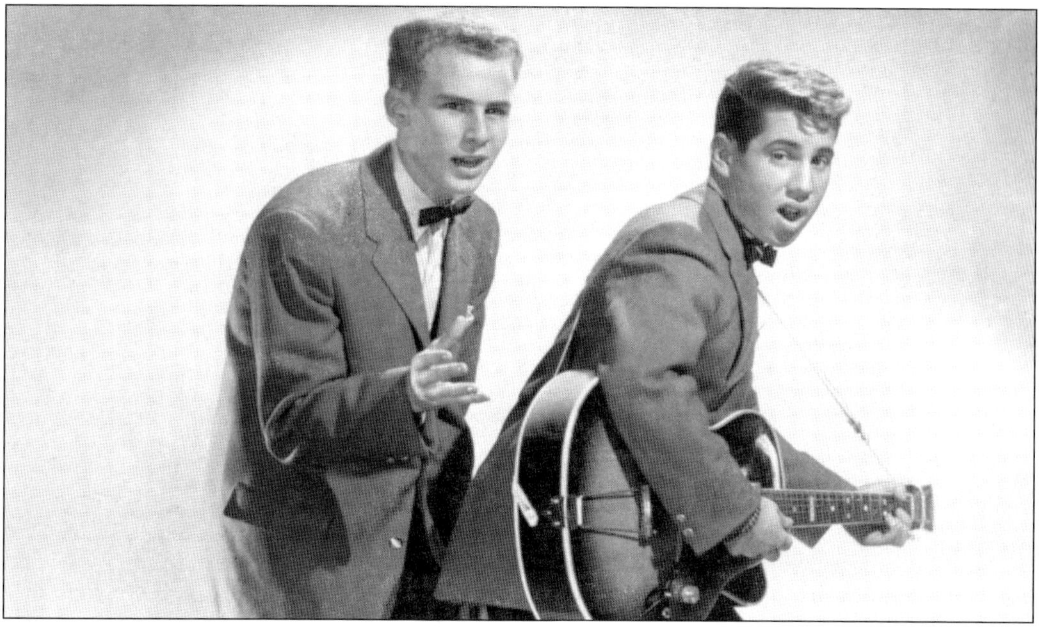

Born within a month of each other in 1941, Kew Garden Hills residents Paul Simon and Arthur Garfunkel bonded over stickball and music while at PS 164. Simon, who lived on Seventieth Road, played guitar, while Seventy-Second Avenue's Garfunkel was a singer. They started performing while at Forest Hills High School as Tom & Jerry. (Garfunkel was Tom Graph because he loved mathematics. Simon used his girlfriend's last name to become Jerry Landis.) Later, as Simon & Garfunkel, they became internationally famous with "The Sound of Silence," "Bridge over Troubled Water," and other hits. They did the soundtrack to the 1968 film *The Graduate* on the way to 10 Grammys. They broke up in 1970, and Simon went on to a long solo career, but he never forgot Queens. His 2016 farewell tour ended with a concert in Flushing Meadows Corona Park. (Both, Alamy.)

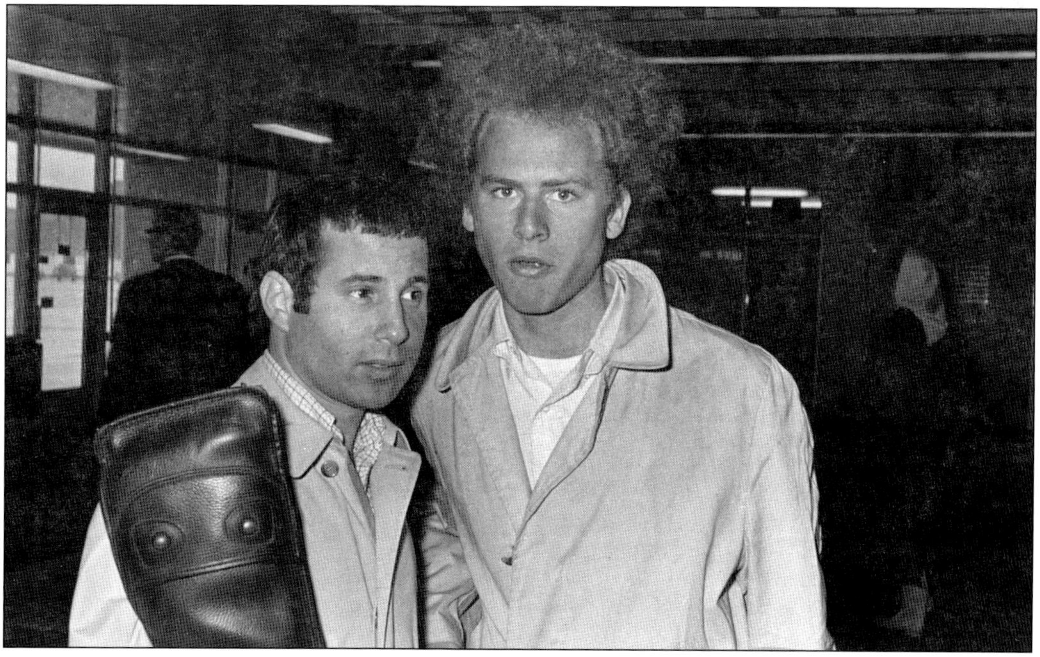

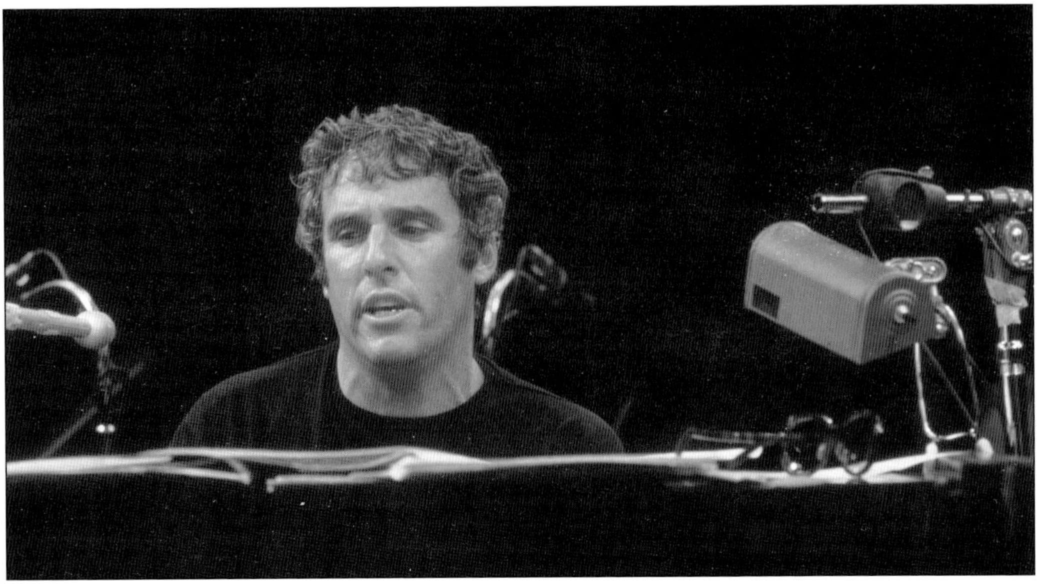

Burt Bacharach founded a 10-piece jazz band while at Forest Hills High School. After graduating in 1946, the Kew Gardens pianist performed all over the place and composed—or cocomposed with Hal David—52 Top 40 hits in the easy listening genre, including "Raindrops Keep Fallin' on My Head" and "That's What Friends Are For." His trophy case features six Grammys and three Oscars. He also wrote ditties for movies such as *Arthur* and *Butch Cassidy and the Sundance Kid*. (LOC.)

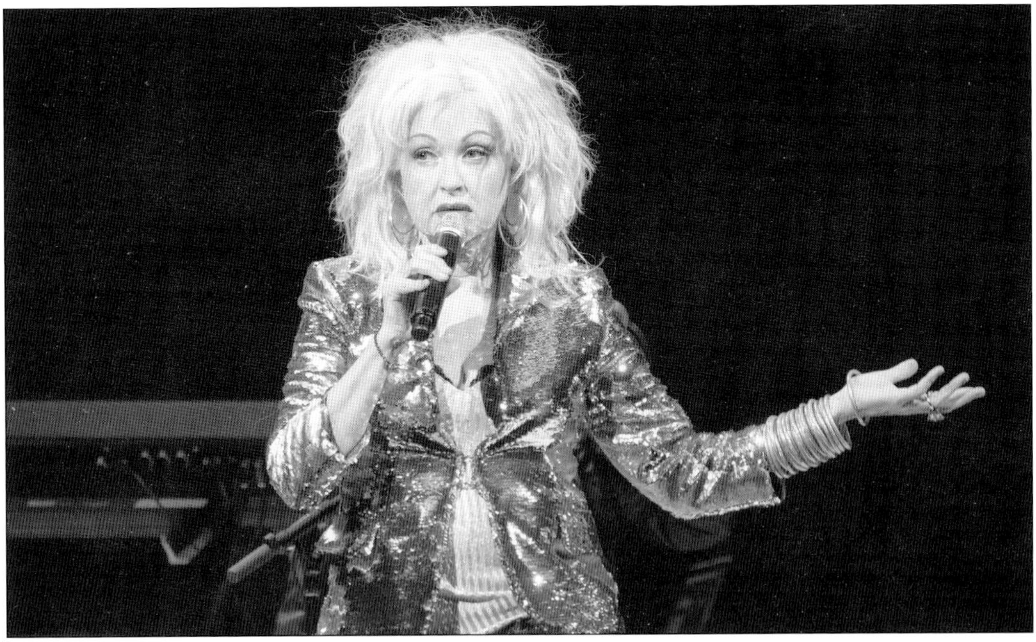

Born in 1953, Cynthia Lauper grew up in Ozone Park. It was not an easy childhood, and she acted out by changing her first name to Cyndi and wearing colorful, waffle-pattern hairstyles and loud thrifted clothing before dropping out of Richmond Hill High School and running away to Canada. She eventually returned and got her break in 1983 with "Girls Just Want to Have Fun." Soon, Lauper was winning Grammy, Tony, Emmy, and American Music Awards. (Depositphotos.)

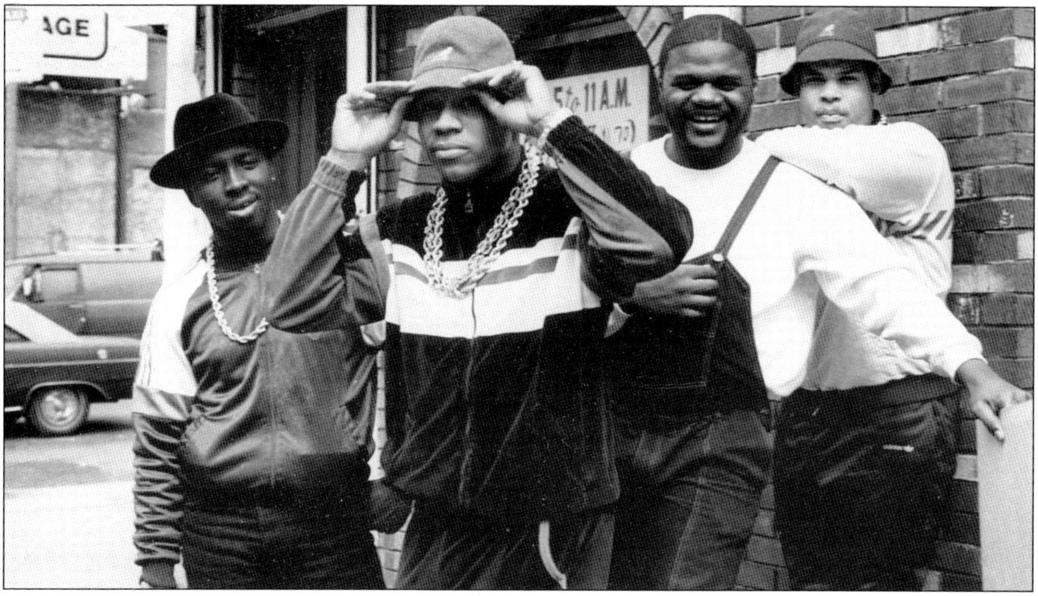

In "Around the Way Girl," LL Cool J fetes "a girl with extensions in her hair, bamboo earrings, at least two pair, a Fendi bag and a bad attitude." Most of the 1990 video was shot in a Long Island City warehouse, but the entertainer, whose initials stand for "Ladies Love Cool James," is referring to women from southeast Queens. Born James Todd Smith in 1968, the two-time Grammy-winning Rock & Roll Hall of Fame inductee grew up with his mother and her parents in St. Albans. The Andrew Jackson High School dropout hit pay dirt with "I Need a Beat" on Def Jam Recordings in 1985. He followed with "Mama Said Knock You Out" while parlaying his talent into an acting career. He is with childhood friends above and the aforementioned Cyndi Lauper (left), Sean Lennon (second from right), and Lenny Kravitz (right) below. (Above, QPL; below, Alamy.)

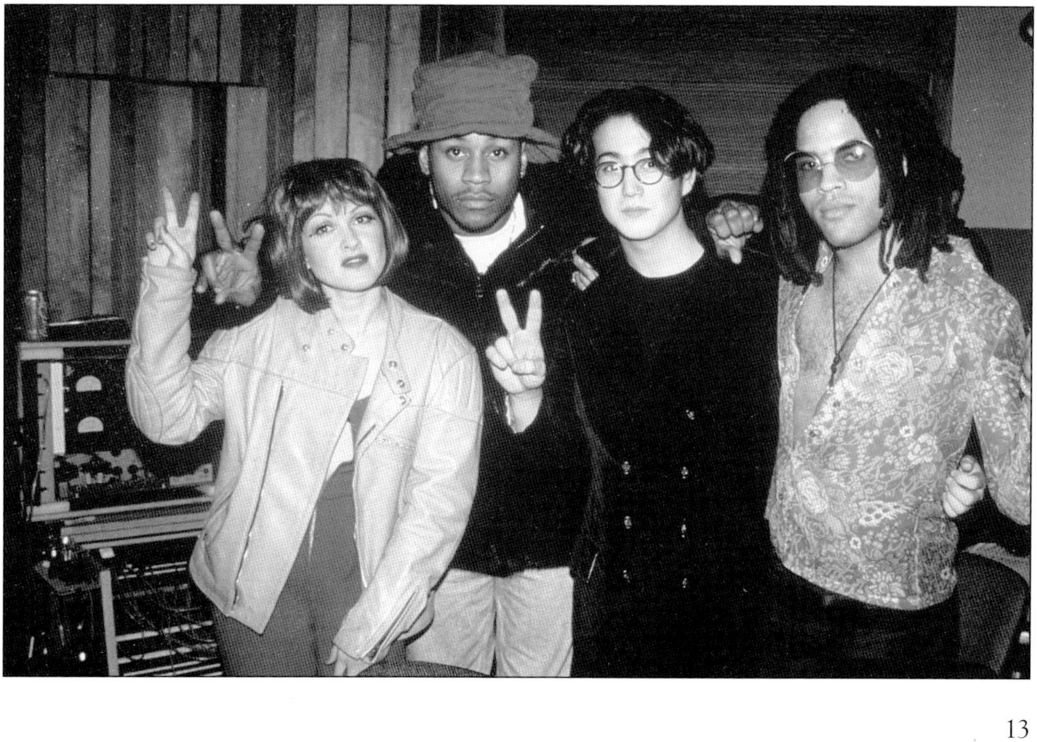

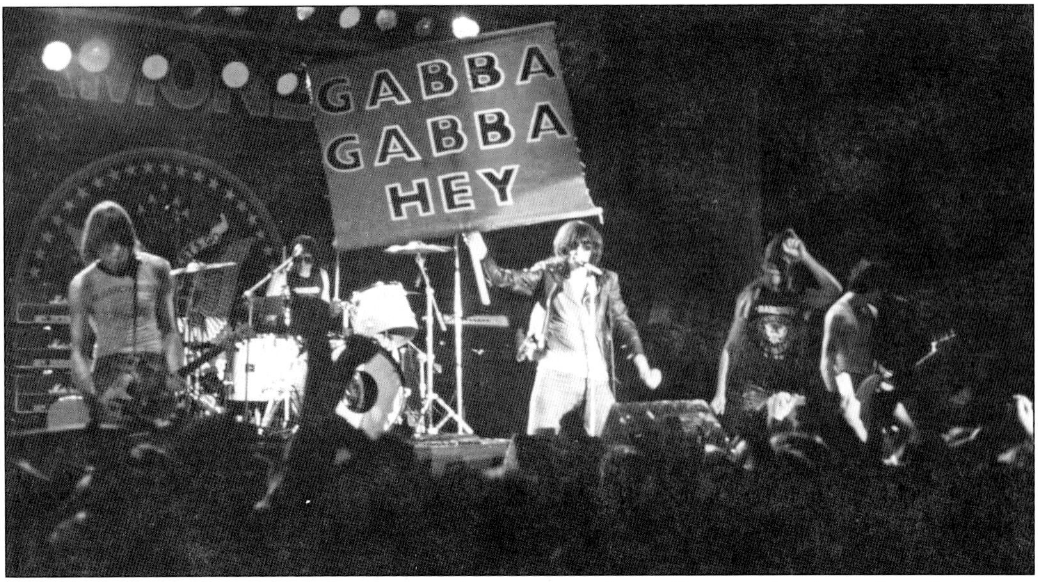


In the 1977 song that made them famous, the Ramones chant, "You can hitch a ride to Rockaway Beach." Dee Dee, the bassist, wrote the tune in homage to the Beach Boys but with his remembrance of how people would stand on Woodhaven Boulevard with their thumbs out to get rides from Forest Hills to Rockaway's surf and sun in the 1970s. He and the other Ramones—Joey (vocals), Johnny (guitar), and Tommy (drums)—attended Forest Hills High School together. The unrelated friends took the same last name before breaking onto the scene with "Blitzkrieg Bop" in 1976. Fans identified with their motorcycle jackets, Converse high-tops, raw lyrics, and punk riffs. They released 14 albums before disbanding in 1996, and although the original members have died of drugs or cancer, the group was inducted into the Rock & Roll Hall of Fame in 2002. The photograph below depicts a mural that Ori Carino created near the Thorneycroft Apartments, where the young pals would hang out and skateboard. (Above, Alamy; below, QTC.)

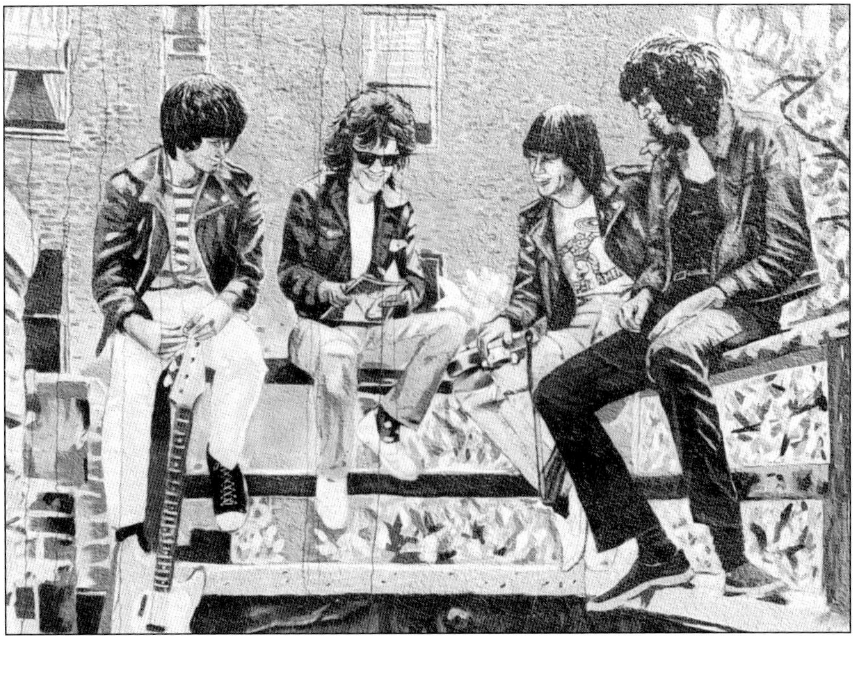

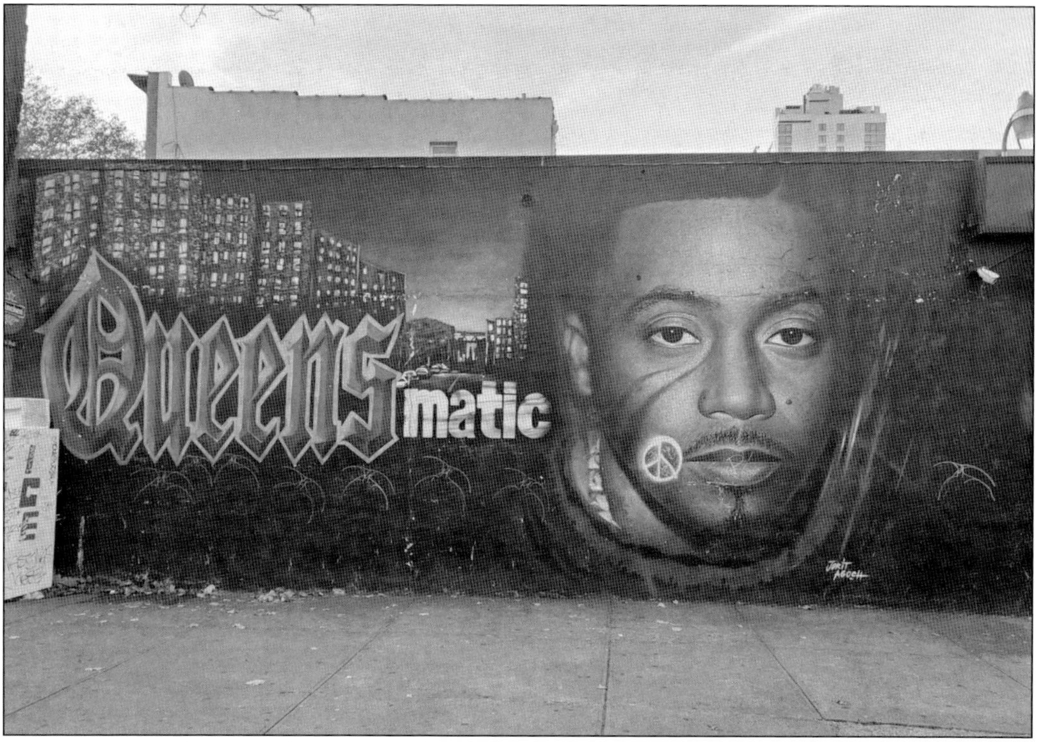


Nasir Jones is cofounder of QueensBridge Venture Partners, which has holdings in more than 40 companies, including Dropbox, Lyft, and Robinhood, but he is better known as the multiplatinum rapper Nas, who grew up in Queensbridge. Born Nasir bin Olu Dara Jones in 1973, the mogul ruled the hip hop scene with the 1994 album *Illmatic*, which features nine tracks about the housing project. The eighth-grade dropout has several homes these days, but he is immortalized on the corner of Twenty-First Street and Fortieth Avenue. (QTC.)

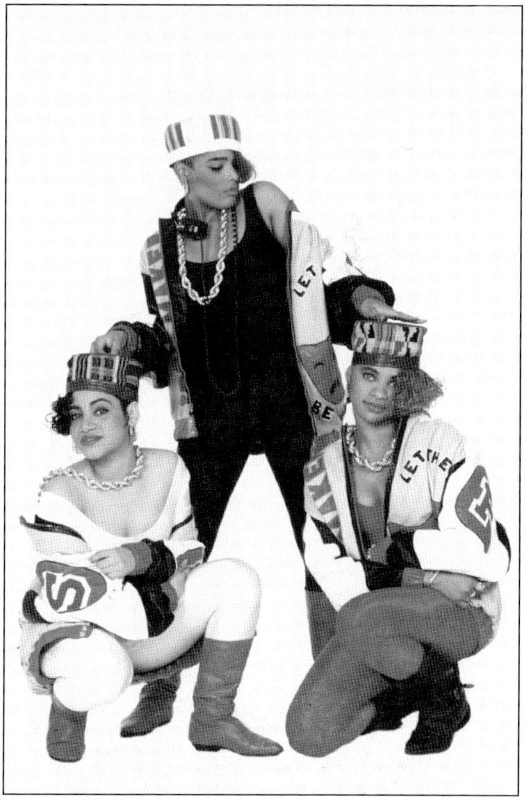

Born in the Caribbean in 1964, Sandra "Pepa" Denton (right) moved to Queens as a child and graduated from Springfield Gardens High School. She met Cheryl "Salt" James (left) while studying nursing at Queensborough Community College in the mid-1980s. They added DJ Spinderella (Deidra Roper, center) and started cranking out hits such as "Push It," "Shoop," and "What a Man" as Salt-N-Pepa. They were the first female rappers to produce gold and platinum albums. (Museum of the City of New York.)

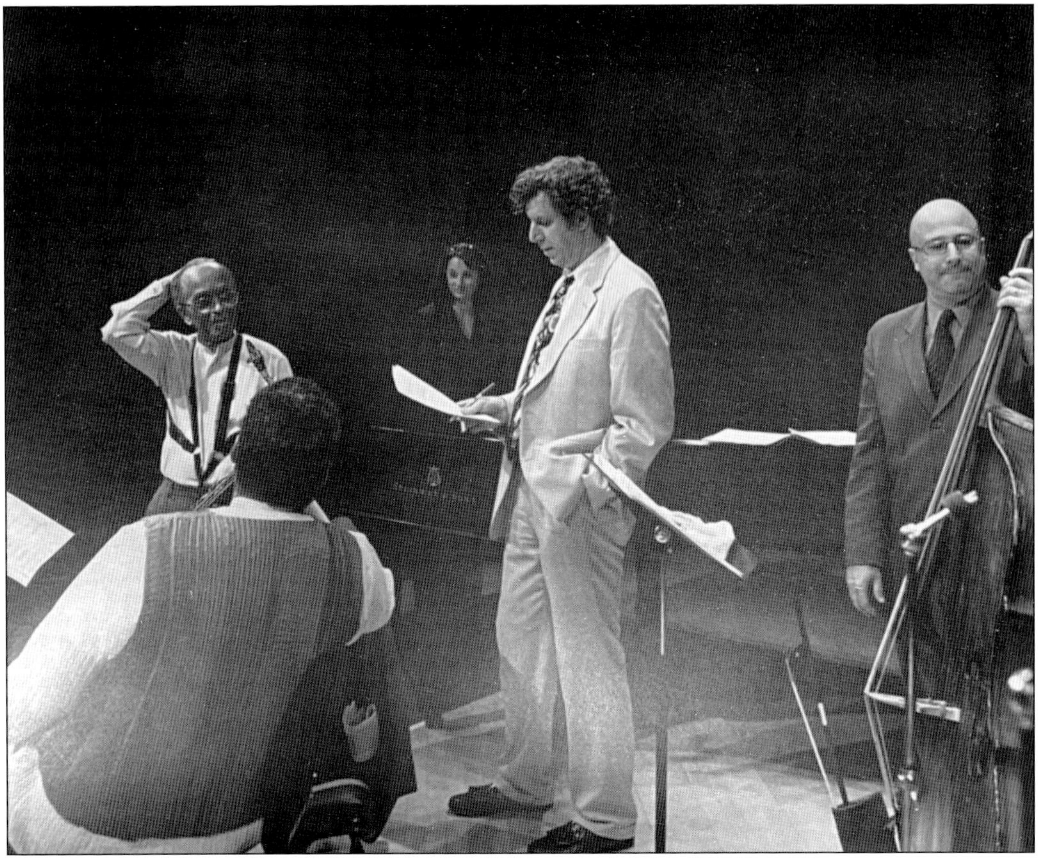

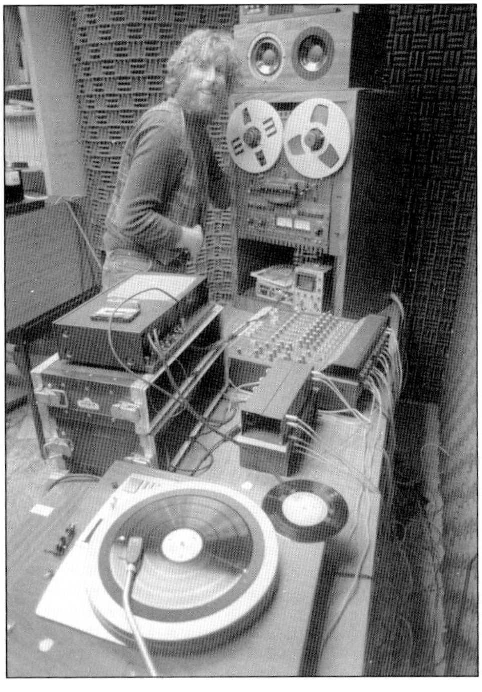

Musicians used to joke that Phil Schaap, who was born in Hollis in 1951, knew more about them than they did, thanks to his encyclopedic memory and lifelong obsession with jazz. On February 2, 1970, the Jamaica High School alum hosted his first radio show on Columbia University's WKCR-FM. By the time he graduated in 1974, he was promoting concerts and managing bands. This led to remastering records as an audio engineer, writing liner notes for CD sets, and working as an archivist for such labels as PolyGram, Sony, and Universal. He also taught at jazz at Lincoln Center, Manhattan School of Music, Princeton University, and The Juilliard School, while winning six Grammys and a prestigious Jazz Master Fellowship with the National Endowment of the Arts. (Both, Oberlin Conservatory Library.)

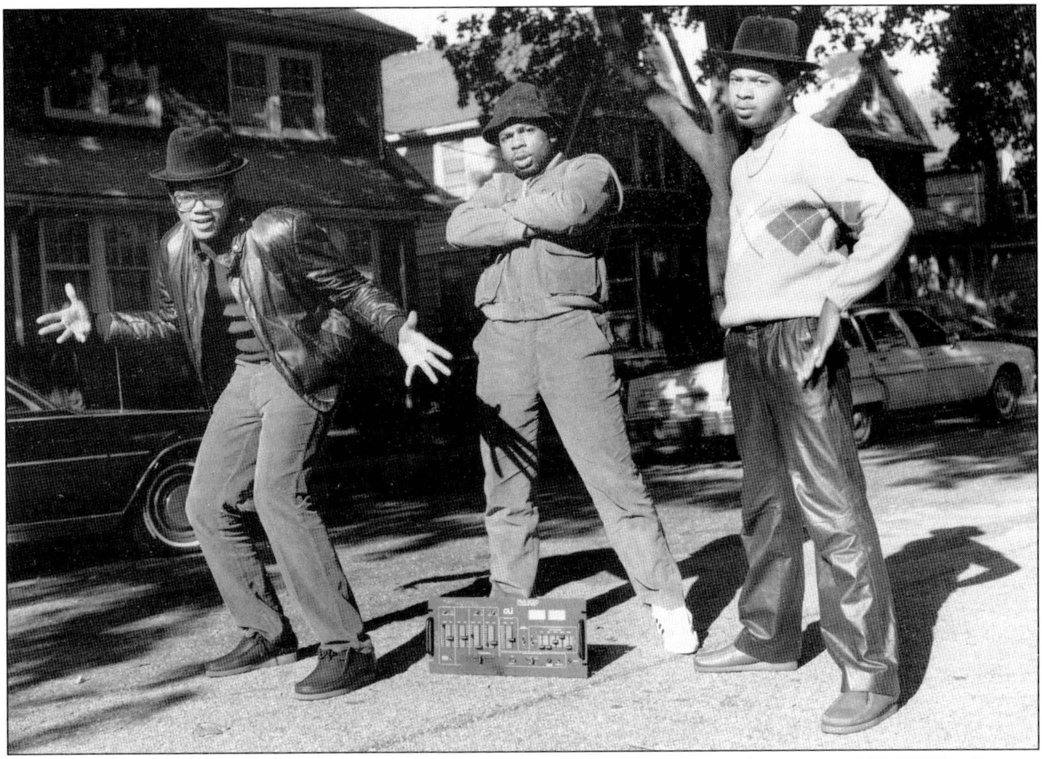

The Hollis intersection of 205th Street and Hollis Avenue was renamed Run-DMC JMJ Way during a festive ceremony led by Queens-bred radio personality Ed Lover on August 30, 2009. Attendees wore thick gold chains, high-top sneakers, and Kangol hats to honor the first rappers to achieve mainstream success. Jason "Jam Master Jay" Mizell grew up there with Joseph "DJ Run" Simmons and Darryl "D.M.C." McDaniels nearby. The pioneers broke out with their hit "It's Like That" in 1983 and crossed over with a rap version of Aerosmith's rock song "Walk This Way" in 1986. They never looked back during a three-decade career that included winning a Lifetime Achievement Grammy and joining the Rock & Roll Hall of Fame. The tune "My Adidas" features the lyrics "standin' on Two-Fifth Street, funky fresh and yes, cold on my feet." Above, the trio is near Mizell's childhood home on 205th Street. Below, a nearby mural memorializes Mizell, who was murdered in 2002. (Above, Janette Beckman; below, QTC.)

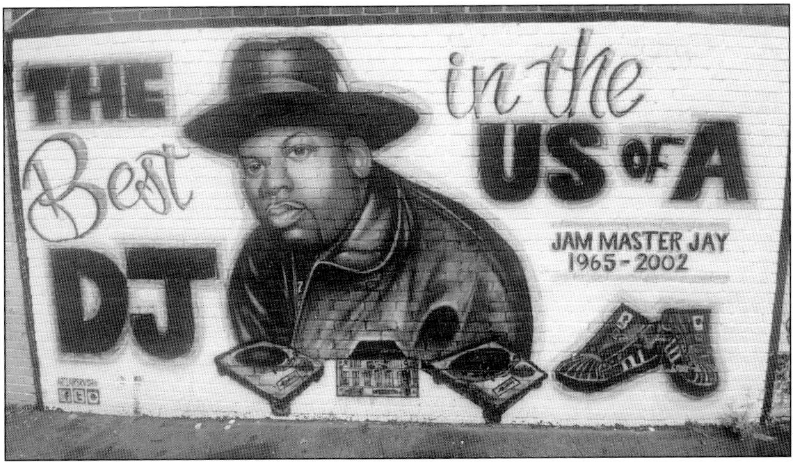

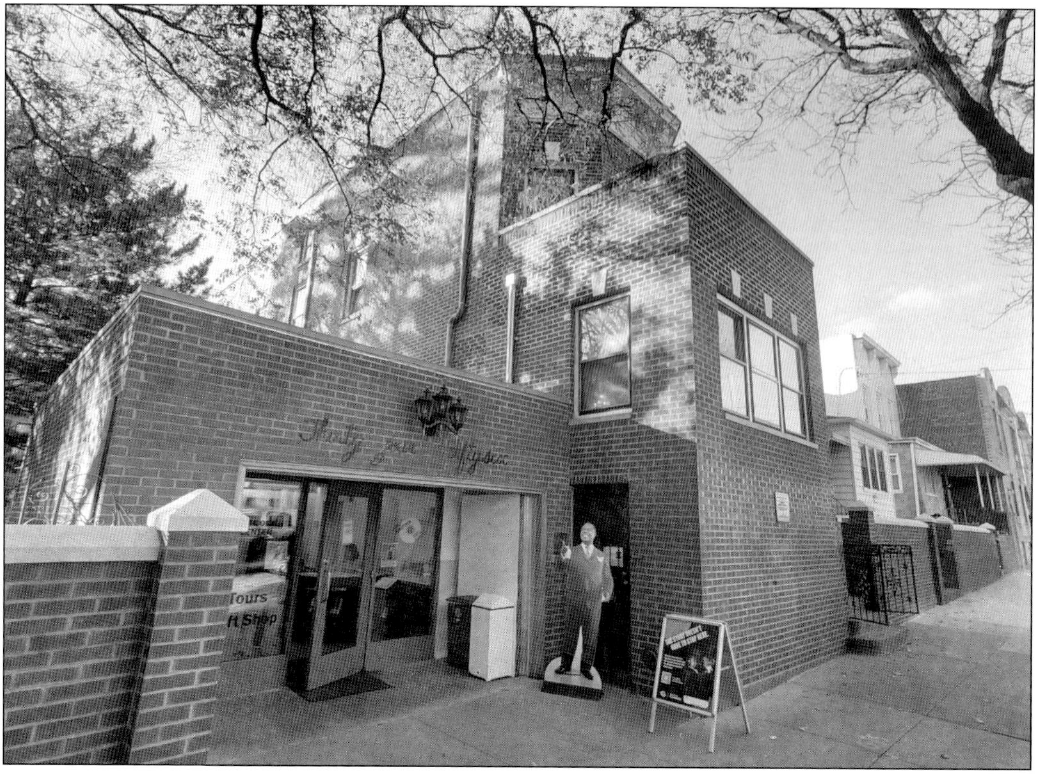

As various public spaces and an airport bear his name, it is obvious that New Orleans is proud of Louis Armstrong. However, the jazz legend left the Big Easy after his difficult childhood there, and the only home he ever owned was in Corona, where he lived with his wife, Lucille (née Wilson), from 1943 until his death in 1971. They bought the unattached brick house (above) for about $8,000 and renovated it to their tastes with a Japanese garden, an all-turquoise kitchen to match the color of Lucille's Cadillac, and a man cave for Satchmo with his recordings, artwork, and items he had collected during his world tours. Lucille donated the property to the city for use as a museum upon her death in 1983. Open to the public, the venue displays Satchmo's entire life, including his trusty trumpet (below). (Both, Rob MacKay.)

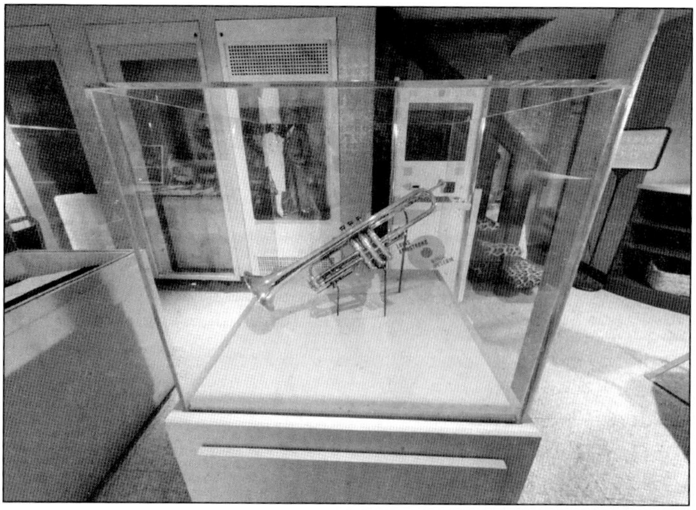

Tony Bennett won two Grammys for "I Left My Heart in San Francisco," but the crooner was born Anthony Benedetto in Astoria in 1926. His father died young, so Tony dropped out of school at 16 to sing in restaurants. After watching him at a Manhattan club in 1949, Bob Hope offered to hire him if he anglicized his last name to "Bennett." He agreed, and his songs topped the charts for six decades. At right, he donates a portrait to a previously mentioned Queens legend. (Alamy.)

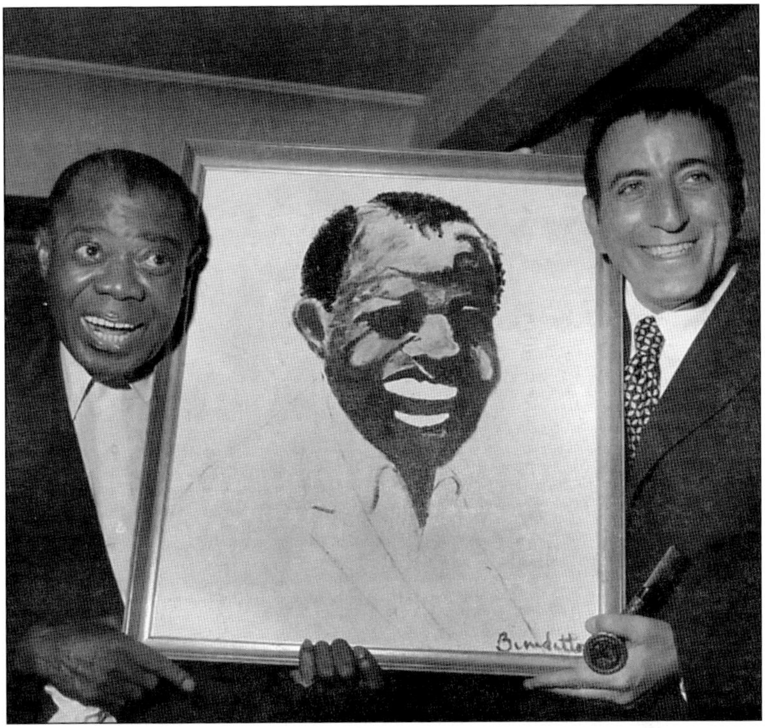

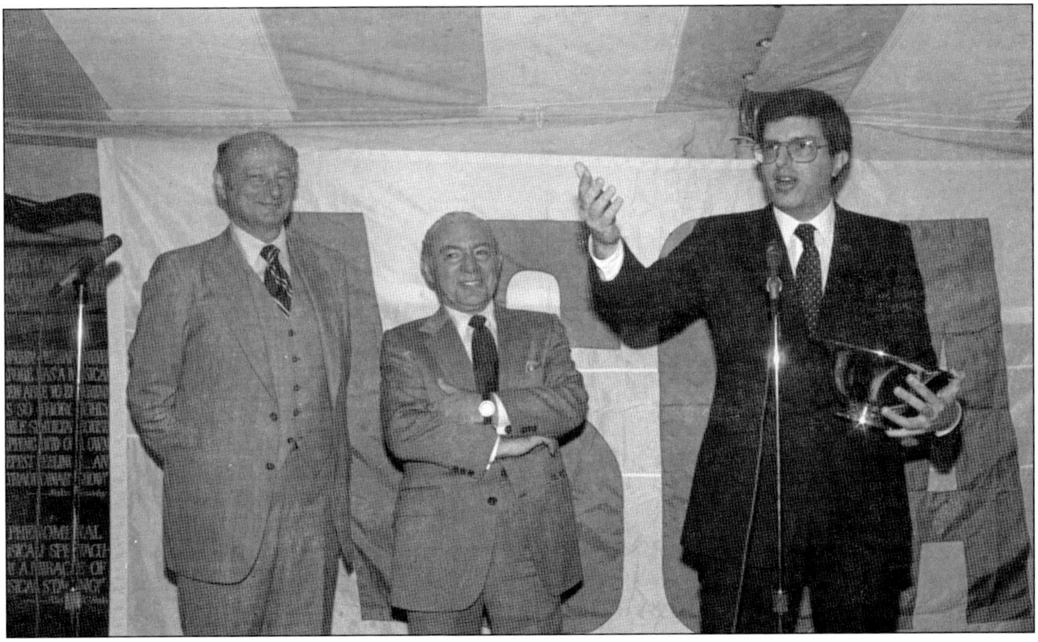

Marvin Hamlisch is one of only three people to complete the PEGOT cycle by winning at least one Pulitzer, Emmy, Grammy, Oscar, and Tony. Born to Viennese Jewish immigrants in 1944, he was the youngest person ever accepted into the Juilliard Pre-College school after transposing "Goodnight Irene" on the keyboard. The 1967 Queens College graduate composed scores for more than 40 motion pictures and Broadway plays. His other focus was symphonies, holding conductor positions in Dallas, Milwaukee, Seattle, and other cities. (New York City Municipal Archives.)

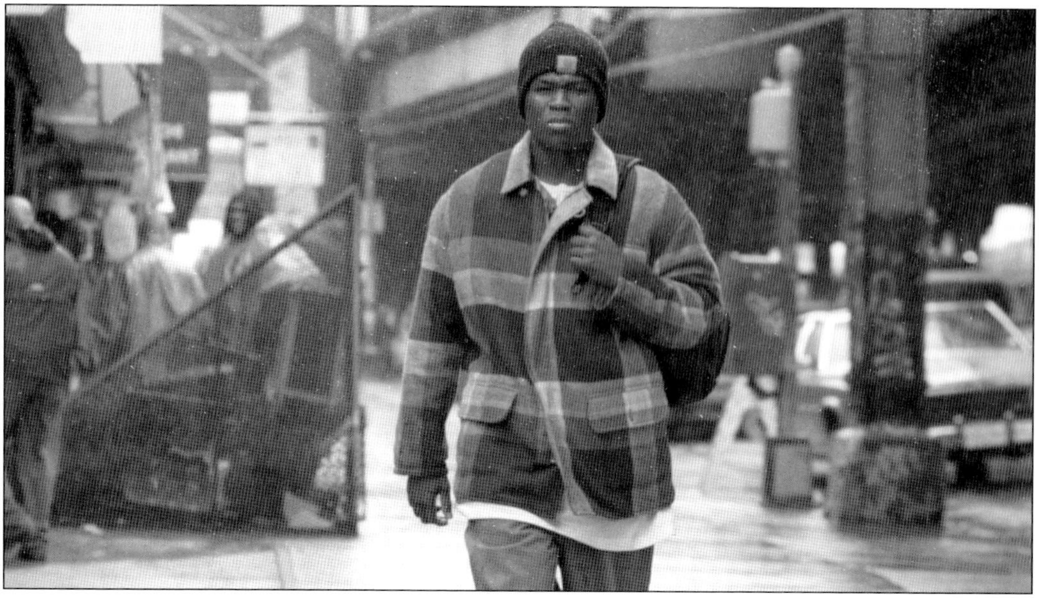

Curtis Jackson grew up in South Jamaica when it was a drug hotbed in the 1980s. His childhood included fathering a son, surviving nine bullets, and prison. Then he busted onto the underground hip hop scene as 50 Cent in 2002. Working with rapper Eminem and producer Dr. Dre, he released *Get Rich or Die Tryin*, the best-selling rap album in 2013. Soon thereafter, he founded his own label, G-Unit Records, on the way to a career in acting, film production, talent management, and event promotion. (Alamy.)

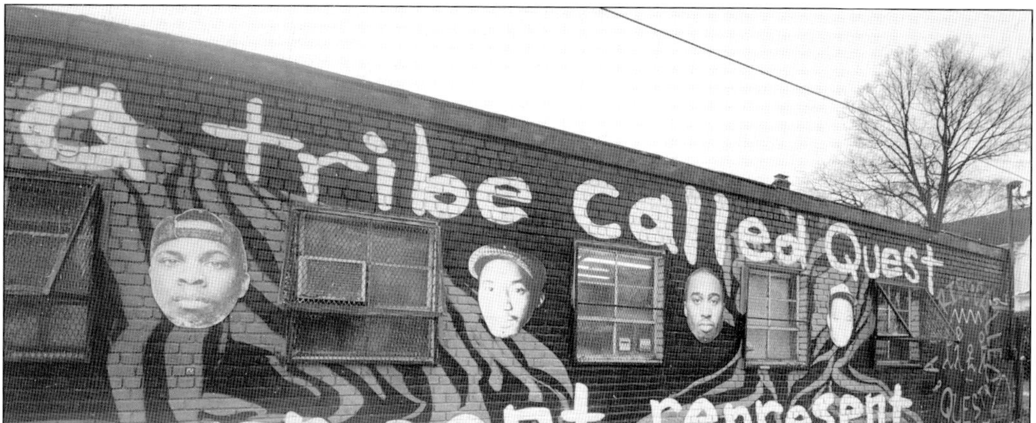


In 2016, Vince Ballentine created a mural on the side of a laundromat at Linden Boulevard and 192nd Street in St. Albans. With a black base, it features red and green drawings inspired by A Tribe Called Quest's album *The Low End Theory* along with head shots of members Q-Tip, Phife Dawg, Ali Shaheed Muhammad, and Jarobi White. On the laundromat's roof in 1991, the southeast Queens quartet performed "Check the Rhime" to an enthusiastic crowd. The rap established A Tribe Called Quest as pioneers of hip hop fused with jazz. (QTC.)

In a video on social media, PS 45 student Onika Tanya Maraj-Petty says she wants to be a nurse when she grows up. The girl, who was born in the Caribbean in 1982 but moved to South Ozone Park at the age of five, started acting in high school. After graduation, she eschewed nursing to launch an entertainment career as Nicki Minaj instead. Good choice! Her trophy case includes eight American Music Awards, five MTV Video Music Awards, and four Billboard Music Awards. (Alamy.)

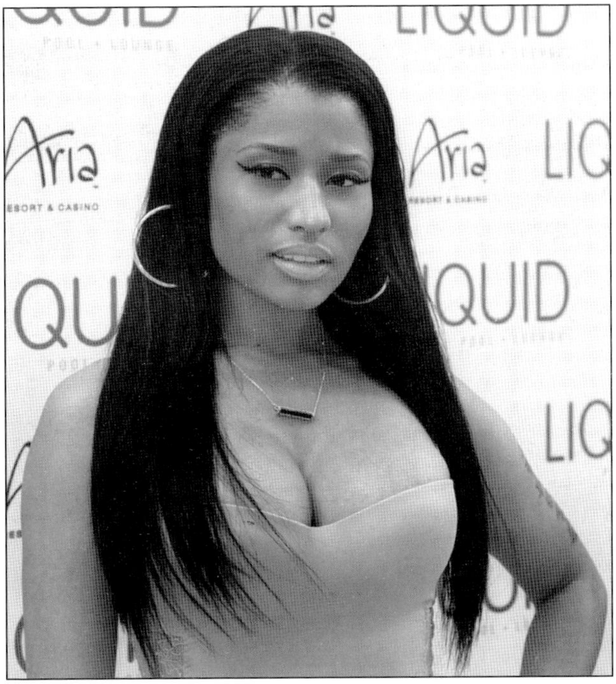


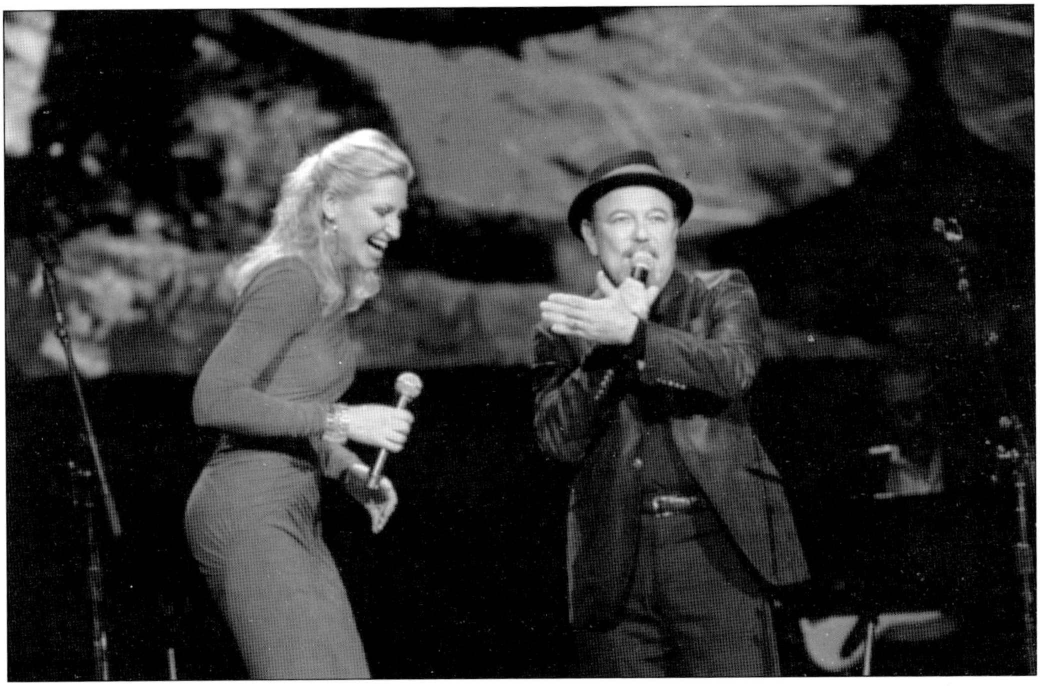

She acts. She writes. She dances. She even invented and trademarked her own musical format, Mixtura, which is a blend of jazz, classical, pop, and world music. Luba Mason (left) was born to Slovakian immigrants in Astoria in 1961. She was in the original Broadway cast of *The Will Rogers Follies* and the first revival of *How to Succeed in Business Without Really Trying*. She was also in *The Capeman*, where she met her husband, multi-Grammy-winner Ruben Blades (right). (Travis Chantar/Luba Mason.)

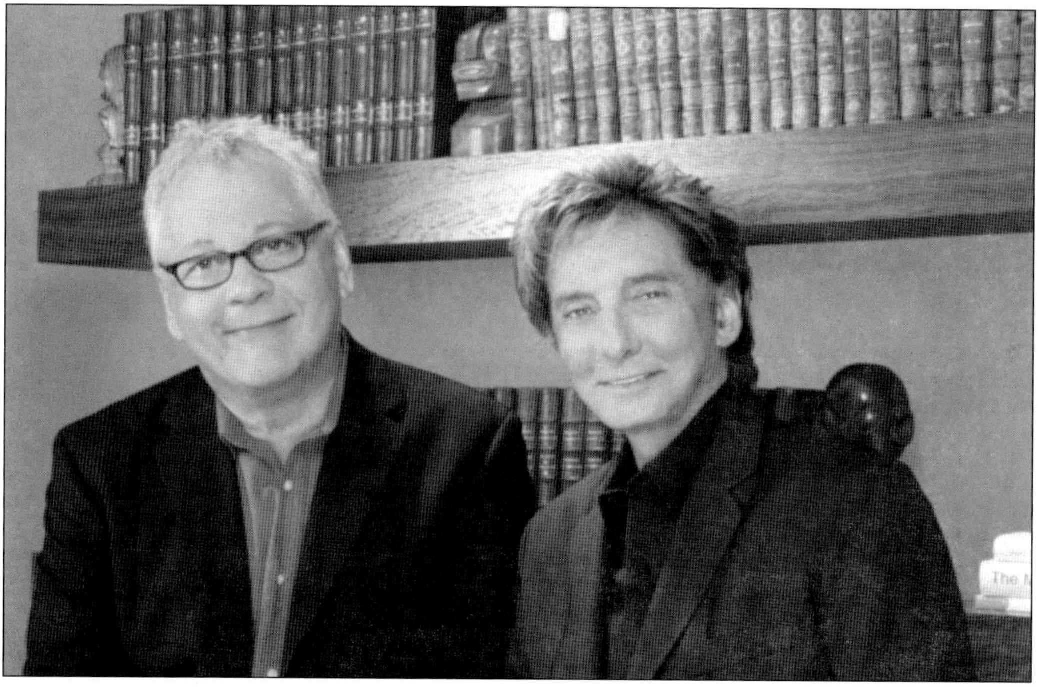

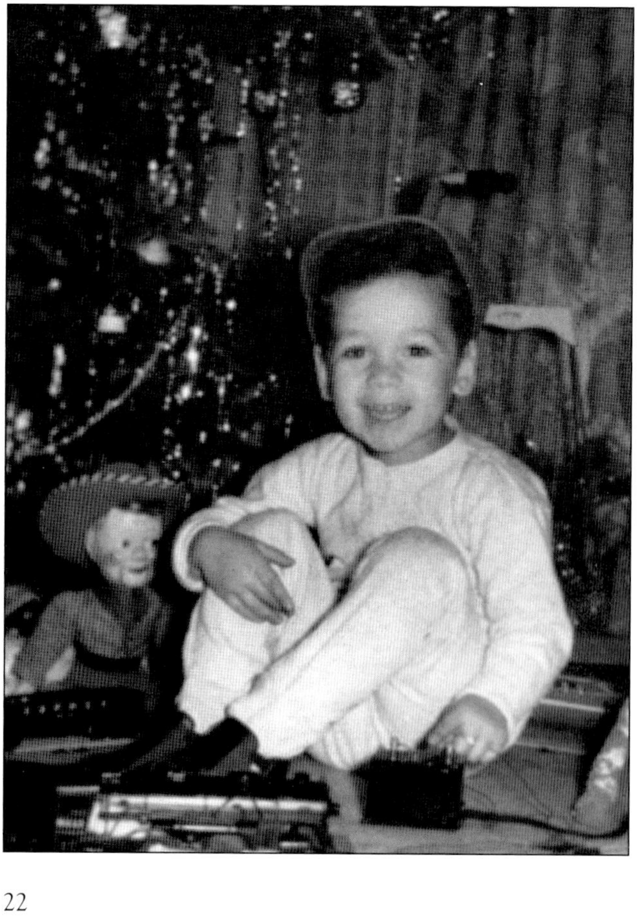

Barry Manilow, who has released 13 platinum and 6 multiplatinum records, needs no introduction. But the voice behind "Mandy" and "Can't Smile Without You" works with a lesser-known lyricist, Bruce Sussman, who grew up in Jackson Heights. Sussman, seen at left in 1950, thought he was going to be a lawyer until he took classes on Shakespeare, music, and religion at Franklin and Marshall College. He was so enthralled that he forced the eastern Pennsylvania college to let him create a first-ever music major. After graduating in 1971, he returned to New York City to work with the BMI Lehman Engel Musical Theatre Workshop. He met Manilow, and they created the Grammy-winning "Copacabana (At the Copa)" in 1978. The ensuing 40-plus-year partnership has produced more than 200 songs, commercial jingles, movie soundtracks, and musicals. (Both, Bruce Sussman.)

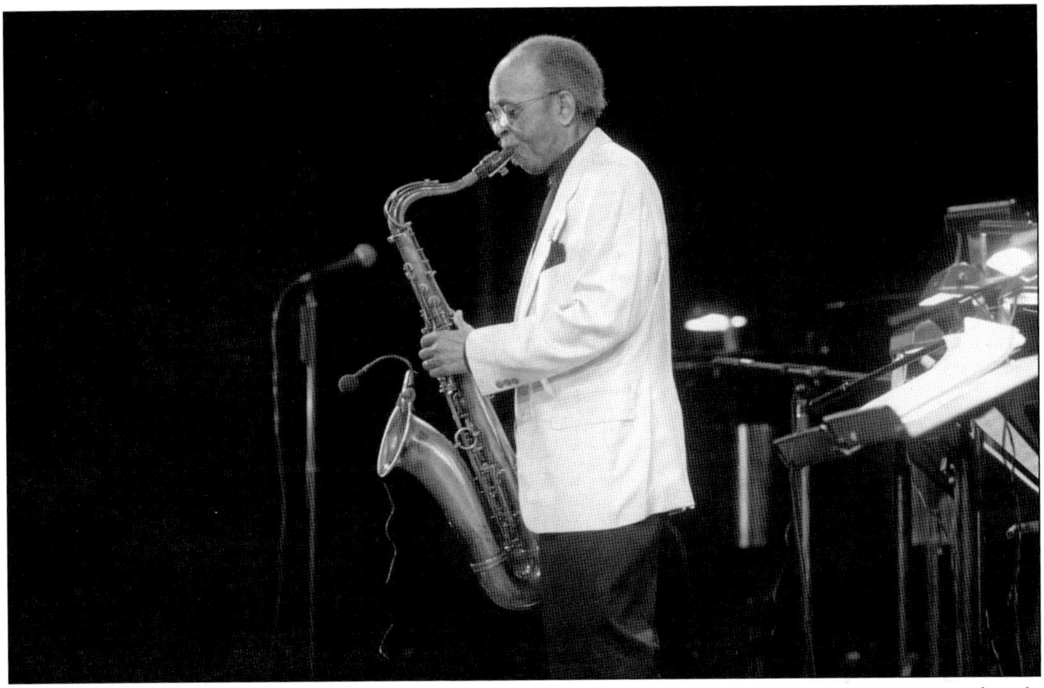

Opened when segregation was the norm in 1953, the Dorie Miller Cooperative Houses immediately attracted a mix of Jewish, African American, and mixed-race families, including many jazz legends who left Harlem for the six-tower Corona complex. Tenor saxophonist Jimmy Heath and his Caucasian wife, Mona (née Brown), were among the pioneers, raising their daughter Roslyn there. While playing in several bands and touring the world on the way to achieving National Endowment for the Arts Master status, Jimmy served on the advisory board of the nearby Louis Armstrong House Museum, founded the Queens College Master of Music in Jazz Studies program (where he taught for almost 25 years), and launched and led Flushing Town Hall's Queens Jazz Orchestra. The Grammy-nominated musician died at the age of 93 in January 2022, and a street corner in the Miller complex was named after him on May 20. At about the same time, Queens College established an endowment fund in his name. (Both, Flushing Town Hall.)

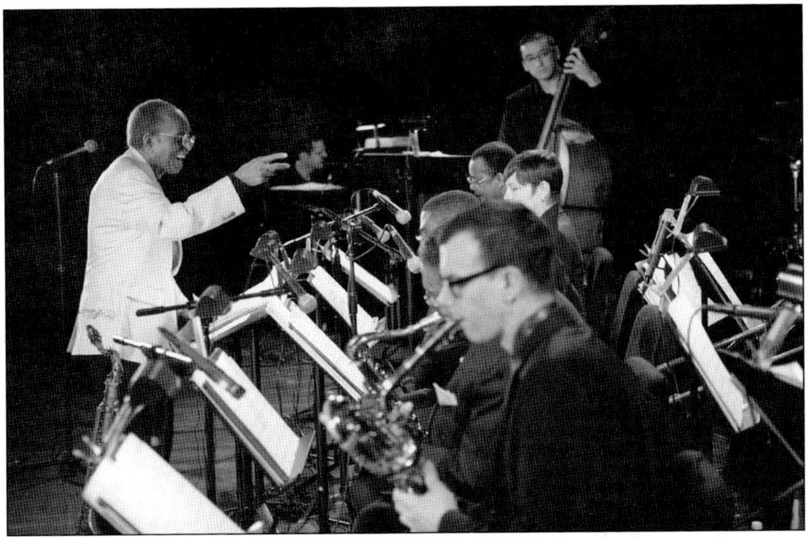

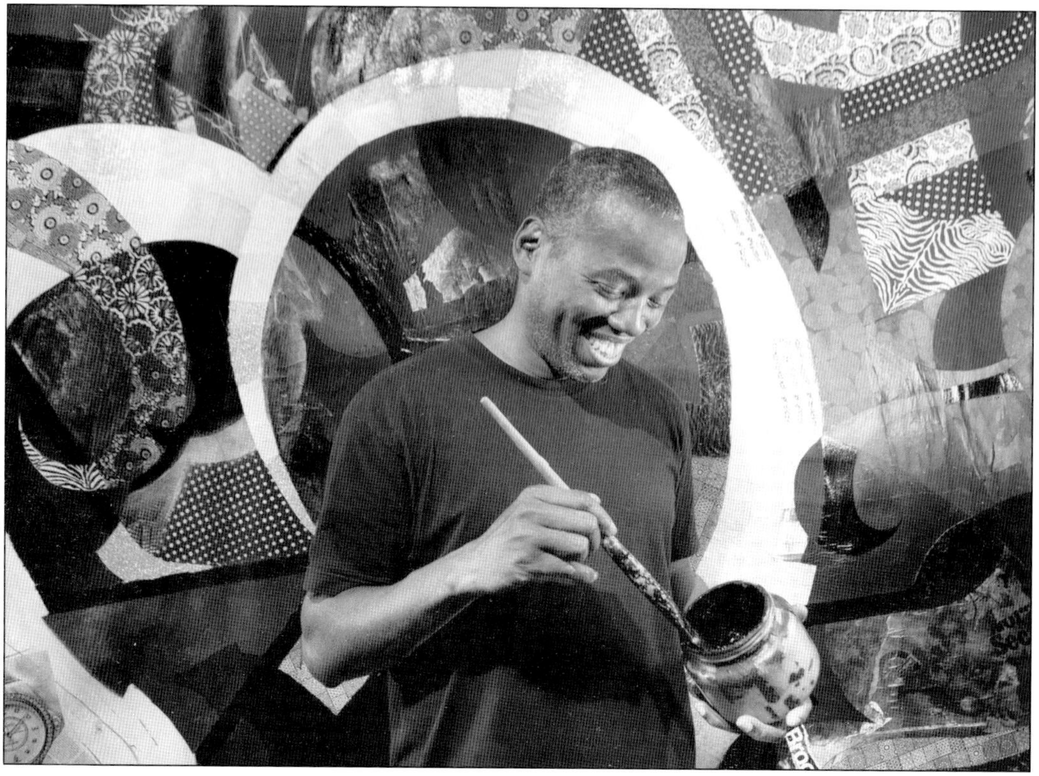

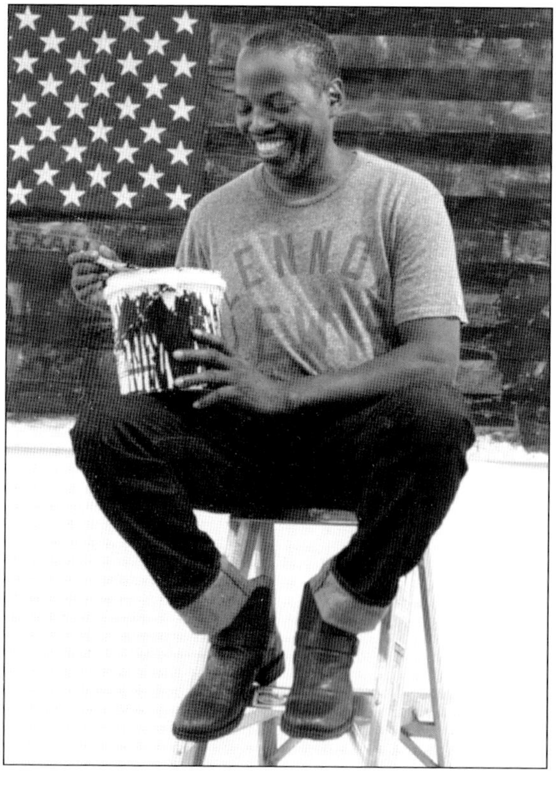

Gifted with many talents and an uncanny ability to reinvent himself, Cey Adams would fit nicely in many of this book's chapters. Born in 1962, the entrepreneur started as a graffiti guy in the late 1970s, when New York City subways were never whitewashed. His southeast Queens home was the center of the hip hop world in the 1980s, and he designed clothes and sneakers for Run-DMC and the Beastie Boys. Soon, he was handling branding for LL Cool J, Jay-Z, Public Enemy, Mary J. Blige, and The Notorious B.I.G. before getting into advertising campaigns for such companies as Levi's, Nike, and Burton Snowboards. In 2001, he designed the logo for Dave Chappelle's show on Comedy Central. In 2016, he contributed a mural to the Smithsonian's National Museum of African American History and Culture. In 2017, he created a Google Doodle. These photographs are by Janette Beckman, who collaborated with Adams on a book project in 2018. (Both, Janette Beckman.)

# *Two*

# Athletic Champs

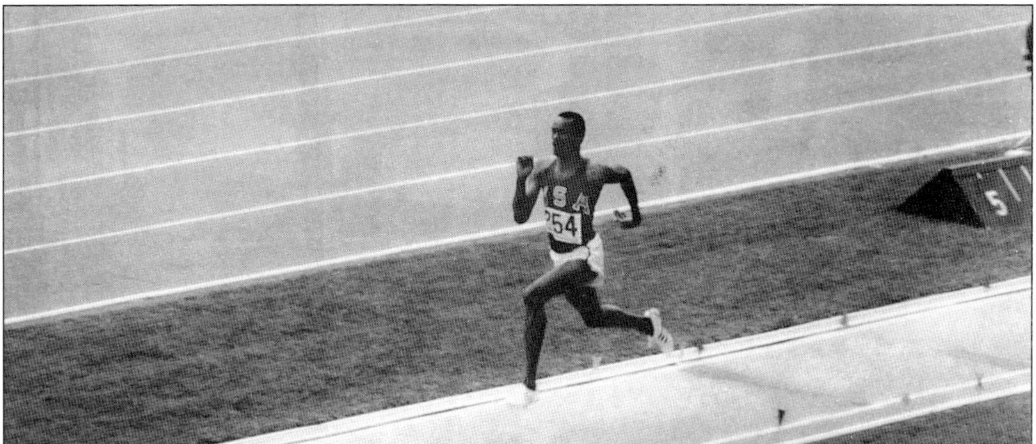

On October 18, 1968, Bob Beamon took a deep breath and started sprinting. After 19 strides, he took off, stretching his legs in the air. Seconds later, the Jamaica High School grad landed in history with a 29-foot, 2.5-inch long jump at the Mexico City Olympic Games. The 22-year-old shattered the previous mark by almost 2 feet. He was inducted into the US Olympic and Paralympic Hall of Fame in 1983. (Bonnay/US Olympic and Paralympic Committee Archives.)

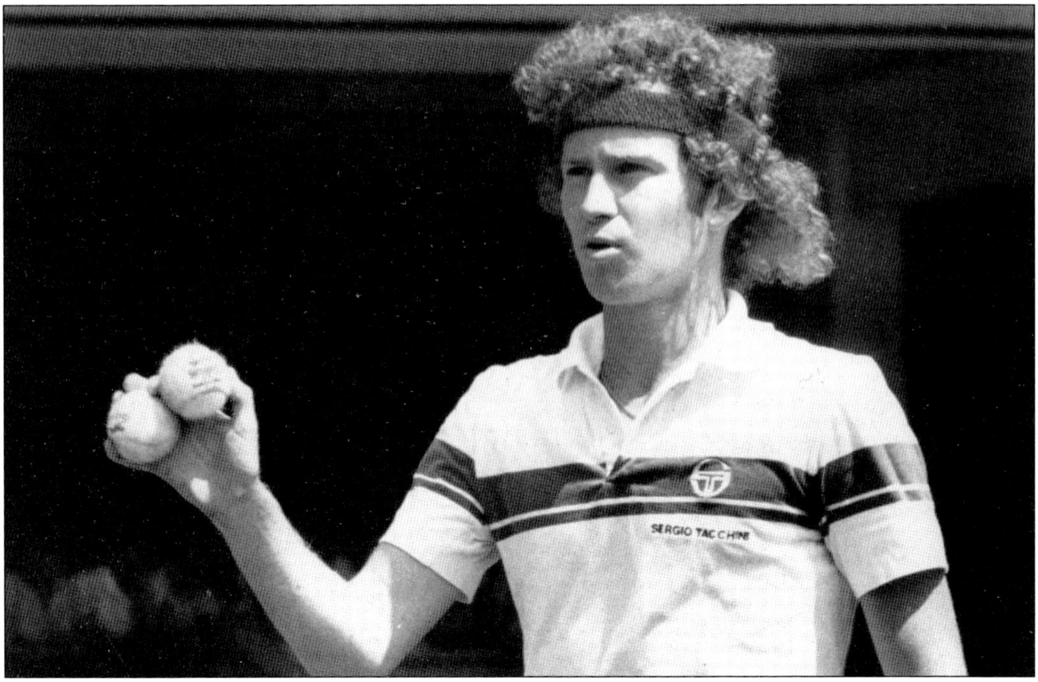


John McEnroe (above) was eight when he started tennis lessons at the Douglaston Club near his childhood home in 1967. A bit later, he worked as a ball boy at the US Open a few miles away. So it should not be a surprise that he won his first Grand Slam singles title at the US Open in 1979. Over his career, he amassed seven Grand Slam singles titles and nine men's doubles titles. He was inducted into the International Tennis Hall of Fame in 1999. The Gerulaitis family fled Lithuania after the 1944 Soviet invasion and eventually settled in Woodhaven, where son Vitas (below) dazzled with fast hands, finesse, and amazing speed on the tennis court. (Like McEnroe, he worked at the US Open as a youth.) After turning pro, the Archbishop Molloy High School grad, a notorious ladies man, was ranked in the singles Top 10 from 1977 to 1982, winning the Australian Open in 1977 and peaking at number three in 1978. (Both, Alamy.)

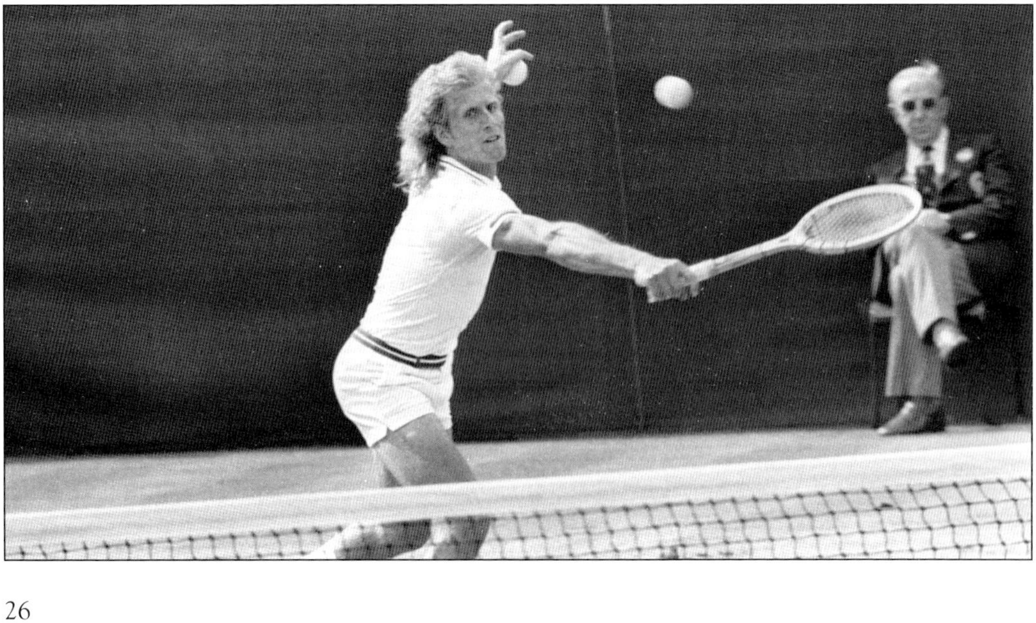

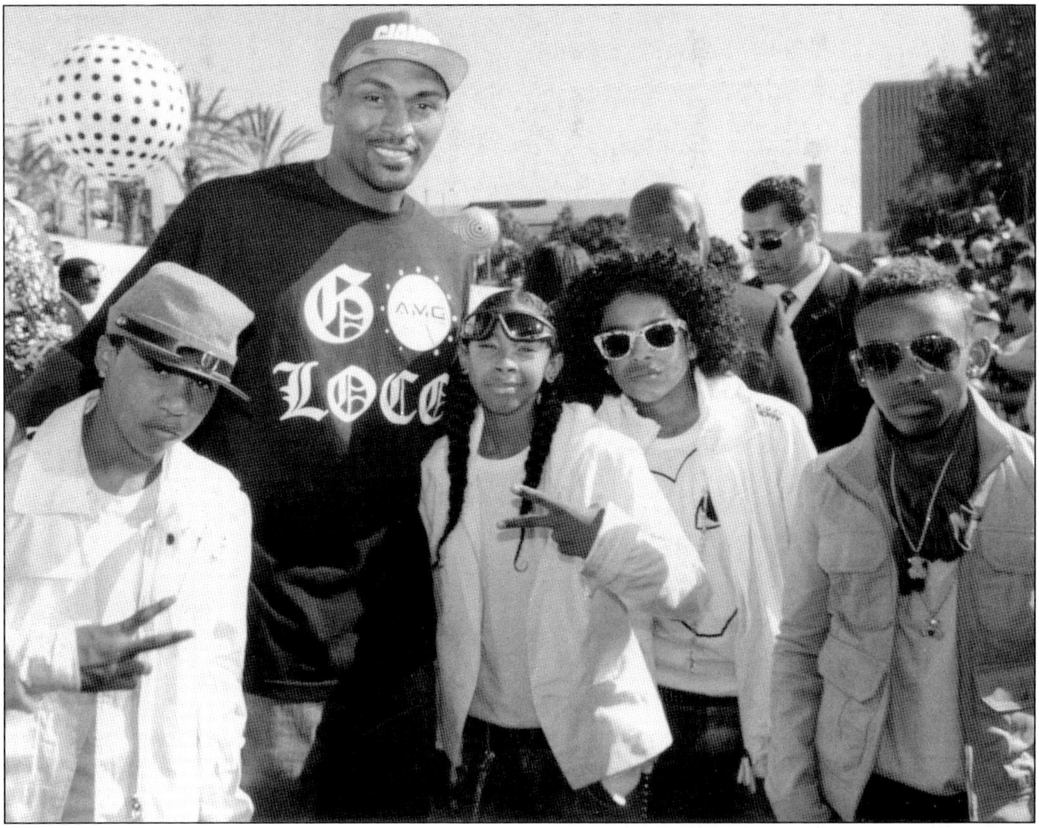

Ron Artest grew up with as many as 17 people in his Queensbridge apartment. He stayed close to home and played college basketball at St. John's University, where he led the team to the 1999 Big East title as a sophomore. He went pro the following year and played on six National Basketball Association (NBA) teams with stints in China and Italy over an 18-year career. His résumé includes a championship with the Los Angeles Lakers, a Defensive Player of the Year Award, and an All-Star Game selection. Artest, standing tall with the rap act Mindless Behavior in Queens above, legally changed his name to Metta World Peace in 2011 after seriously considering the name Queensbridge. (Above, SJU; right, QPL.)

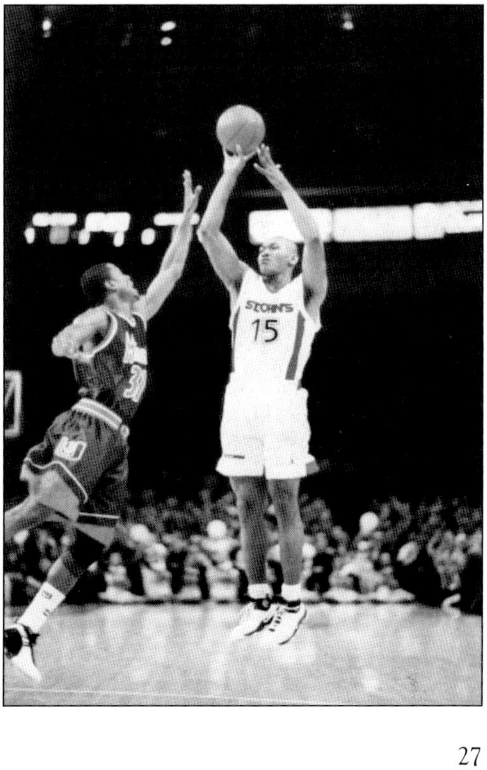

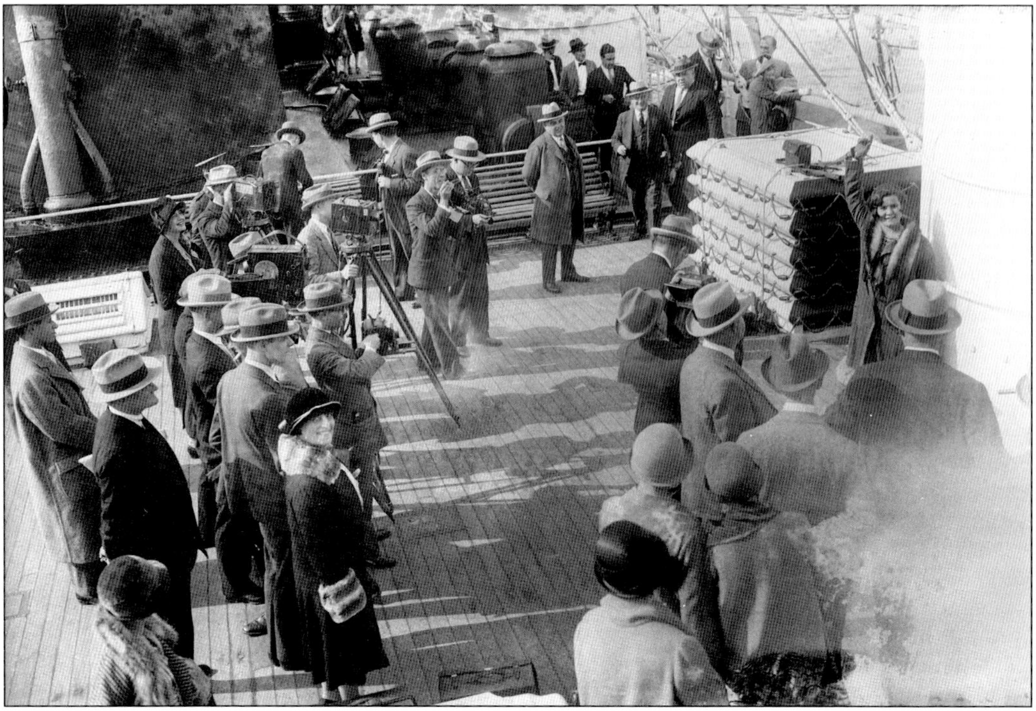

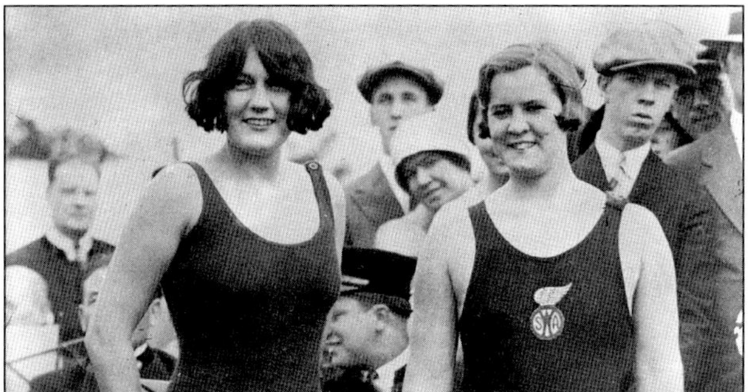


Gertrude Ederle (above, at right with arm raised) was comfortable in two places: the Flushing house where she lived for almost 60 years and the water. Born in 1906, she was the daughter of a German butcher and set her first swimming world record at the age of 12. Over the following years, she accumulated 29 world or national records. On August 6, 1926, the 19-year-old donned a two-piece bathing suit her sister had designed and became the first woman to swim the English Channel. For a while, she replaced Babe Ruth as the country's most popular athlete, with Irving Berlin composing "Trudy" for her and Pres. Calvin Coolidge calling her "America's Best Girl." On August 27, 1926, she was the first woman to be celebrated with a ticker-tape parade in downtown Manhattan. Her memory lives on via Ederle Terrace, a public space in Flushing Meadows Corona Park. (Both, LOC.)

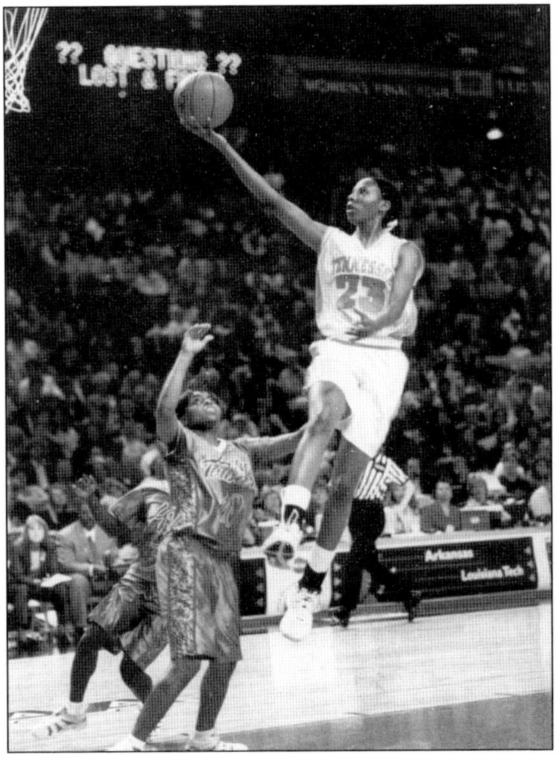

Her Queensbridge nickname was "Flat Out" because she would flat out abandon whatever she was doing to shoot hoops. Born in 1977, Chamique Holdsclaw won four state championships with Middle Village's Christ the King Regional High School and three NCAA championships at the University of Tennessee at Knoxville, where she was known as "The Claw." After success in the Women's National Basketball Association (WNBA), the lightning-quick six-foot, two-inch star joined the Women's Basketball Hall of Fame in 2018. (Both, WBHF.)

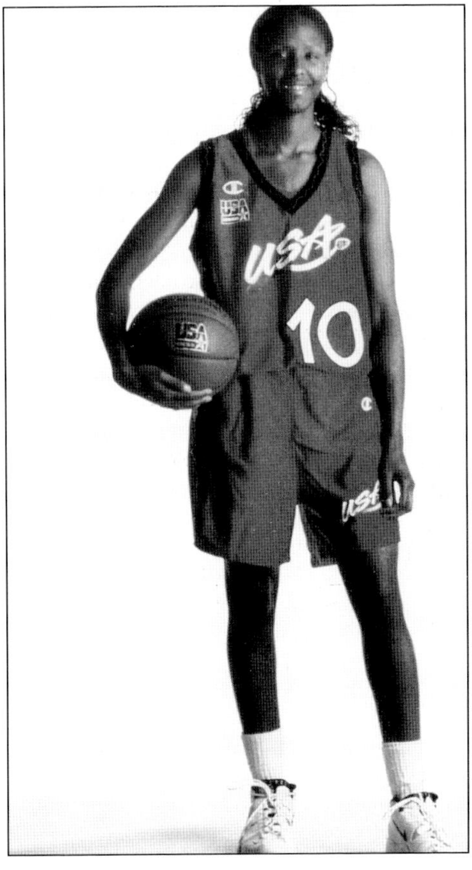

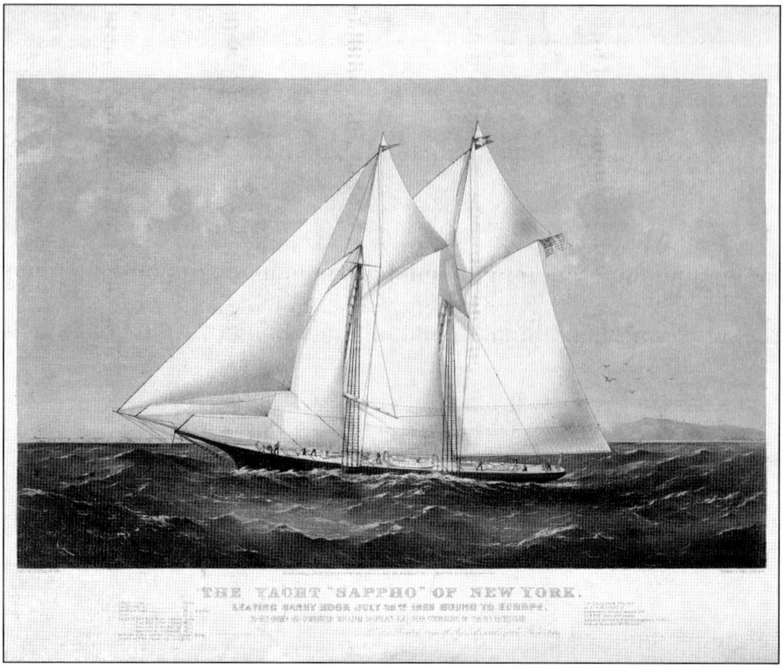


A scion of the family who owned much of Douglas Manor, William P. Douglas grew up sailing on Little Neck Bay. In 1868, the 24-year-old Douglas purchased *Sappho* (seen in this 1869 Currier & Ives print) and hired Capt. Bob Fisk. They sailed to England, where they competed against British railroad tycoon James Ashbury in races around the Isle of Wight just after the America's Cup tradition began. (LOC.)

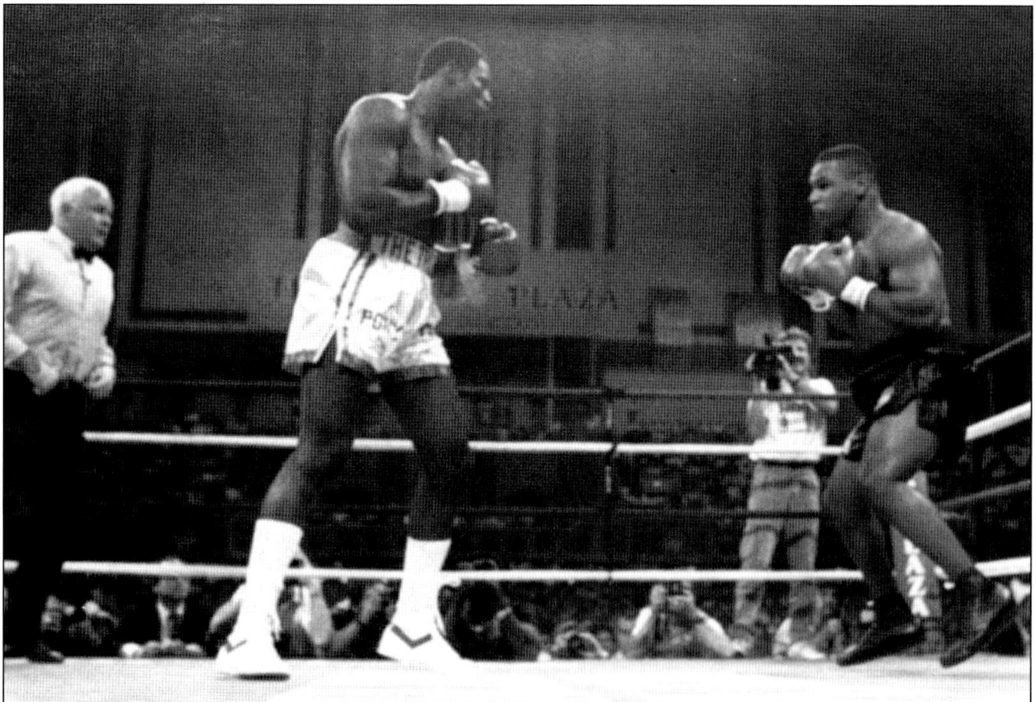


After his beloved grandmother died when he was 19, Carl Williams started walking six miles to a St. Albans gym to learn boxing. He won New York Golden Gloves championships in 1980 and 1981 and picked up the nickname "The Truth" because his lethal right hand made opponents believe. In 1982, the heavyweight turned professional, starting off with 16 straight victories. Then he lost world champion bouts to Larry Holmes and Mike Tyson. (Getty Images.)

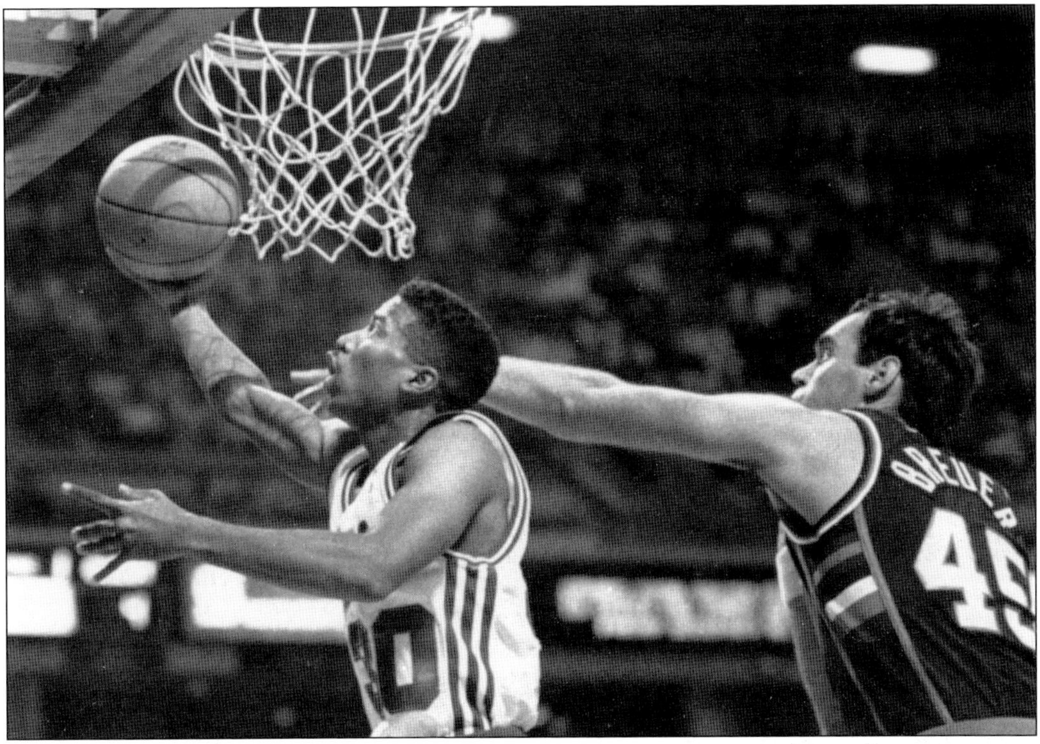


Point guards Kenny Smith (above) and Kenny Anderson (right in 1988) were playground legends in LeFrak City and All-Americans at Archbishop Molloy High School in Briarwood. Known as "Jet" because of his speed and jumping ability, Smith starred alongside Michael Jordan at the University of North Carolina before playing in the NBA from 1987 to 1997. Jet won back-to-back championships with the Houston Rockets in 1994 and 1995 before retiring to become a sports analyst. Growing up a bit later, the skinny Anderson was known as "Mr. Chibbs." With dazzling ball-handling skills, quickness, and shooting ability, he broke the New York state high school scoring record with 2,621 points and was the 1989 Gatorade National Player of the Year as a senior. Mr. Chibbs played for Georgia Tech for two years before the NBA's New Jersey Nets drafted him in 1991. He played for nine teams over 14 seasons. (Above, Alamy; right, AMHS.)

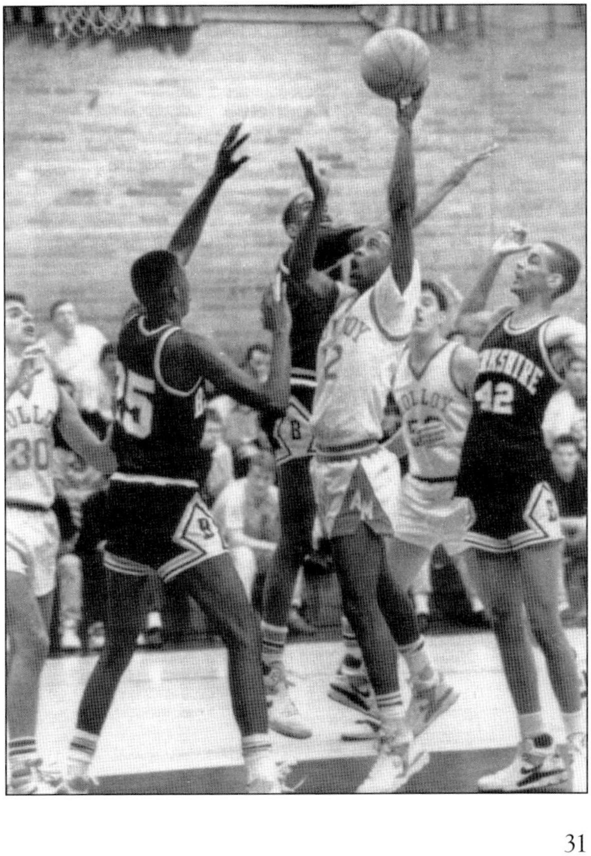

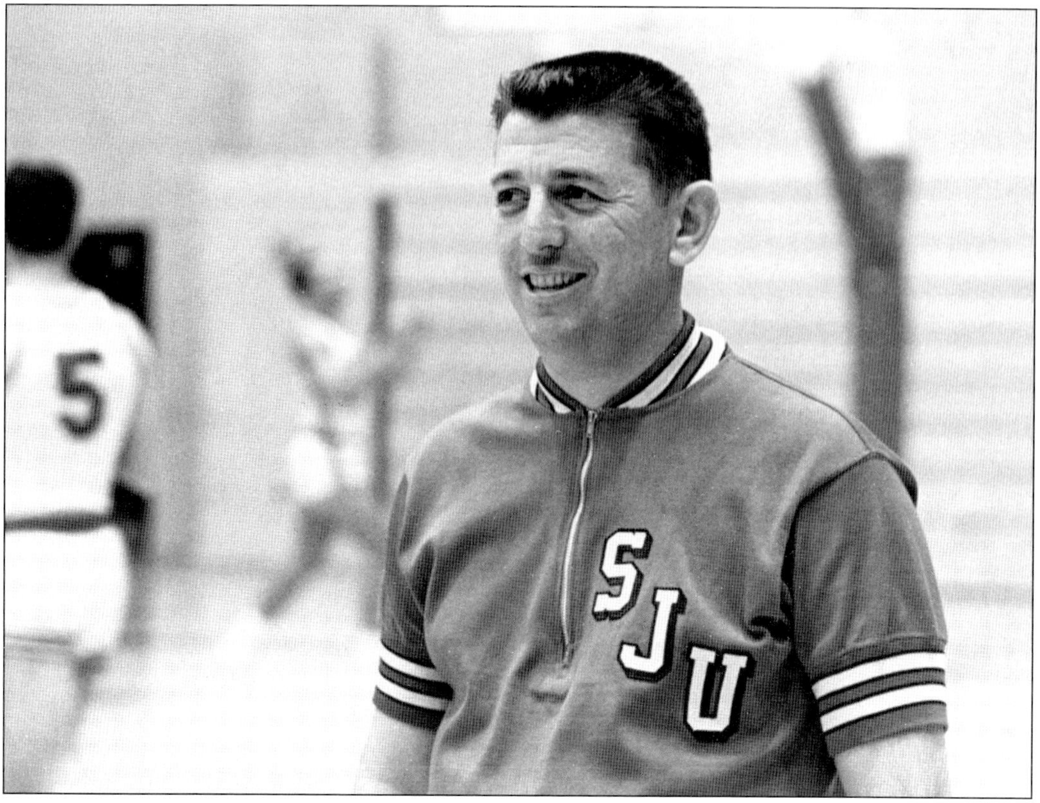


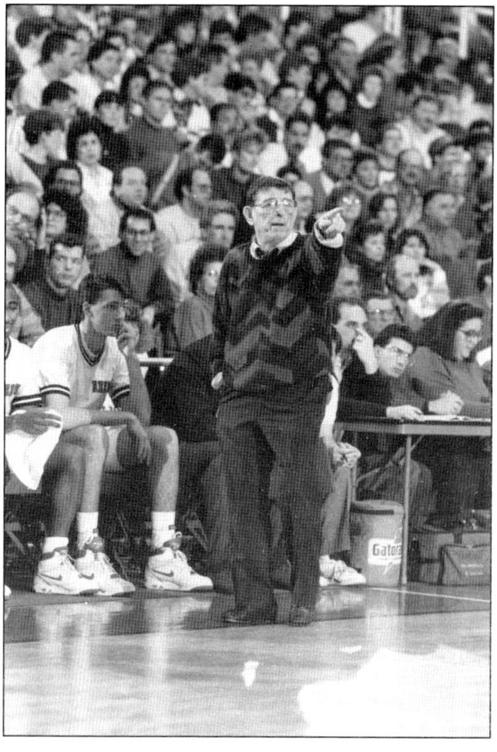

Lou Carnesecca's Tudor-style home on Midland Parkway in Jamaica Estates is a few blocks from St. John's University's basketball complex. But he would leave early to get to practice on time because he would trade pleasantries, talk hoops, and share his never-ending trove of stories with everybody on the way. The coach/father figure, who was born Luigi to Italian immigrants in 1925, loved the school, and the school loved him—despite his hideous sweaters. His record was 526-200 with two Big East titles over 24 seasons (1965–1970 and 1973–1992) at St. John's. He was selected as National Coach of the Year in 1983 and 1985 by the US Basketball Writers Association and inducted into the Naismith Memorial Basketball Hall of Fame in 1992. The complex where he ran his practices was renamed Carnesecca Arena in 2004. (Both, SJU.)

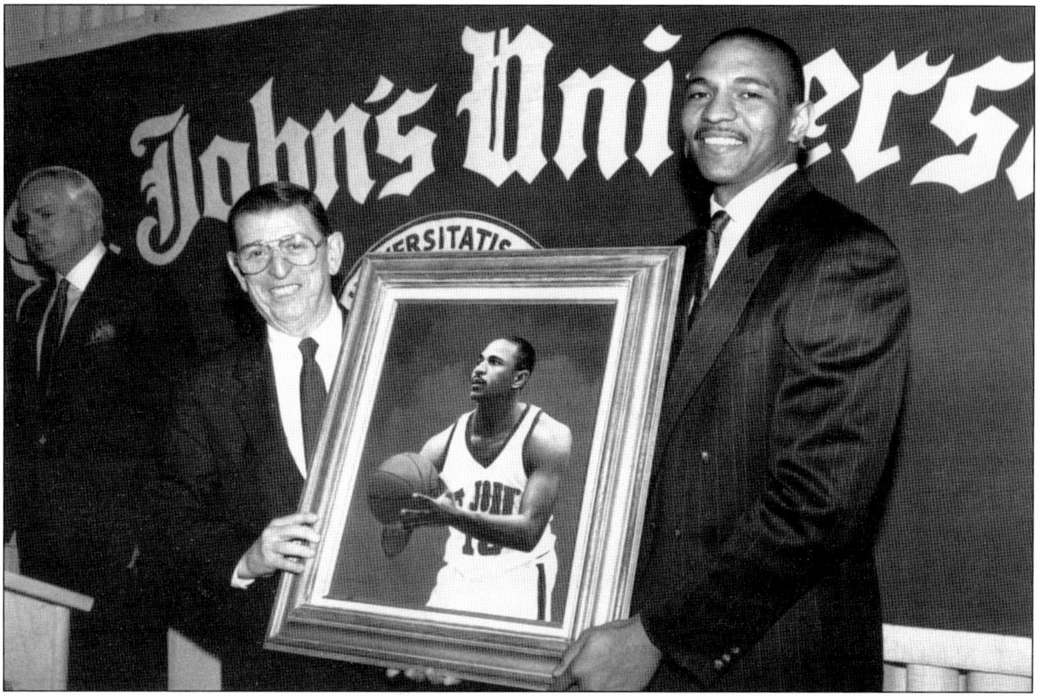


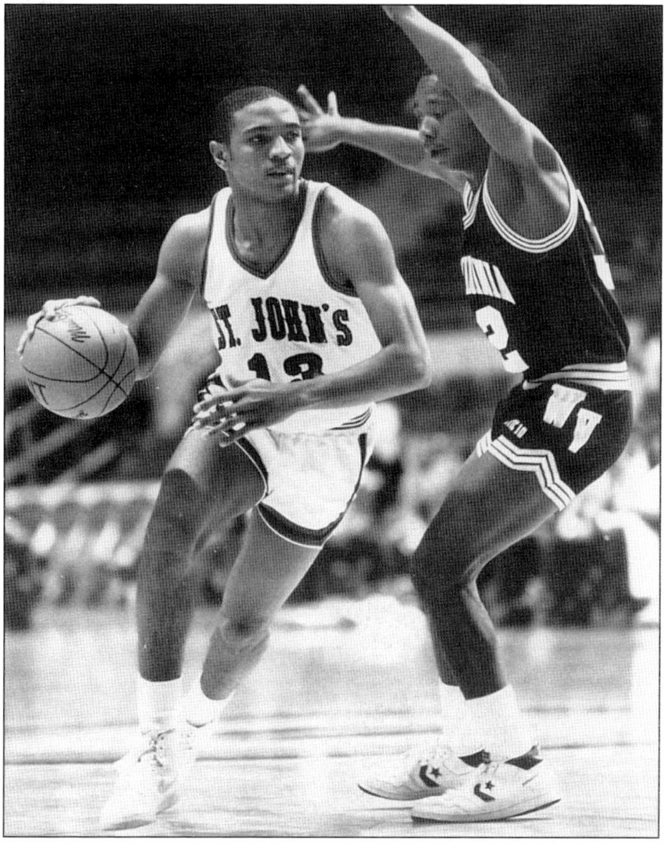


It is hard to believe now, but Mark Jackson (born April 1, 1965) was a horrible basketball player in junior high school. Friends remember him as the last person chosen during pickup games in Daniel M. O'Connell Park in St. Albans, where he grew up. But then he sprouted to about six feet, three inches and developed an uncanny streetball sense. After playing college ball at St. John's University, he got to live every New York City kid's hoop dream when he was drafted by the New York Knicks in 1987. With his family traveling to Madison Square Garden for home games, he won the NBA Rookie of the Year Award in 1988 and had some solid years before being traded to the Los Angeles Clippers. He retired in 2004 after playing for seven teams. Though he never won an NBA championship, he made one NBA All-Star Game. (Both, SJU.)

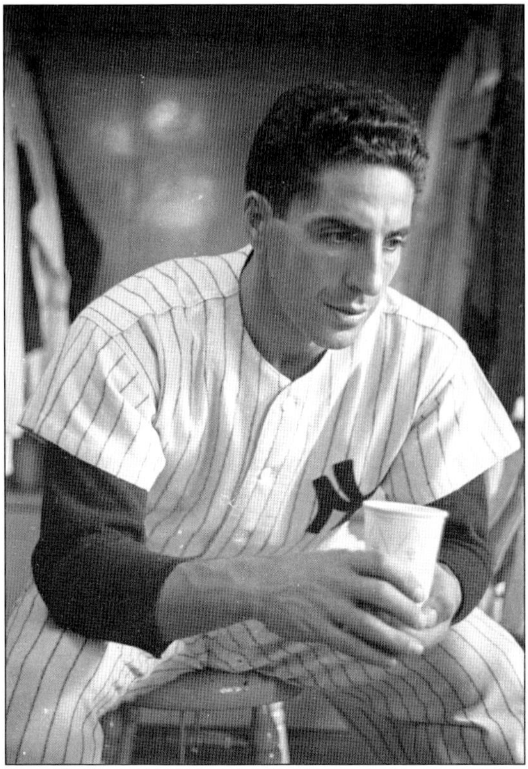

Born in 1917, Phil Rizzuto grew up in a Glendale house, where his sister Mary lived until her 1993 death. He played baseball at PS 58 and Richmond Hill High School, where he learned to say "Holy Cow" instead of cursing. His beloved Brooklyn Dodgers took no interest in him, as he stood only five feet, six inches and weighed about 150 pounds, but the Yankees drafted him in 1937. The smallest player in the major leagues quickly became a star shortstop, leading the Bronx Bombers to seven World Series championships in 12 seasons. Seen at left in 1949, he made the MLB All-Star Game five times and won the MVP award in 1950 while gaining fame as the game's best bunter and obtaining the nickname "Scooter" for his running style. After his 2008 death, Richmond Hill's Smokey Oval Park was conamed Phil "Scooter" Rizzuto Park. (Left, LOC; below, QTC.)

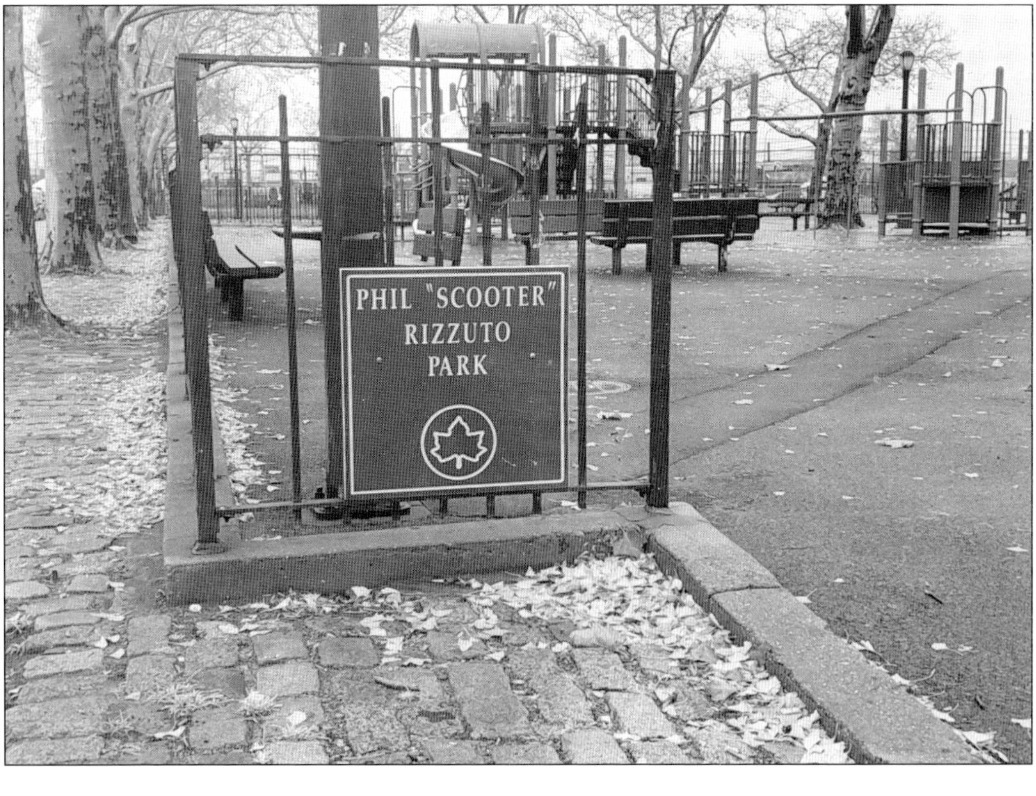

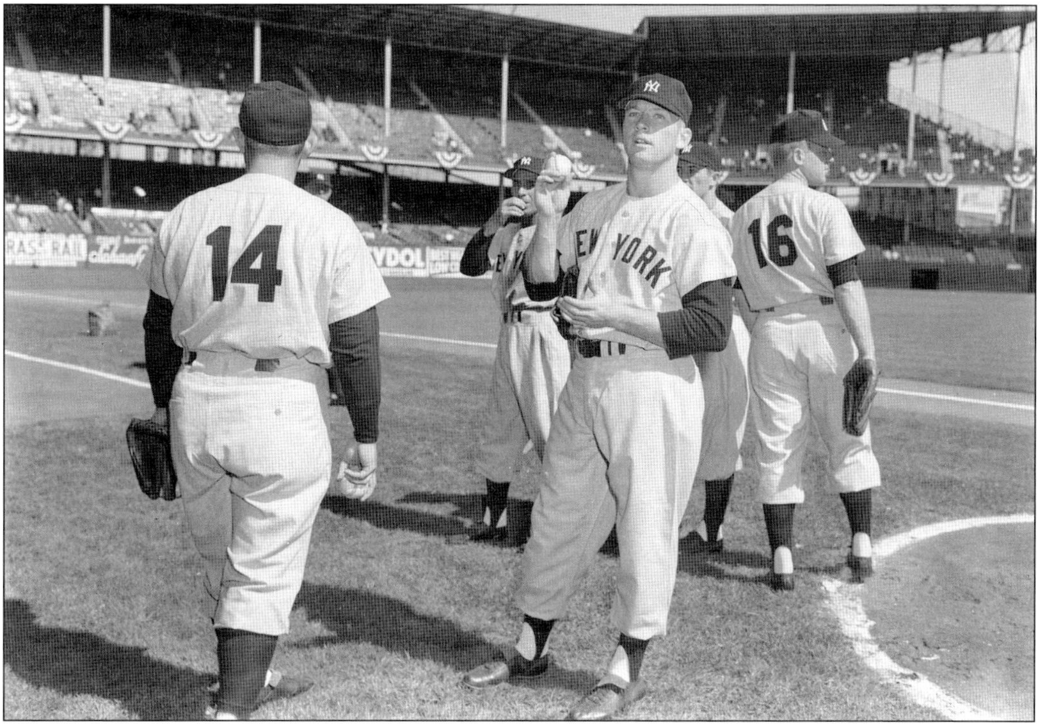


On September 20, 2021, New York City conamed the Astoria stretch of Forty-Third Street between Thirty-Fourth and Thirty-Fifth Avenues as Edwards Charles "Whitey" Ford Way. The legendary Yankees pitcher grew up on the block (31–53 Thirty-Fourth Street to be exact) with his mother, Edna, and his father, James, who worked for Con Ed and co-owned a bar. Born in 1928, he grew up playing first base with the Thirty-Fourth Avenue boys in Astoria sandlots and Manhattan's School of Aviation Trades before joining the Bronx Bombers in 1947 and receiving the nickname "Whitey" due to his blond hair. The southpaw pitcher was dominant for 16 years, winning six World Series championships and a Cy Young Award and making 10 MLB All-Star Games. (Above, NBHFM; below, official New York City Council photograph by Emil Cohen.)

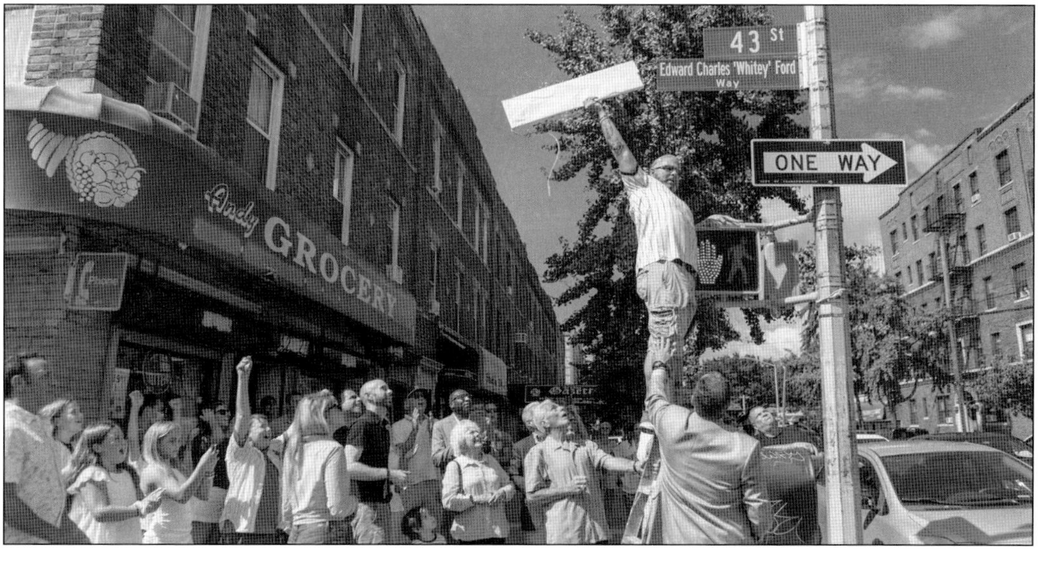

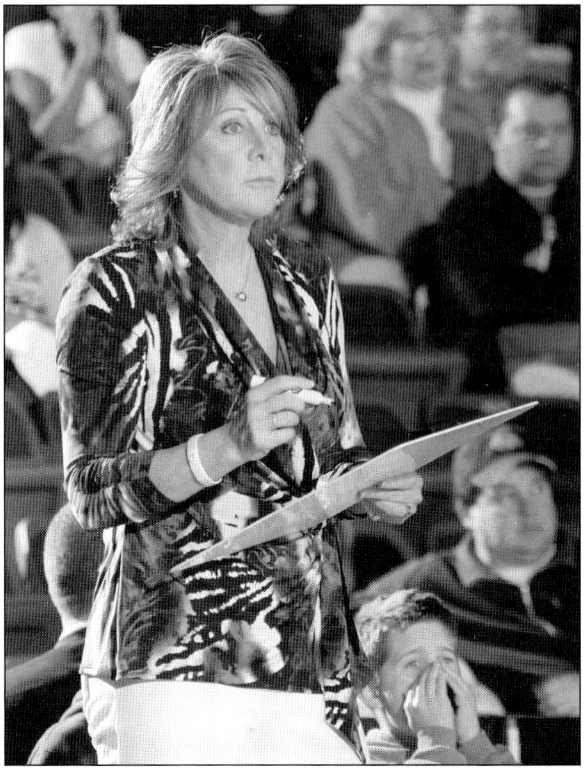

In 1986, Nancy Lieberman became the first woman to play on a professional men's basketball team when she suited up for the Springfield Fame of the United States Basketball League (USBL). It was just another day at the office for "Lady Magic," who spent her youth banging it out with males in Rockaway parks. Born in 1958, the five-foot, ten-inch point guard was a three-time All-American at Far Rockaway High School before winning two NCAA championships with Old Dominion University. Her pro career began with the Dallas Diamonds of the Women's Pro Basketball League (WBL) in 1980. She won the championship, took Rookie of the Year, and made the All-Pro team. However, the league disbanded the following year. She went on to play in three other female leagues and for the Harlem Globetrotters before being inducted into the Naismith Memorial Basketball Hall of Fame in 1996. (Both, WBHF.)

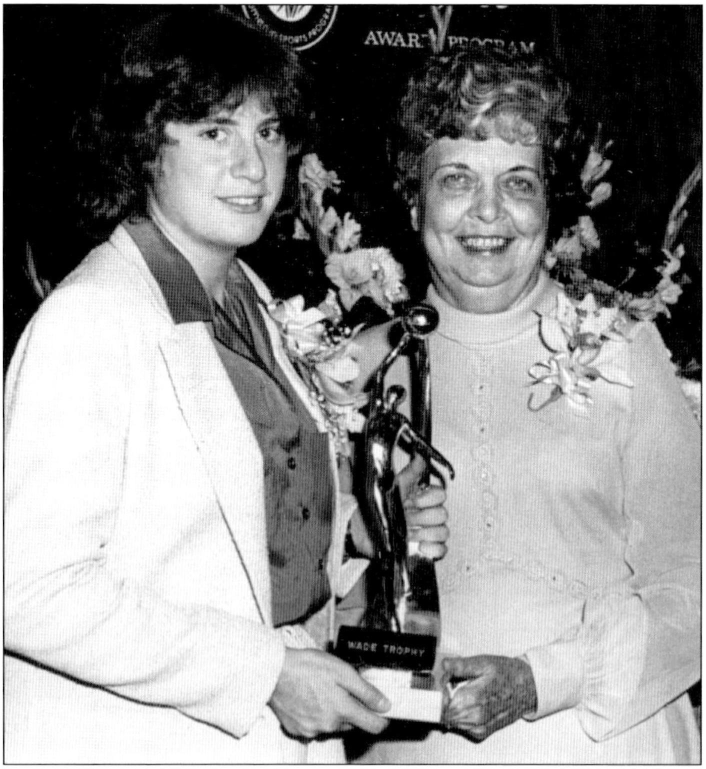

Bob Cousy was cut from Andrew Jackson High School's basketball team twice but led the varsity to a Queens championship as a senior. This led to a scholarship at College of the Holy Cross, where the late bloomer from St. Albans made the NCAA All-American team. He starred with the Boston Celtics from 1950 to 1963, leading the NBA in assists for eight straight years and winning six NBA championships. The Celtics retired his number 14 jersey in 1971. (LOC.)

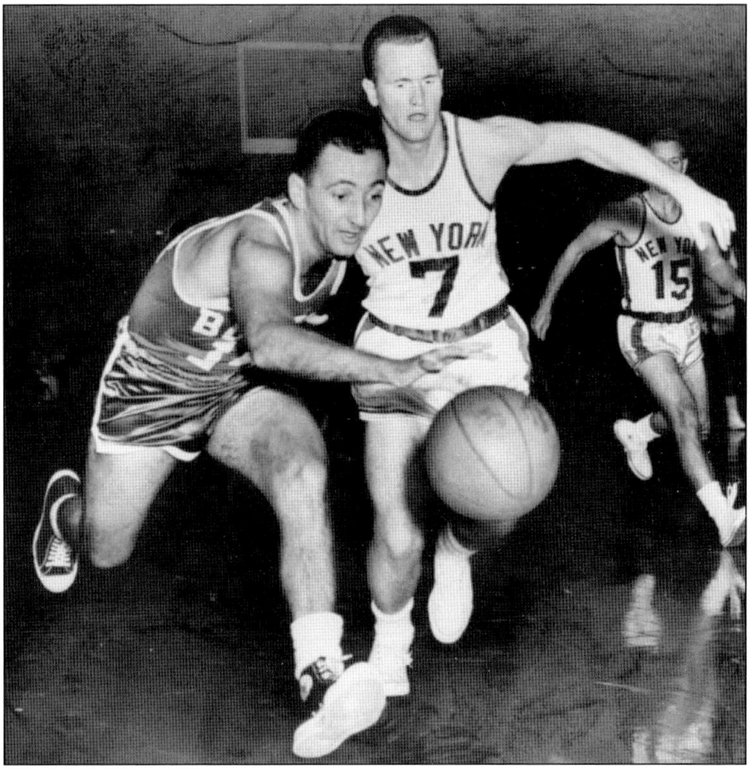


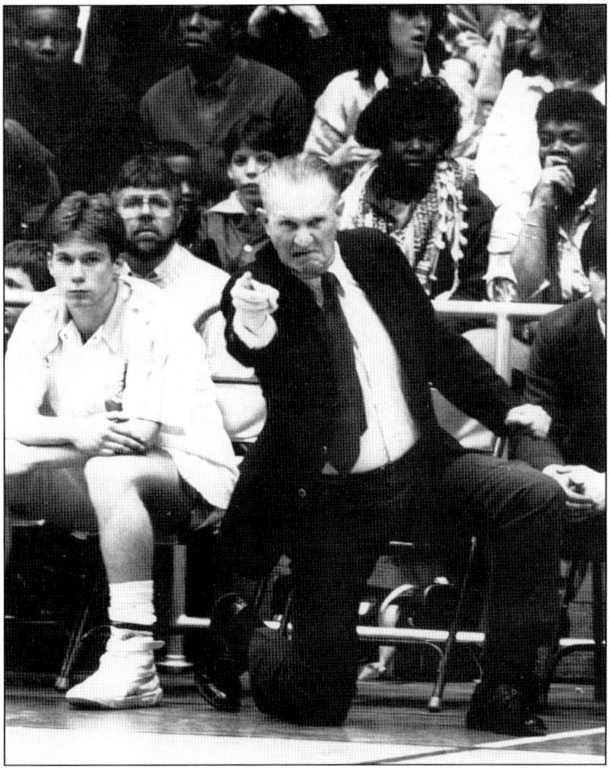

There are great coaches, legendary coaches, and Jack Curran, who has the most wins—2,680—in high school history. This record might last forever because he double dipped, running Archbishop Molloy High School's boys basketball and baseball programs for 55 years. Born in 1930, this New York Police Department cop's son played college hoops before returning to Molloy in 1958. Curran has 22 Catholic High School Athletic Association Coach of the Year Awards in basketball. In baseball, he won the honor 25 times. (AMHS.)

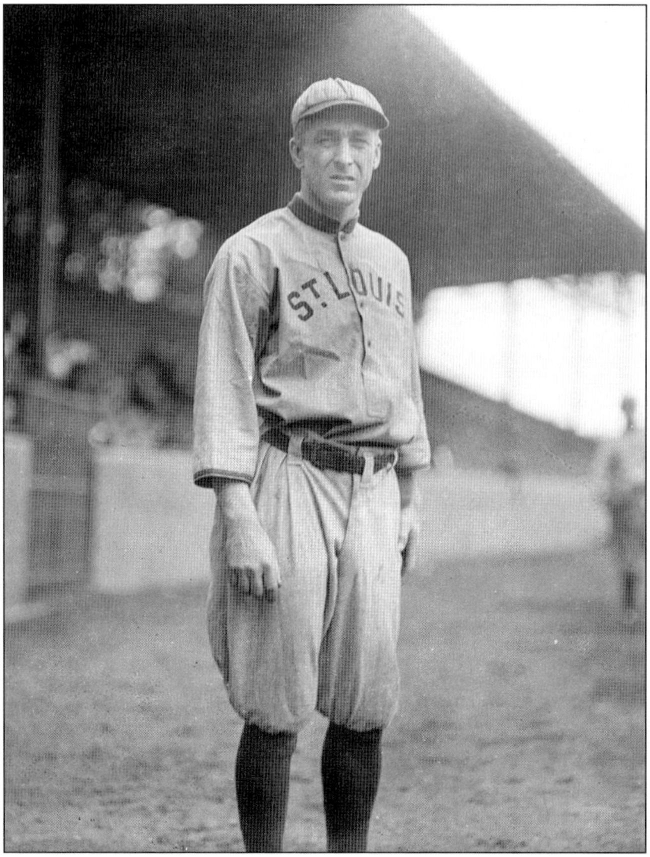


Despite their different backgrounds and talents, Branch Rickey and Jackie Robinson are forever bonded by their roles in breaking Major League Baseball's color barrier. After a short, modest career as a catcher with the St. Louis Browns and the New York Yankees, Rickey (left) got into sports management, helping design baseball's farm system. In 1942, the Ohio native became general manager and president of the Brooklyn Dodgers. Three years later, he signed Robinson (below in Birmingham, Alabama, in 1963), who had excelled in baseball, basketball, football, and track at the University of California, Los Angeles before playing with the Kansas City Monarchs in the Negro Baseball League. After a stint in the minors with the Montreal Royals, Robinson made his major-league debut as a Dodger on April 15, 1947. (Both, LOC.)

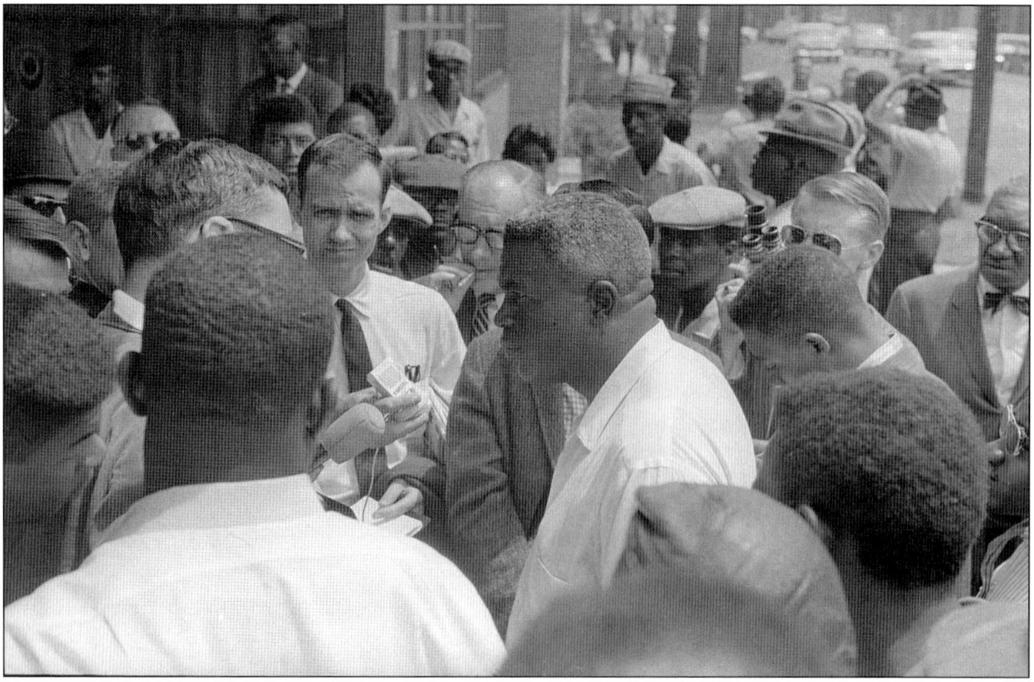

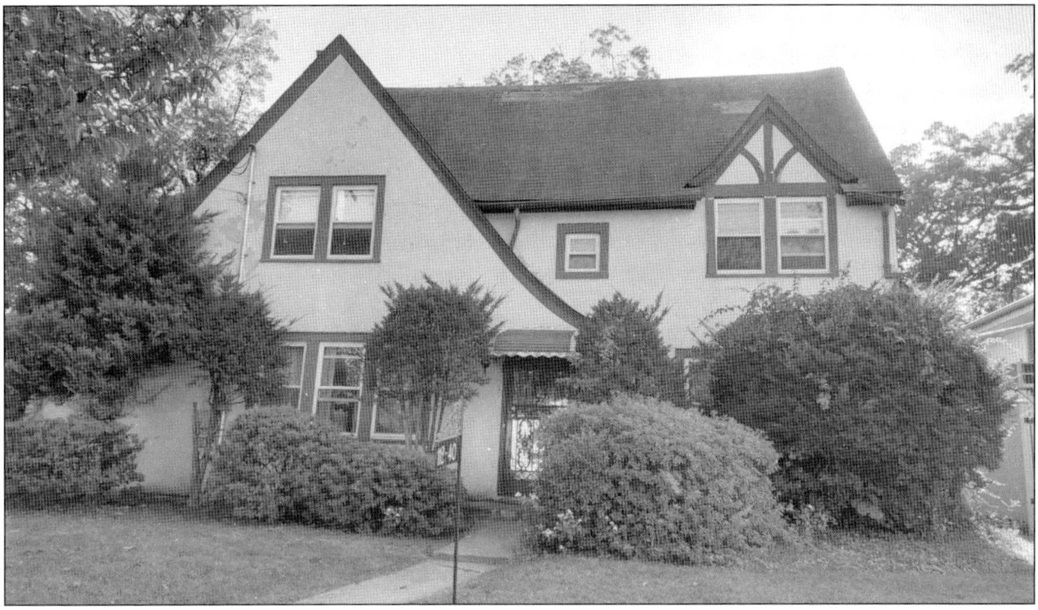

Though the Dodgers played their home games at Brooklyn's Ebbets Field, Rickey and Robinson lived in Queens. Robinson resided in Addisleigh Park, a small, landmarked portion of western St. Albans that was once called "Black Hollywood East" because so many prominent African Americans lived there. His house is shown above. Count Basie, Ella Fitzgerald, Lena Horne, and even boxer Joe Louis are among the famous residents of Addisleigh Park. Rickey, who was a very religious man, lived in Forest Hills Gardens, where he was an active member of the Church-in-the-Gardens. His dwelling is pictured below. (Both, QTC.)

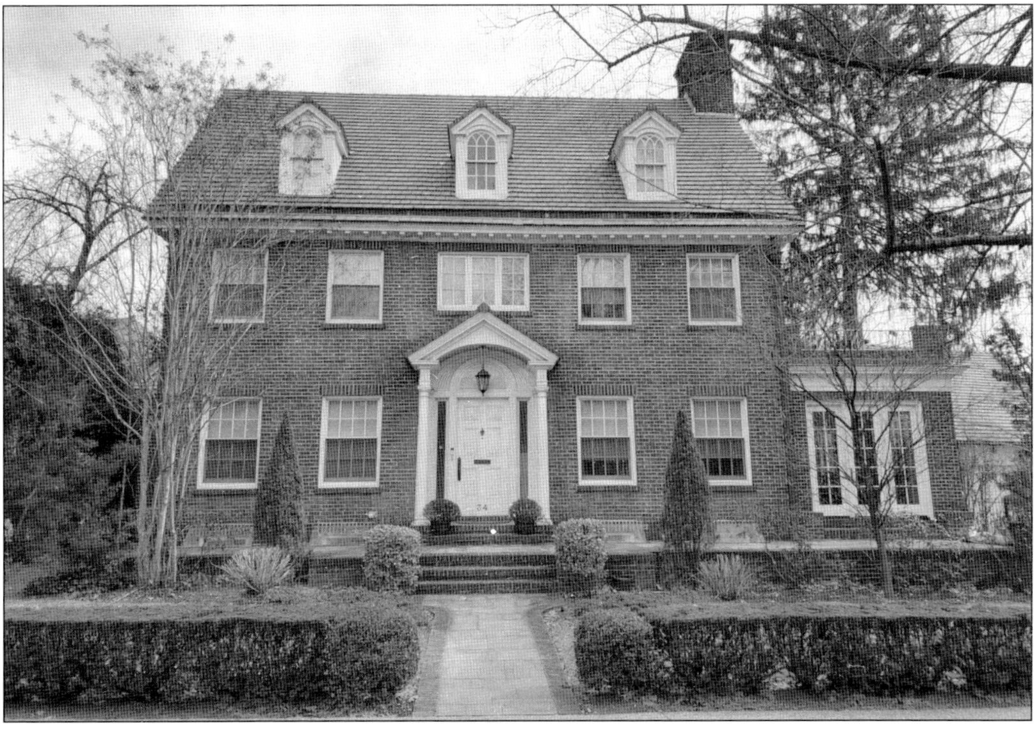

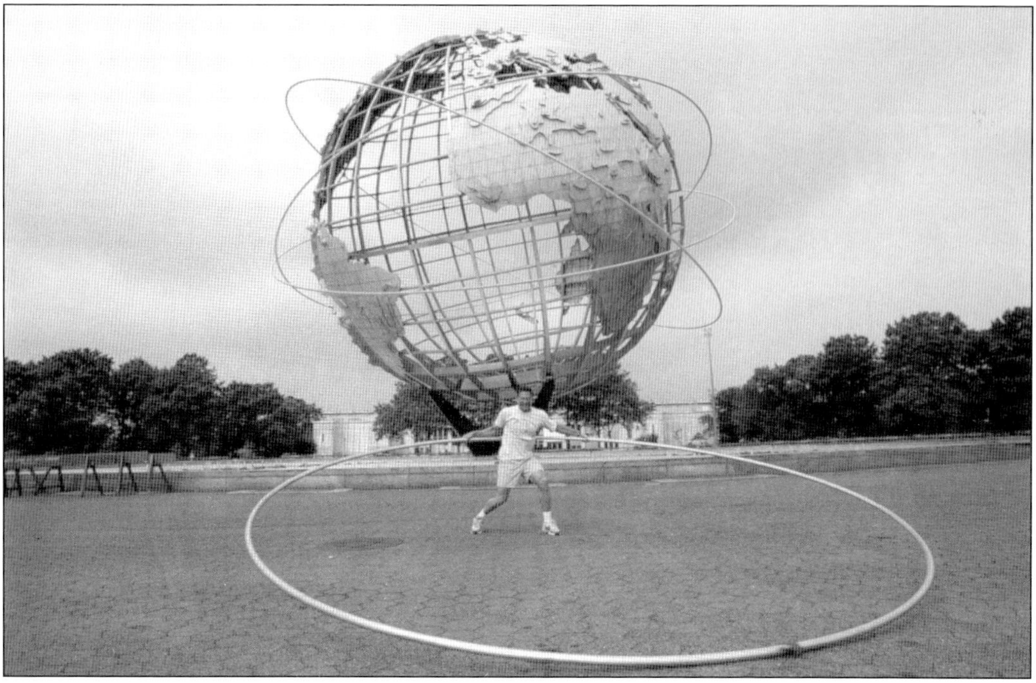

Ashrita Furman might hold the Guinness record for holding Guinness records! He has set more than 600 official records—of which more than 200 still stand. Born in 1954, he grew up in Kew Gardens Hills as Kevin before following Sri Chinmoy, a Hindu guru who founded a spiritual community in Jamaica Hills. Chinmoy gave Furman the name "Ashrita," which means "Protected by God." He also preached that everything is possible for those with the right mental state. So in 1979, Ashrita did 27,000 jumping jacks to set his first Guinness record. This led to such feats as balancing a pool cue while walking the longest distance ever at the Egyptian pyramids, bouncing the fastest mile ever on a kangaroo ball along the Great Wall of China, and Hula-Hooping the fastest mile ever at Ayers Rock in Australia. (Above, Alamy; below, Sri Chinmoy Centre.)

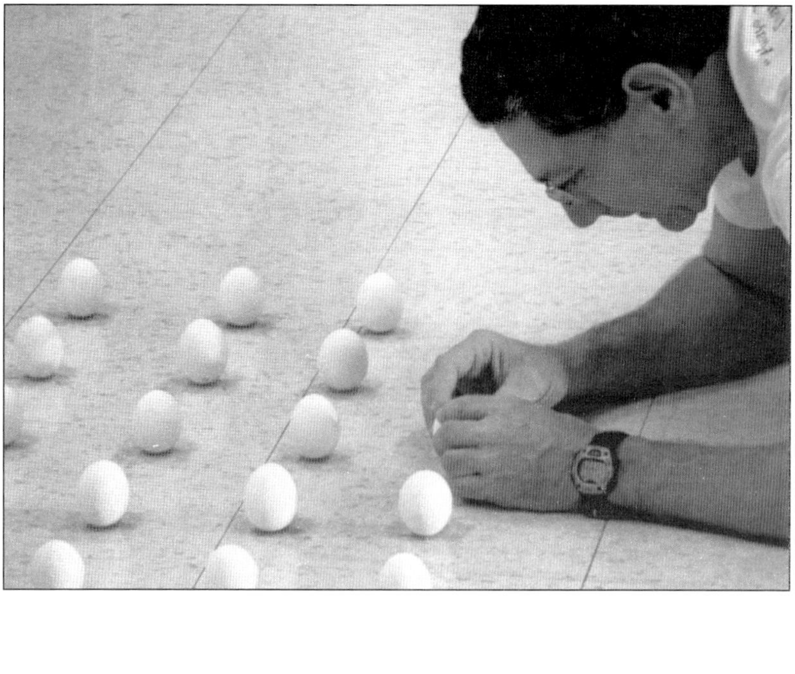

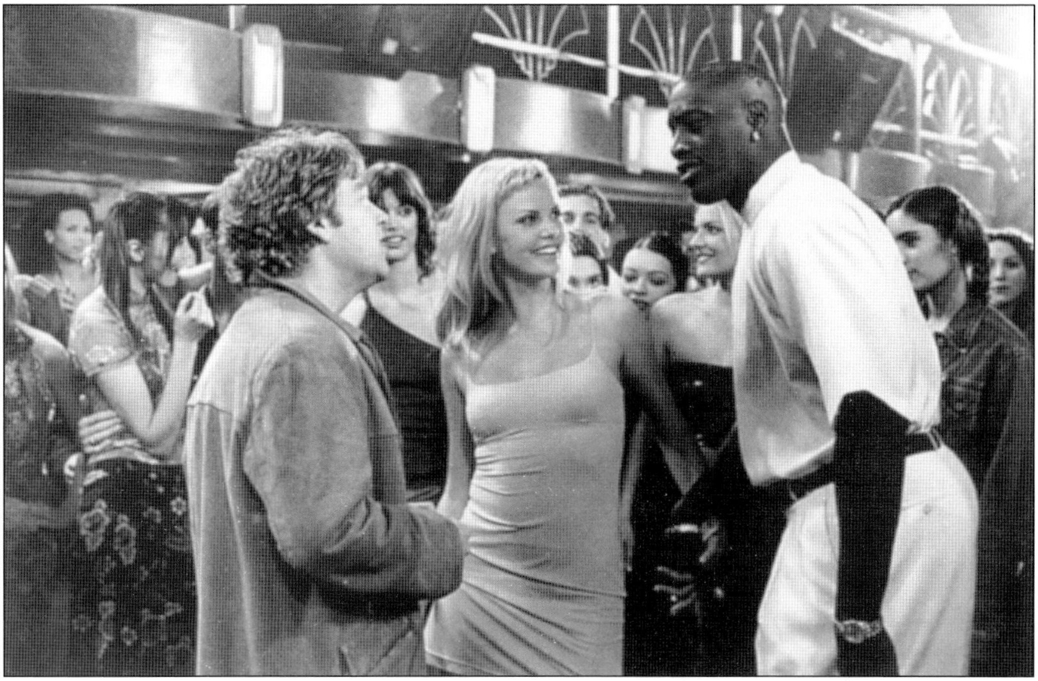

Not super talented, Anthony Mason's grittiness made him a quintessential New York Knick during the 1990s. The 1984 Springfield Gardens High School grad (seen here with Charlize Theron) would cut "Mase" in his hair before games. The Beastie Boys honored the barrel-chested baller with the rap line "I got my hair cut correct like Anthony Mason, Then I ride the IRT right up to Penn Station" in the song "B-Boys Makin' with the Freak Freak." His high school gym was named Mase Court in 2015. (Alamy.)

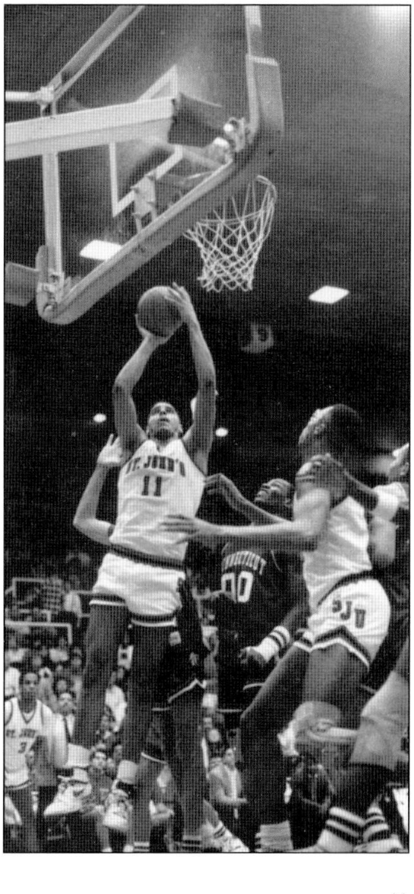

It is easy to criticize Jayson Williams for his off-court history, which includes bar fights and a prison sentence. But there is another side to the basketball player, who founded a Florida rehabilitation center in 2017. Born in 1968, the public housing kid starred at Christ the King Regional High School before heading to St. John's to play for Lou Carnesecca, a father figure. Drafted in 1990, he played professionally for nine seasons, leading the NBA in offensive rebounds in 1998. (SJU.)

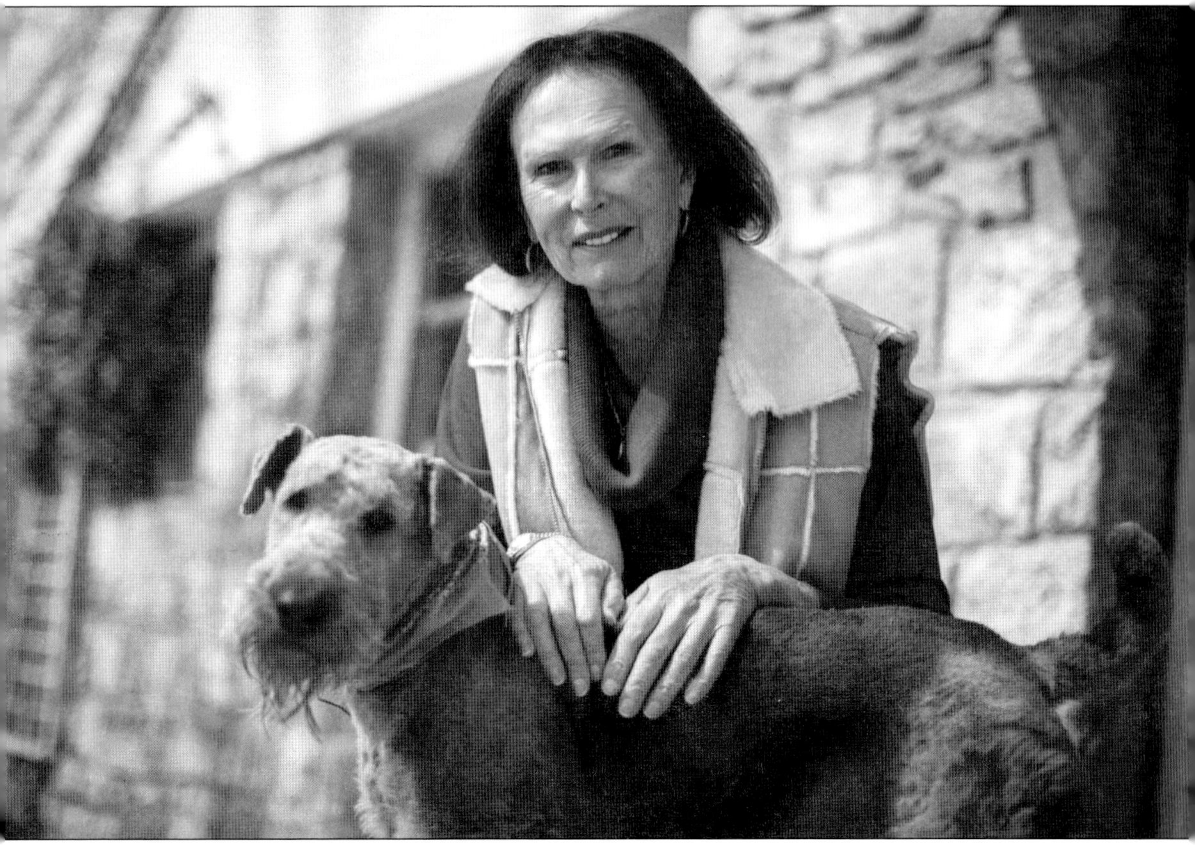

Born to two Russian immigrant doctors in 1934, Richard Raskind grew up in Forest Hills. He captained Yale University's tennis team before going to medical school. While practicing ophthalmology, he played in the US Open five times. In 1975, the 41-year-old underwent gender reassignment surgery to become Dr. Renée (French for "reborn") Richards. After winning a court case, she played professional women's tennis for four years before retiring—from tennis, not ophthalmology—at 47. (Alamy.)

# *Three*

# Business Boomers

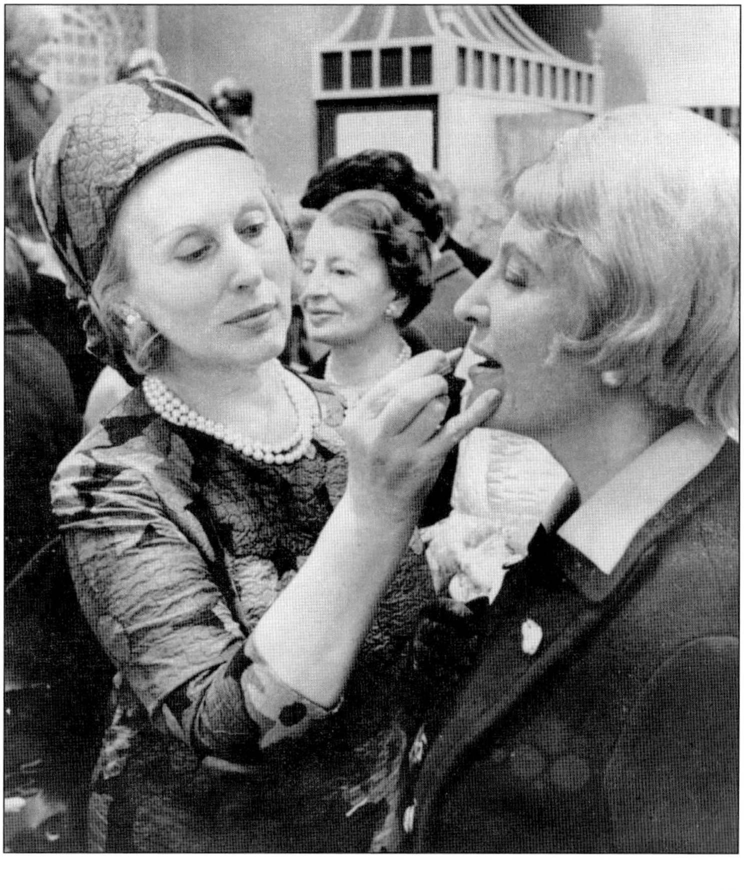

John Schotz fled war-torn Hungary for his sister's Corona house in 1914. The chemist started manufacturing perfumes, lotions, and creams (with names like Dr. Schotz's Viennese Cream) that his niece Josephine Esther Mentzer would then sell at Newtown High School. She married Joseph Lauder, and they founded Estée Lauder, using her nickname. They created products like Aramis for Men and Clinique. When the company went public in 1995, it was worth about $2 billion. (LOC.)

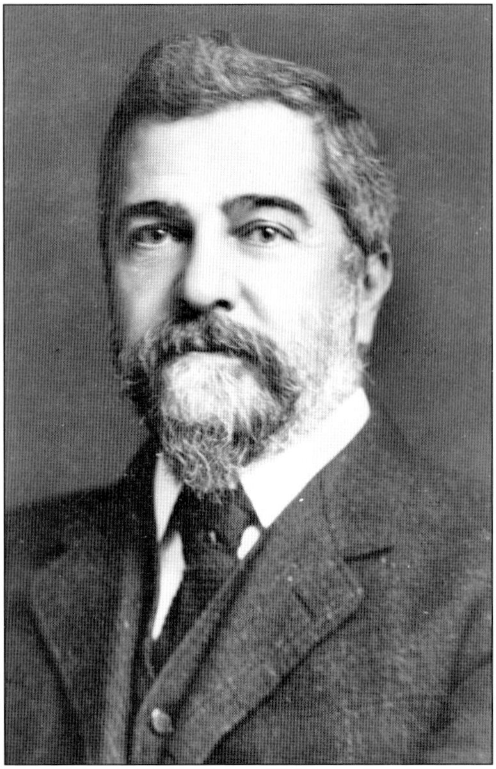

Louis Comfort Tiffany (1848–1933) created innovative ceramics, glassware, jewelry, lamps, leaded-glass windows, metalwork, mosaics, and textiles. Many clients, including Pres. Chester Arthur and Mark Twain, were wealthy individuals looking to adorn their mansions. But his best work came from Corona, where he and Arthur Nash founded the Stourbridge Glass Company in 1893. It disbanded during the Great Depression, and the factory is now PS 315, but some of his works are on display at the Neustadt Gallery at the Queens Museum about one mile away. (Left, LOC; below, The Neustadt Collection of Tiffany Glass.)

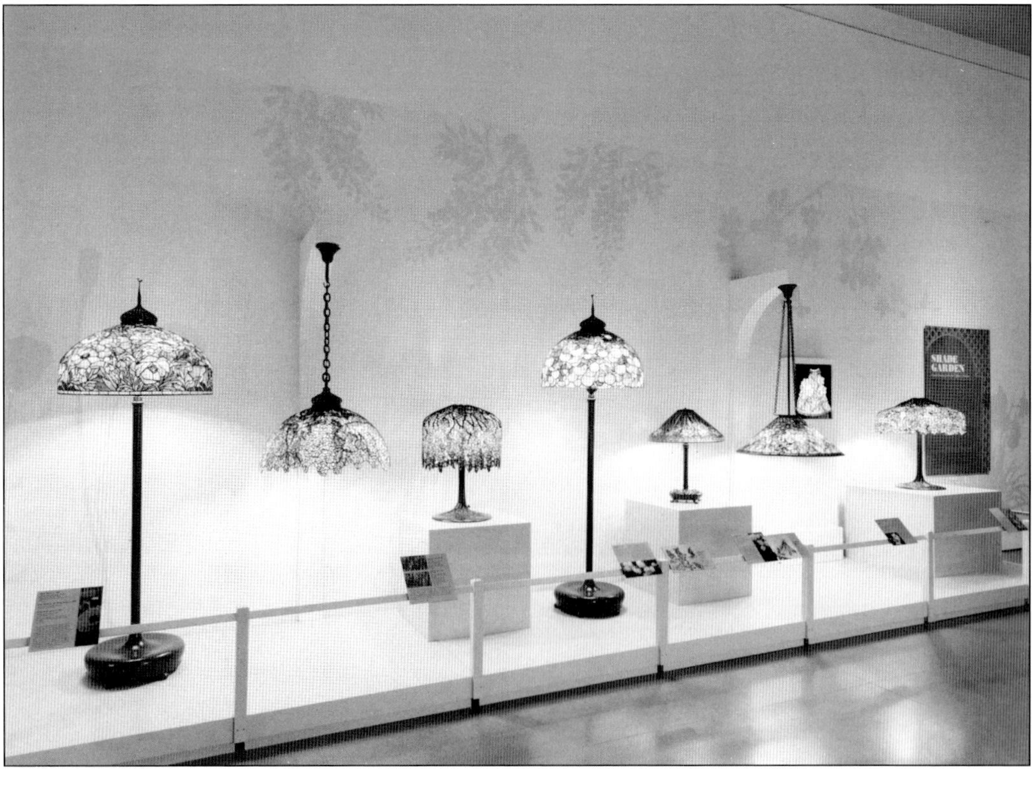

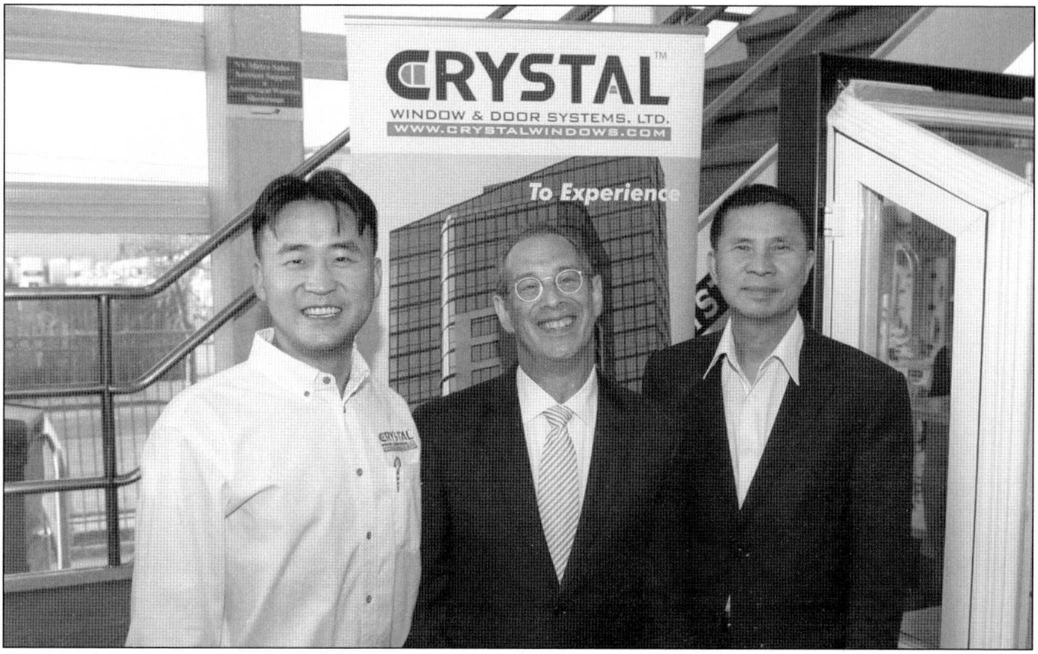


Thomas Chen (right) has not woken from his American Dream. After leaving rural Taiwan with little English and less money in 1982, he worked menial jobs and saved before launching a small manufacturing company in 1990. Crystal Window & Door Systems grew until it became a national leader with factories in California, Illinois, Missouri, and Pennsylvania and employed more than 400 people. Thomas and his son Steve (left) then got involved in philanthropy, supporting the Queens Museum, Queens Theatre, Queensborough Community College, and Flushing Town Hall, among other entities. In 2021, the Chens established a $1,105,000 endowment for Queens College's School of the Arts. They are pictured above with Queens Economic Development Corporation executive director Seth Bornstein. Below is Crystal's 215,000-square-foot main production facility in College Point. (Above, Dominick Totino; below, QTC.)

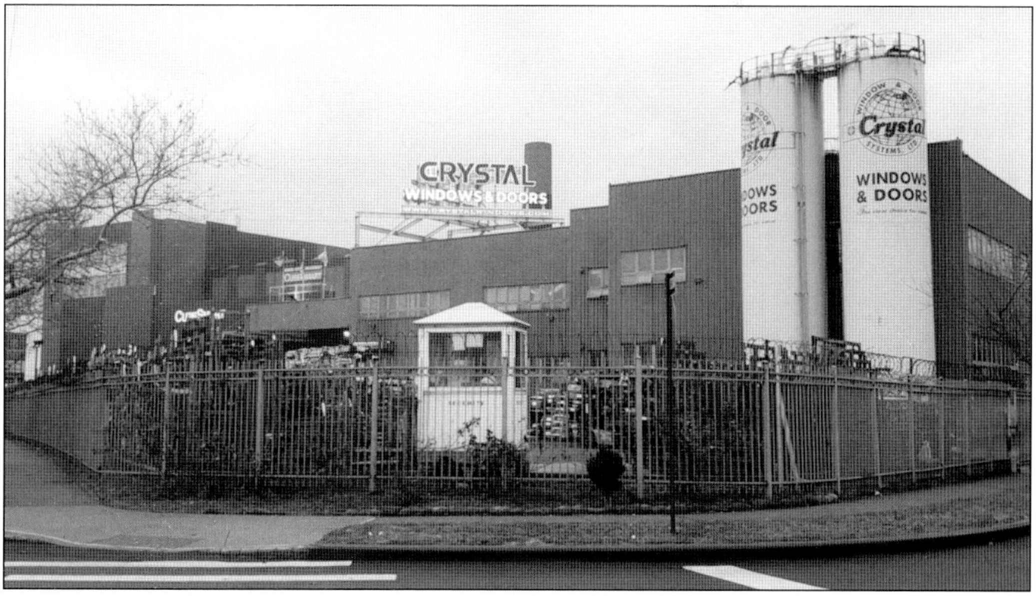

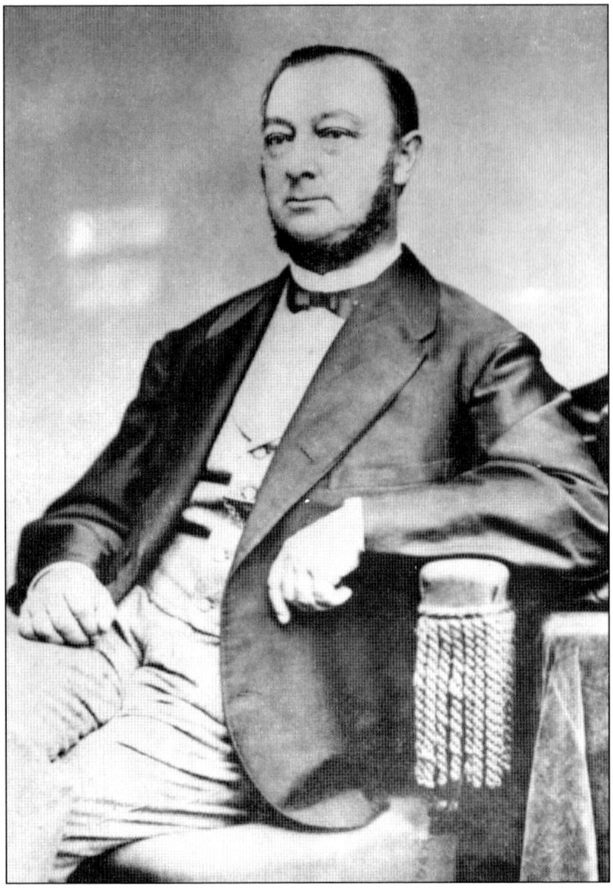

He put robber barons to shame. Born in Hamburg in 1818, Conrad Poppenhusen immigrated to Manhattan in 1842 after a fire destroyed his German hometown. In 1852, he got a license to use Charles Goodyear's process to vulcanize rubber and started manufacturing everything from caster wheels to brushes. Enterprise Rubber Works boomed, and Poppenhusen moved it to then-rural College Point. His mostly German employees followed him. Using his own money, Poppenhusen drained marshes, paved roads, planted trees, constructed a railroad station, installed sewers, and laid water and gas lines. He also created the Poppenhusen Institute, which housed the country's first free kindergarten (established in 1870), a vocational high school, courthouse, jail, bank, library, and ballroom. He retired in 1871, and unfortunately for him—and College Point—his sons squandered the fortune. He declared bankruptcy shortly before his 1883 death. (Both, QPL.)

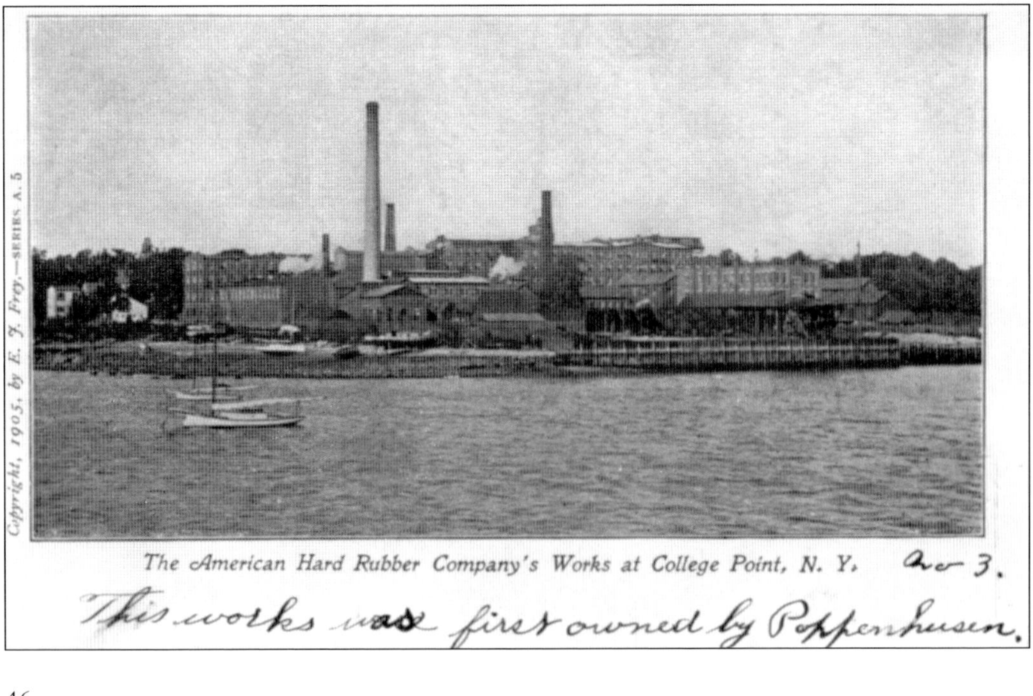

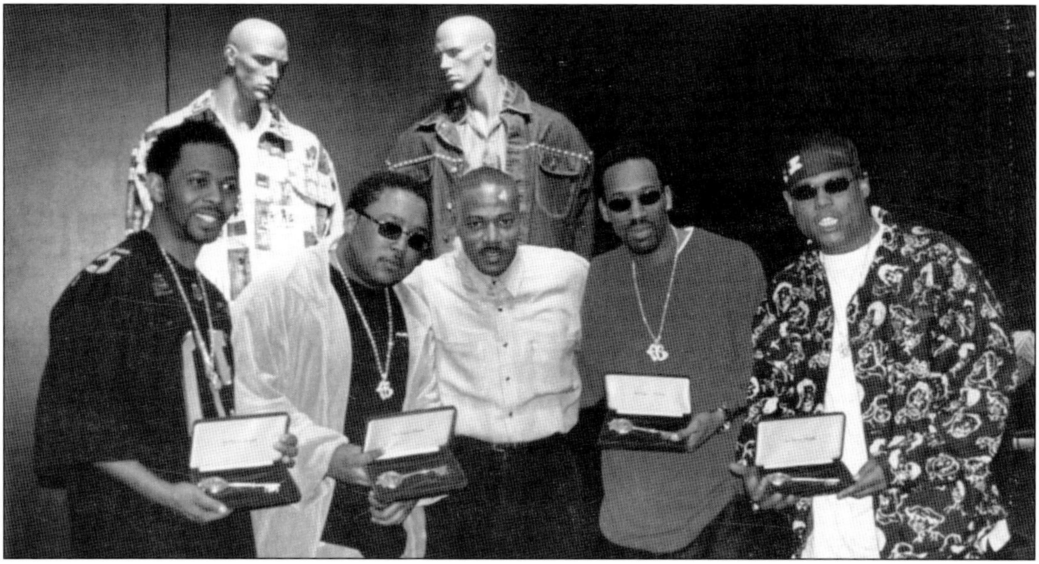

Daymond John launched FUBU (For Us, By Us) from his mother's Hollis garage in 1992. The 20-something John made hats, jerseys, and shirts. The label exploded into a $6-plus-billion empire that defines modern urban style. John, in the middle of this Queens Public Library photograph, currently owns more than 900 companies. The child of West Indian immigrants is also a household name due to his participation as a judge on the Emmy-winning ABC television program *Shark Tank*. (QPL.)

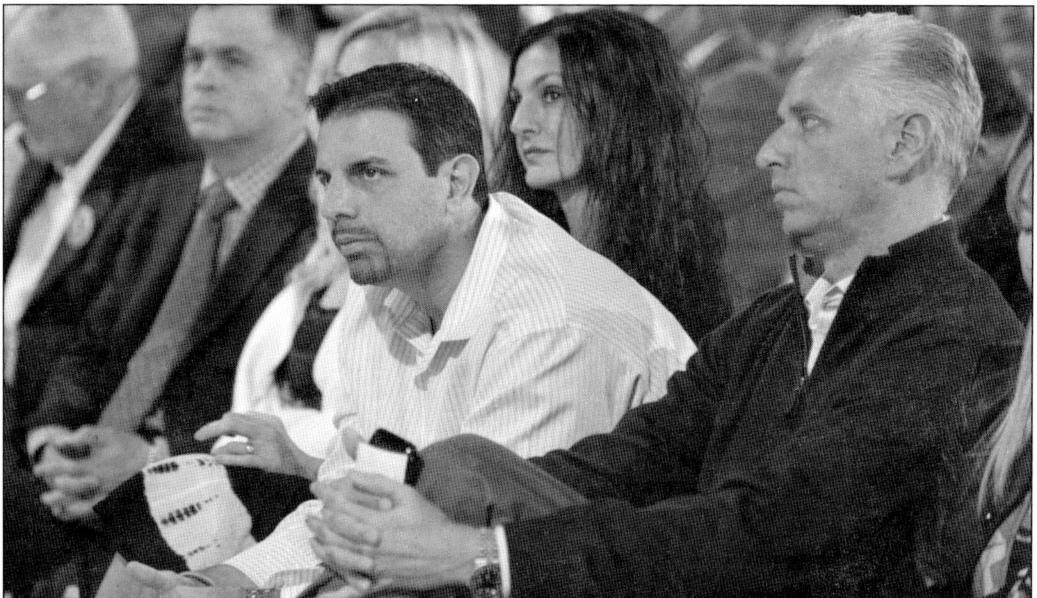

In 1999, Middle Village native Mike Repole (center, white shirt) and J. Darius Bikoff founded Energy Brands with Smartwater and Vitaminwater as their big products. They sold the company to Coca-Cola for $4.1 billion in 2007. Two years later, Repole helped Pirate Brands quadruple sales in less than five years before B&G Foods bought it for almost $200 million in 2013. Next up was BodyArmor Sports Drink, which Repole helped grow before Coca-Cola purchased it for $5.6 billion in 2021. (Alamy.)

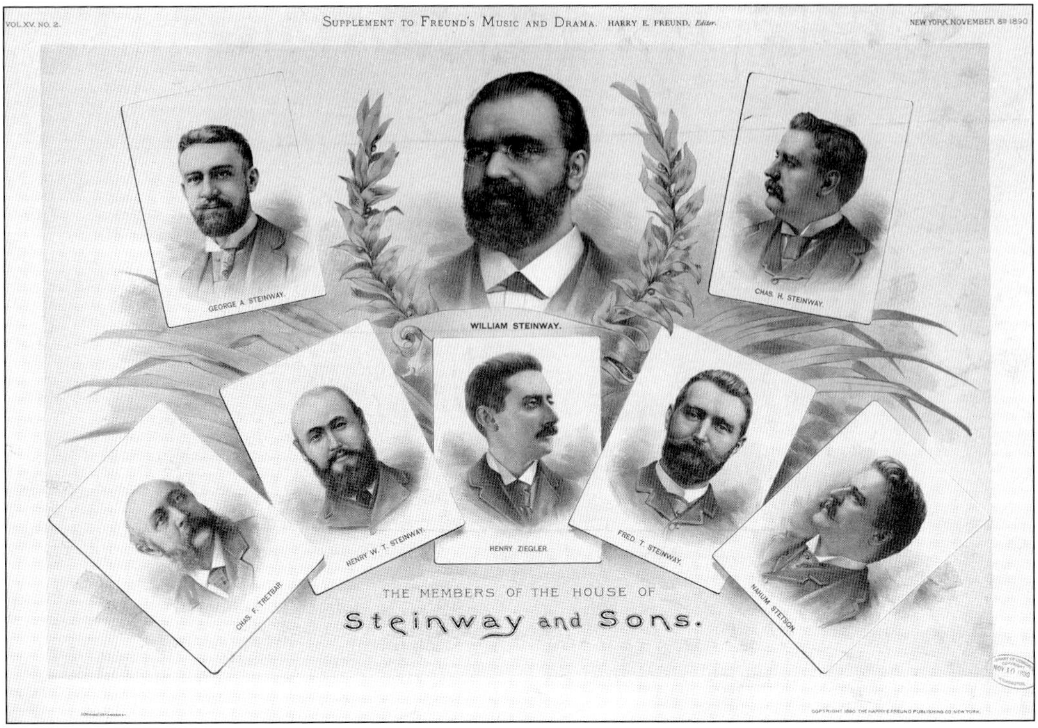


He was born Wilhelm Steinweg in Braunschweig, Germany, in 1835, but he achieved musical and manufacturing immortality as William Steinway in Astoria. In 1850, his father, Heinrich Engelhard Steinweg, who made pianos at home, moved the family to Manhattan. Three years later, he founded Steinway & Sons to make pianos. William, the fourth son, was the marketing genius of the family. He obtained dozens of patents, including one for cross-stringing grand pianos, which changed the tone, and took a gold medal at the 1855 American Institute Fair and another at the International Exposition of 1867 in Paris for his work. As his product sizzled, he constructed Steinway Hall on East Fourteenth Street in Manhattan. Part performance venue, part showroom, Charles Dickens did a reading there in 1867. (Both, LOC.)

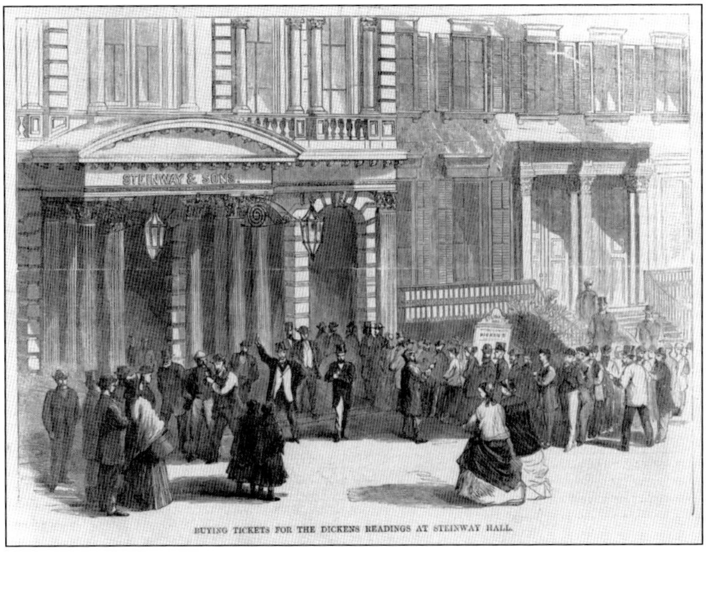

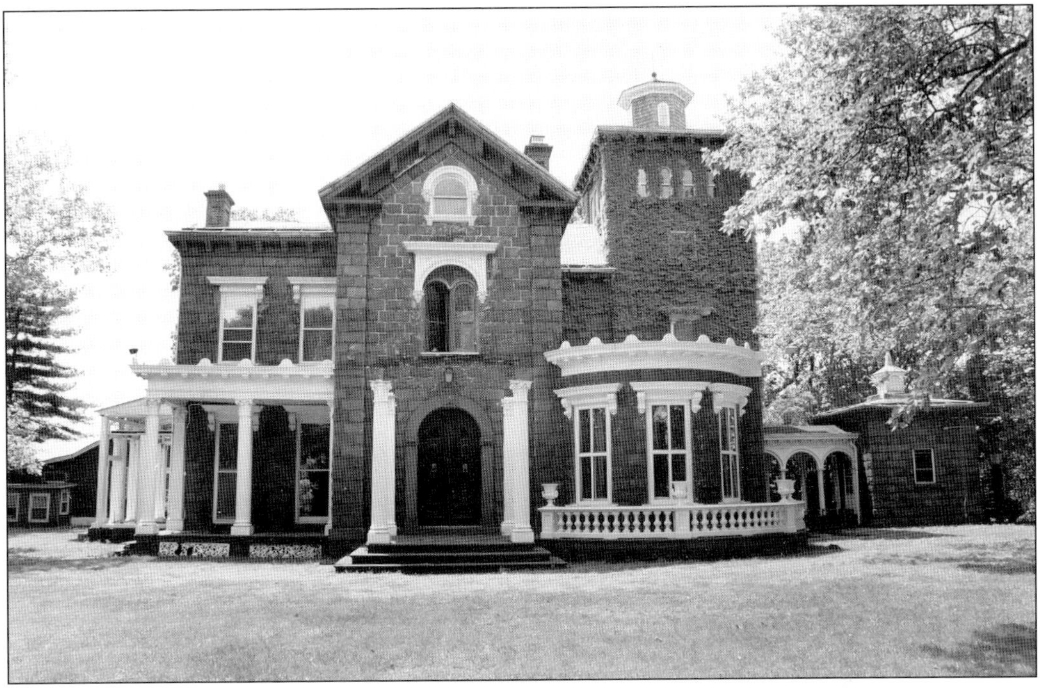

In 1870, William Steinway bought a 27-room, granite-and-bluestone Italianate villa and 440 acres in northern Astoria, which was largely salt meadows at the time. He built the Steinway Piano Factory, a sawmill, and a foundry where he could cast his own piano frames and saw lumber. He also established a de facto corporate town, Steinway Village, nearby. He designed redbrick houses, planted shade trees, and donated land for a church, public school, firehouse, and post office. The factory is still operating in the same place—it made its 600,000th piano in 2015—but the Steinway family sold the company in 1972. (Above, GAHS; right, LOC.)

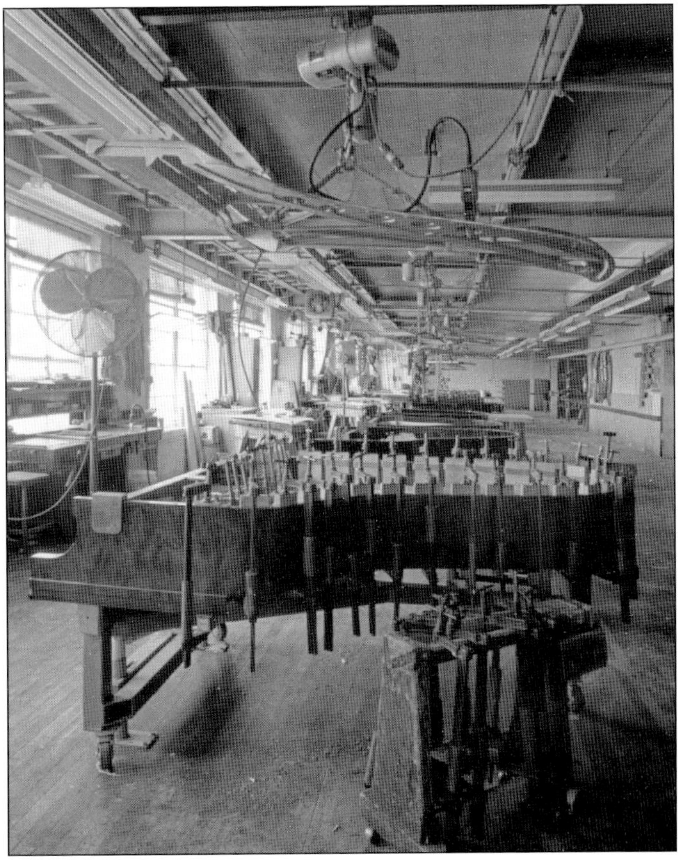

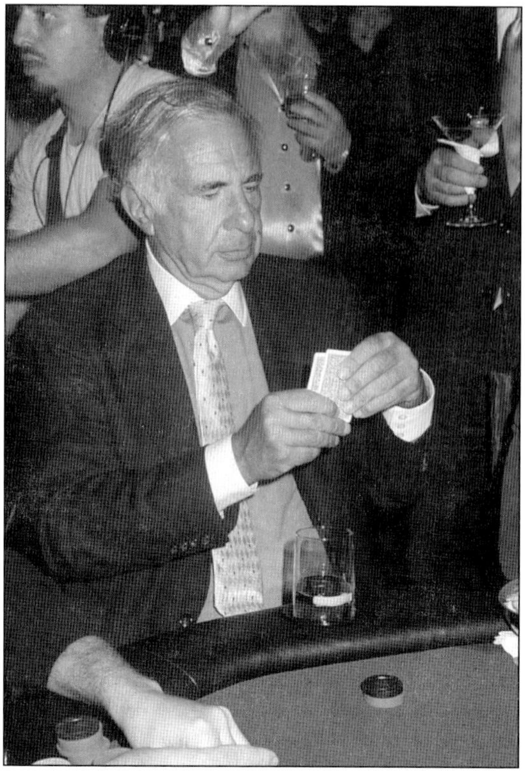

Carl Icahn's traditional, middle-class childhood preceded an untraditional, high-finance adulthood on the Forbes 400 with an estimated wealth of $17-$22 billion. Born to two teachers in 1936, the Far Rockaway native allegedly paid his room and board at Princeton University through poker winnings. In 1961, he became a stockbroker, and he later founded companies and invested in everything from oil to telecommunications with exceptional savvy. In 2010, he pledged to give away half of his fortune. (Alamy.)

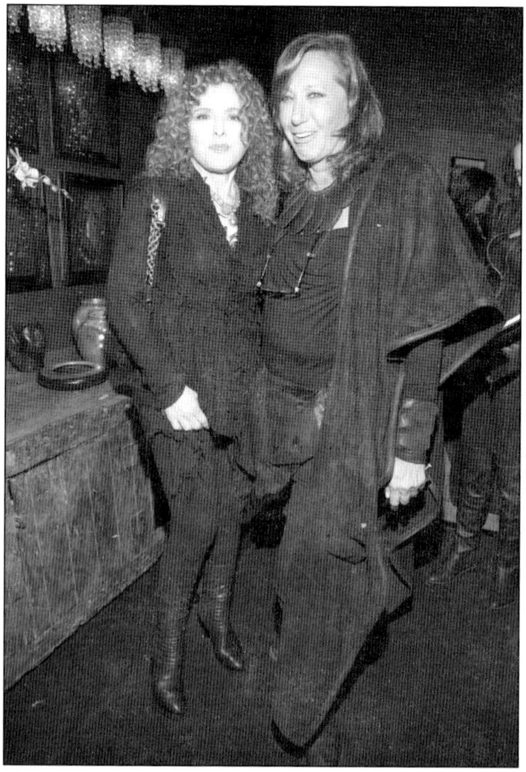

Donna Faske (right) grew up in a two-bedroom apartment in Kew Gardens. Her mother, Helen, was a saleswoman in the Garment District, where her father, Gabby, sold custom suits. In the 1960s, she left Parsons School of Design to work for fashion maven Anne Klein. After marrying Mark Karan, she launched Donna Karan New York in 1985. The clothing company was so successful that people called her "The Queen of Seventh Avenue." In this photograph, she is with Queens native Bernadette Peters (left), who is shown in chapter four. (Alamy.)

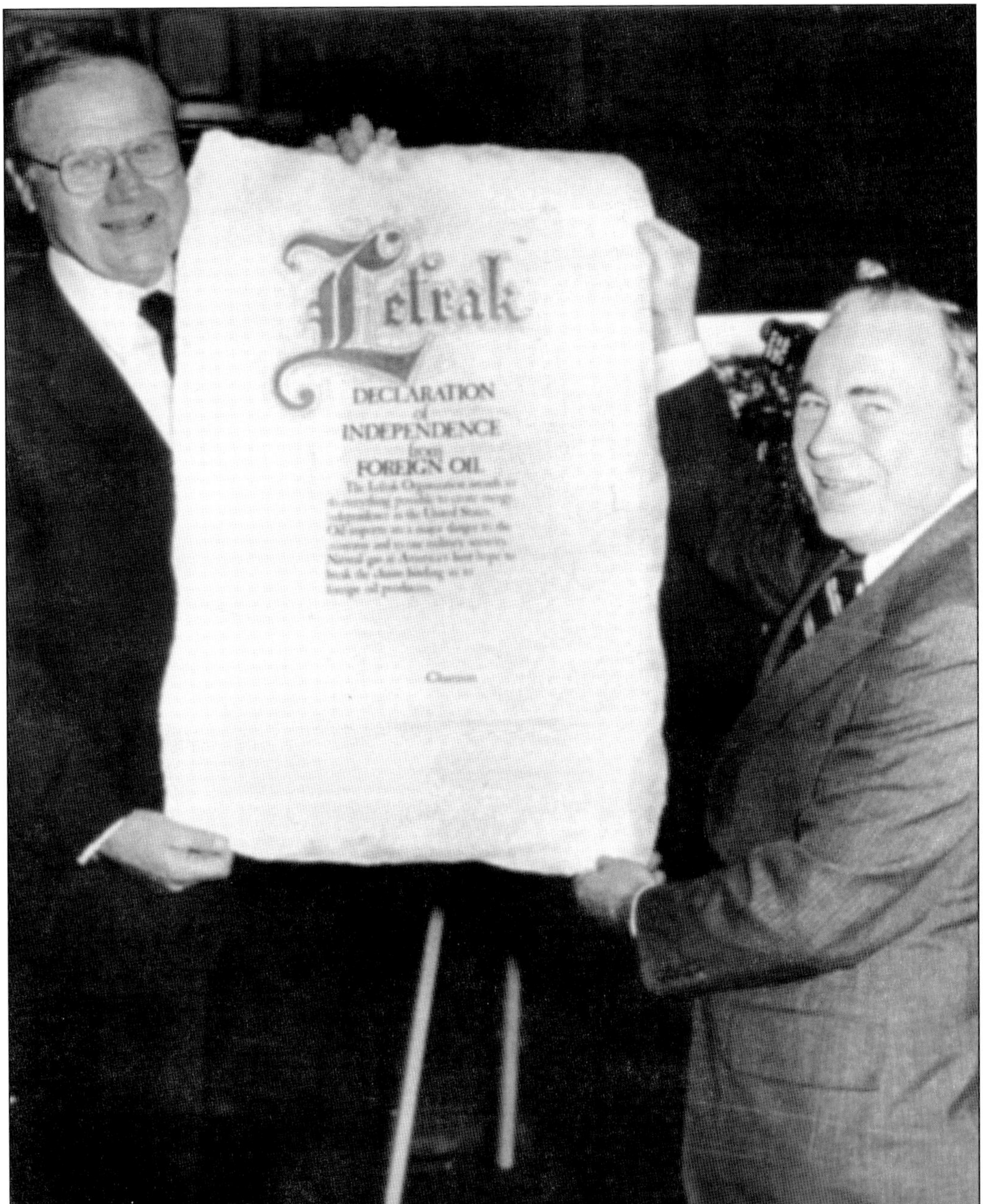


As a fourth-generation developer whose great-grandfather built houses in France in the 1800s, Sam LeFrak (left, with Brooklyn Union Gas CEO Eugene Luntey) joked that cement poured through his veins. Well, he certainly poured a lot of cement for his megaprojects, such as Manhattan's Battery Park City and Newport in Jersey City. One major one, LeFrak City, lies over 40 acres in Rego Park. Completed in 1971, the complex has 20 seventeen-story buildings with more than 4,600 apartments and an outdoor pool, a great lawn, basketball courts, a library branch, and a security force. (Michael Perlman and Jeff Gotlieb.)

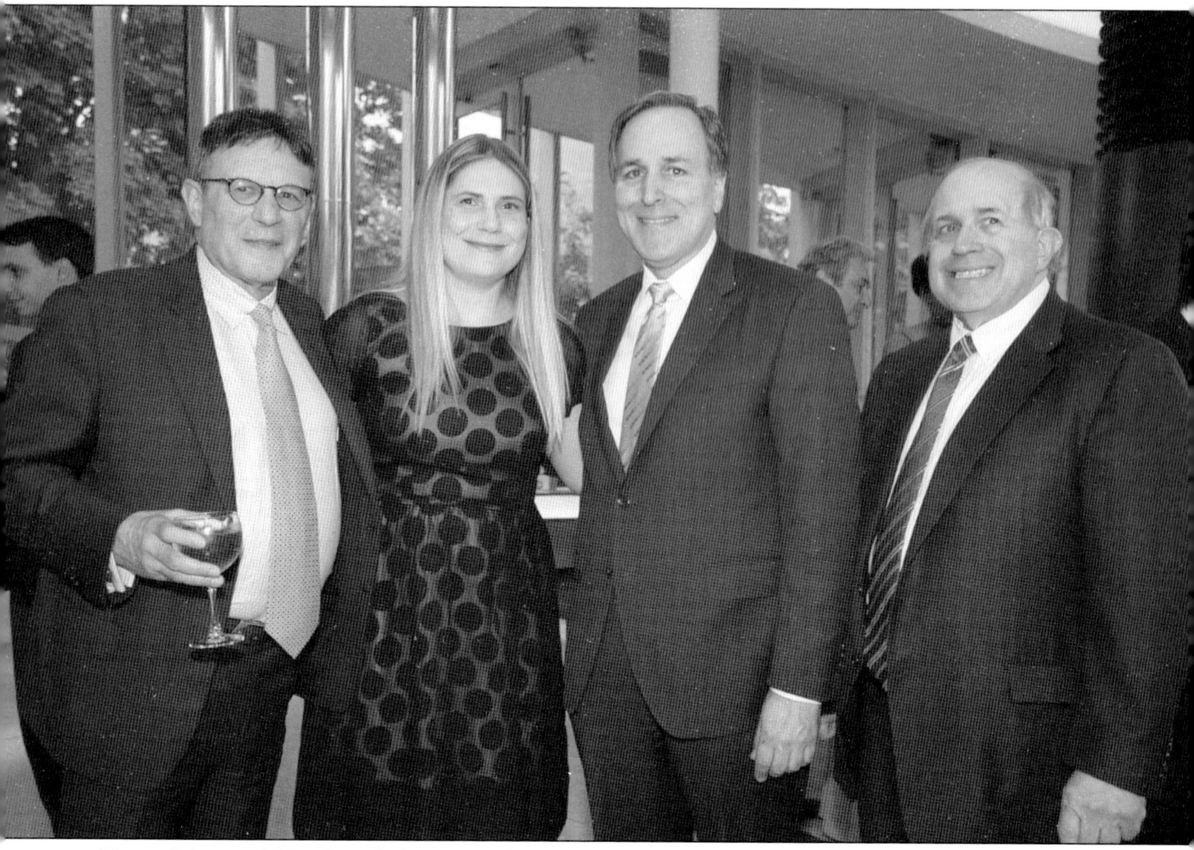

Twins Max and Ken Kupferberg were born to Romanian immigrants in Flushing in 1919. They graduated from Flushing High School in 1937 and were in the first-ever class at Queens College, where they majored in physics. In 1946, they founded electronic equipment manufacturer Kepco Inc. with brothers Jesse and Jack. The Flushing company grew into a multimillion-dollar industry leader that is involved in research and development as well as manufacturing and sales. The brothers' philanthropy grew simultaneously. Over the years, the Kupferberg Foundation has donated several million dollars to more than 40 borough organizations, including Flushing Hospital Medical Center, Queens Botanical Garden, and the New York Hall of Science. Queens College has the Selma and Max Kupferberg Center for the Visual and Performing Arts, while the Harriet and Kenneth Kupferberg Holocaust Center is at Queensborough Community College, City University of New York. The next generation (from left to right, Seth, Martin, and Mark) are with Queens Theatre executive director Taryn Sacramone in this photograph. (Dominick Totino.)

No entity contributed to the borough's rural-to-urban conversion as much as the Cord Meyer Company. In 1893, German immigrant Cord Meyer (right) purchased land from Samuel Lord of Lord & Taylor in the farming community of Newtown. He formed a partnership with his brothers Christian and John, and they laid out streets, set up sewers, and constructed houses. After planting elm trees, they renamed the community Elmhurst. In the early 1900s, the brothers moved east, buying farms in Whitepot and building a variety of residential dwellings. They changed the area's name to Forest Hills. The Cord Meyer Company remained family-owned until 2003, when brothers Charles and George, great-grandsons of the founder, ceded control to Sal Panico and Anthony Colletti. (Both, GAHS.)

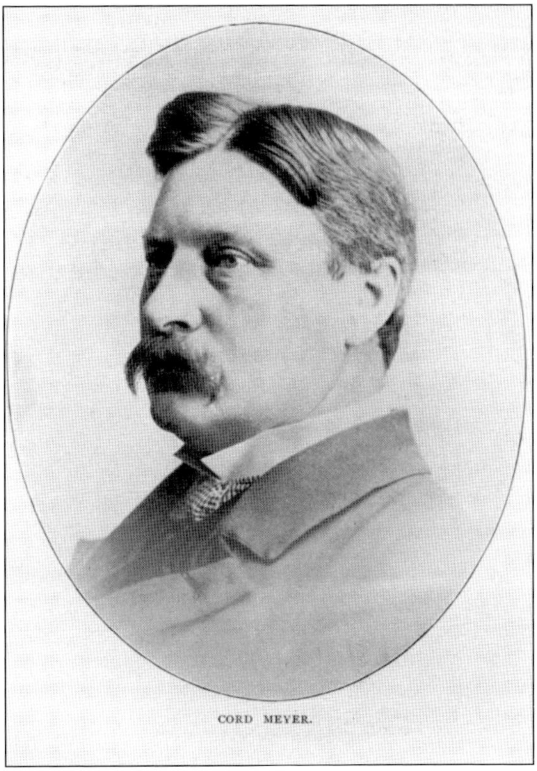


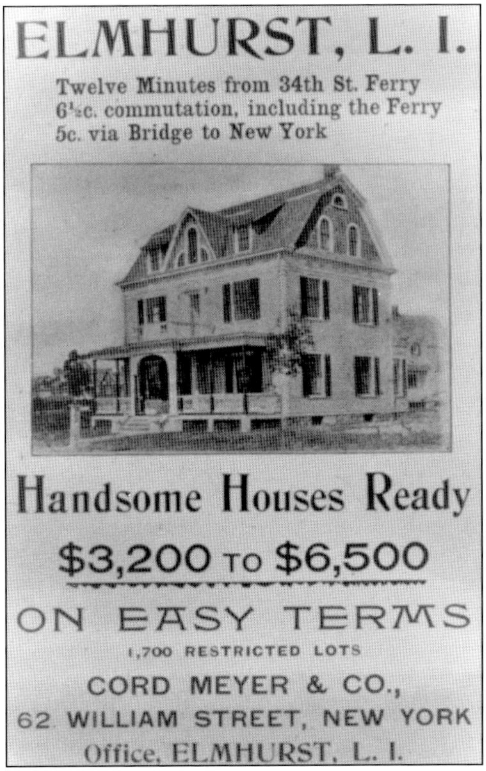

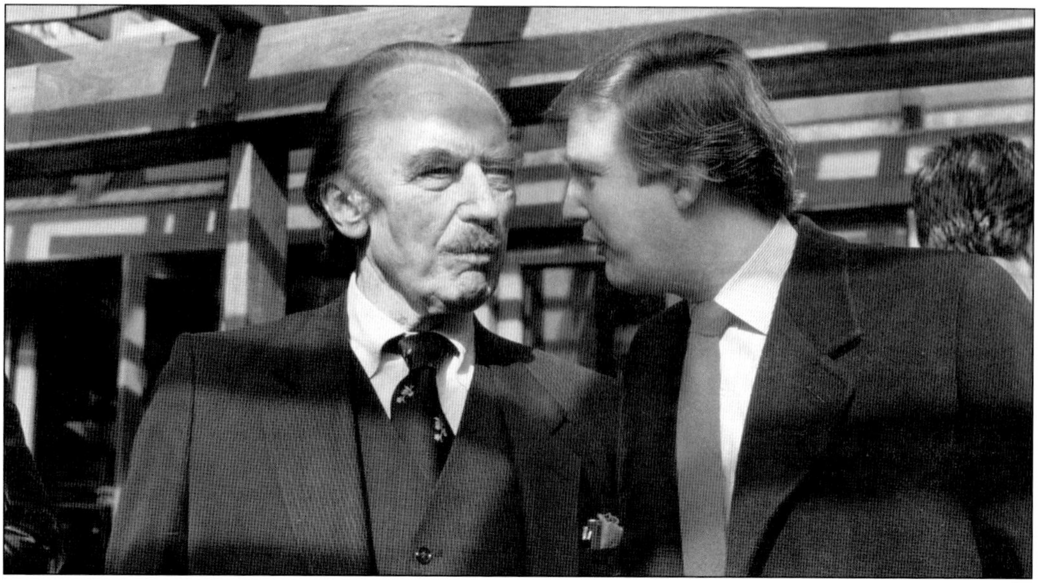

Friedrich Christ Trump Sr. was a barber in Kallstadt, Germany, who made a small fortune running a restaurant (and probably a brothel) for prospectors during the Klondike Gold Rush in Yukon Territory in the late 1890s. Due to issues with the German government, he stayed in the United States, and Frederick Christ Trump Jr. (above) was born in 1905. Growing up in Woodhaven, Fred Jr. was a workaholic, founding a construction company at the age of 15. Because he was a minor, he partnered with his mother, Elizabeth, and called the entity E. Trump & Son. He started with garages, and within two years of graduating from Richmond Hill High School, he built his first house. He never stopped, creating roughly 2,700 middle-class units, mostly in Brooklyn, Queens, and Staten Island. As per the marker below, he also established one of the country's first supermarkets, Trump Market, in Woodhaven during the Great Depression. (Above, LOC; below, QTC.)

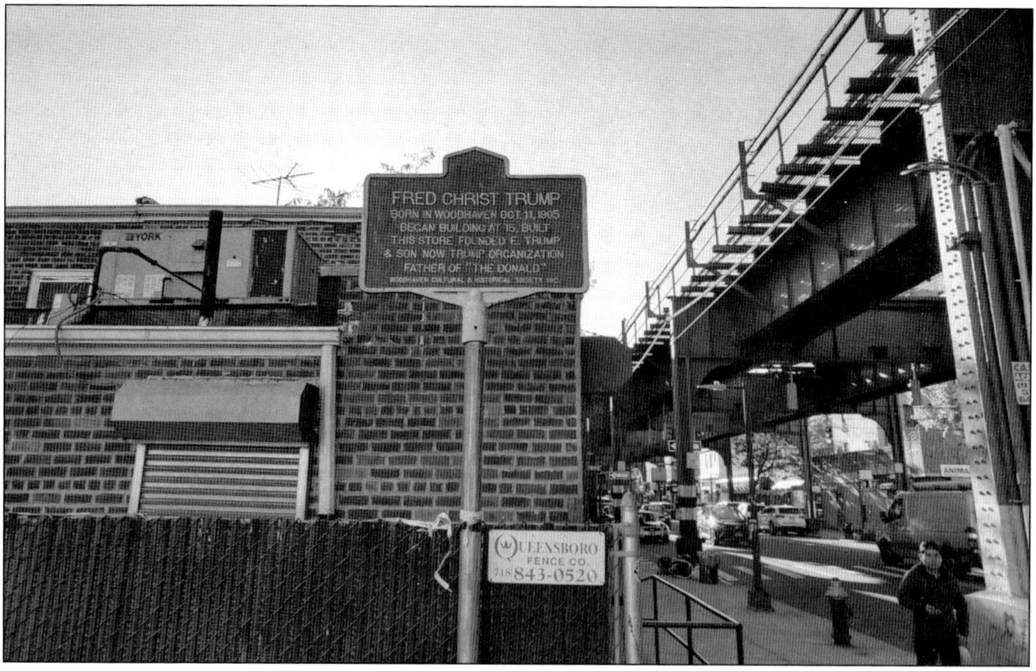

Fred Jr. married Scottish immigrant Mary Anne MacLeod in 1936, and they settled in Jamaica Estates, where they raised five children. Donald was born in 1946. After graduating from The Wharton School of the University of Pennsylvania in 1968, Donald took the family business to Manhattan and beyond, building luxury apartments, skyscrapers, casinos, resorts, and golf courses. He also licensed his name to other ventures and coproduced and hosted the NBC reality show *The Apprentice* from 2004 to 2017. Having to deal with government officials during projects, he had a disdain for them. He flirted with elected office with various political parties before entering the 2016 presidential campaign as a Republican, winning the nomination and the general election on November 8, 2016. From January 20, 2017, to January 20, 2021, he served as the country's 45th president. (Right, LOC; below, QTC.)

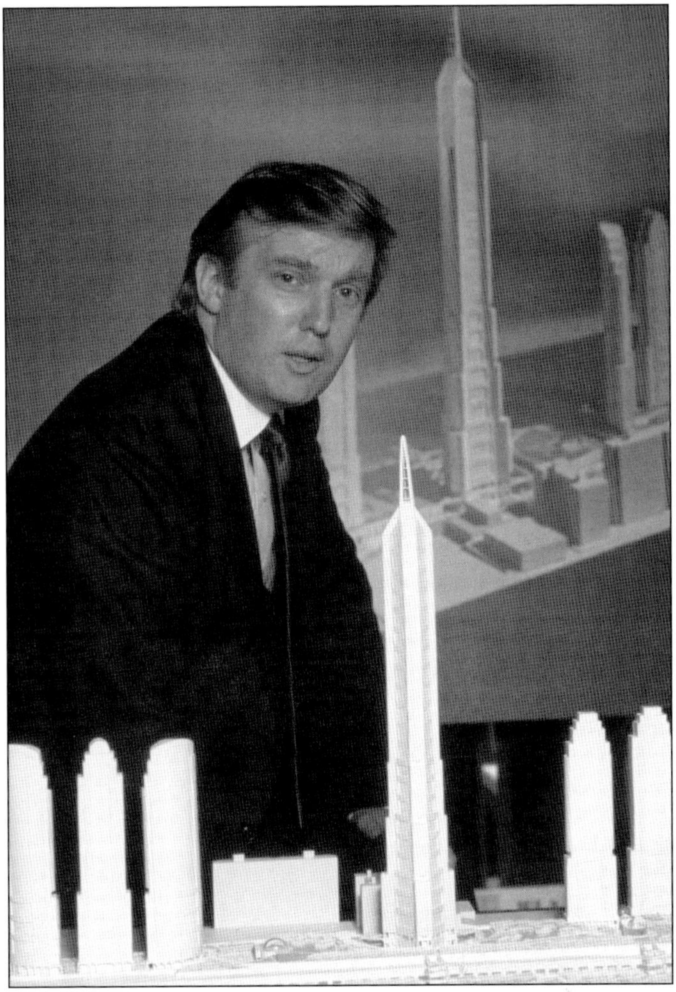

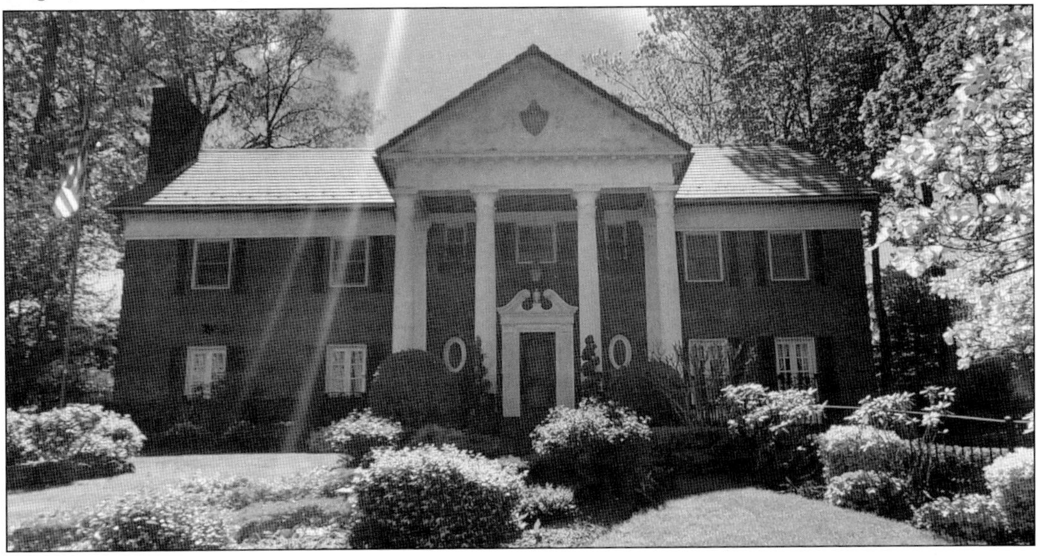

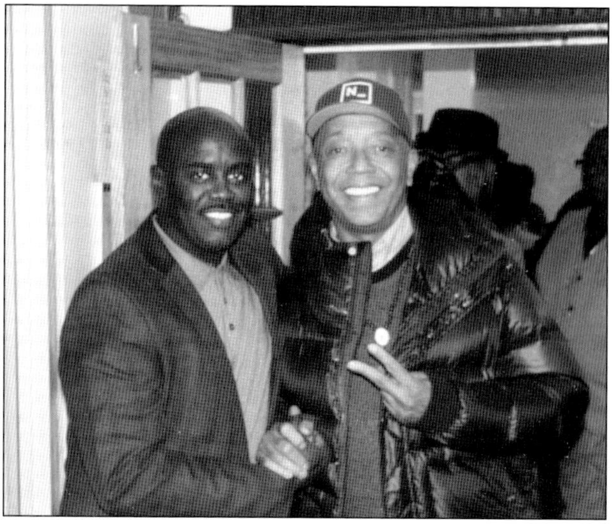

Russell Simmons (right) cofounded the music label Def Jam Recordings in 1984 before launching Rush Communications and the Argyleculture, Phat Farm, and Tantris clothing lines. After tremendous financial success, he established the Rush Philanthropic Arts Foundation in 1995. However, the Hollis native, a brother of Joseph "DJ Run" Simmons of Run-DMC (see chapter one), stepped down from his positions after several women accused him of rape. Simmons, pictured with music promoter Tony Moore (left), denied the allegations. (QPL.)

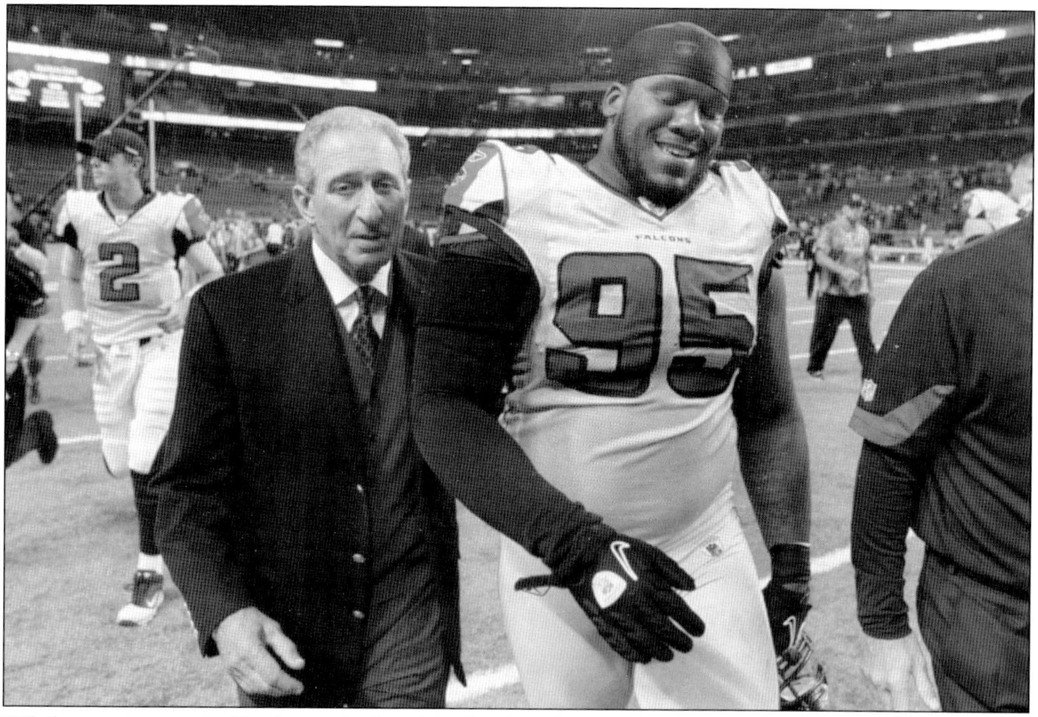

While growing up in Flushing, Arthur Blank adored sports, especially the Brooklyn Dodgers. In 1963, he graduated from Babson College and entered the workforce in the accounting/finance area. After 15 years with Handy Dan Home Improvement Centers, he launched The Home Depot with Bernard Marcus. Both became billionaires. Blank retired in 2001 and bought the Atlanta Falcons, the Arena Football League's Georgia Force, and Atlanta United, a Major League Soccer team. He is shown here at left with Falcons defensive lineman Jonathan Babineaux. (Alamy.)

When Harry Van Arsdale Jr. was born on November 23, 1905, a labor dispute was raging within the New York City building and construction industries. His father, a union electrician, was unemployed due to a 33-month lockout. About two decades later, Van Arsdale graduated from Flushing's Townsend Harris High School and joined his father's union, Local 3 of the International Brotherhood of Electrical Workers (IBEW), as a helper, installing telephone switchboards and new technology for sound movies. He quickly advanced, becoming a manager in 1933, but he never forgot his father's struggles. In 1950, he spearheaded construction of Electchester, a 103-acre, 38-building residential complex with about 2,500 affordable apartments for IBEW members in South Flushing/Pomonok. (His bust is in the management lobby.) In 1957, he was elected president of the New York City Central Labor Council AFL-CIO. (Right, LOC; below, QTC.)

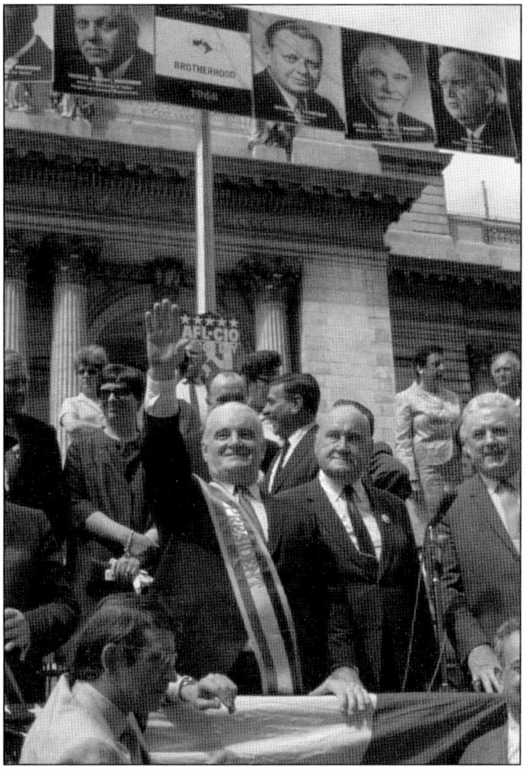


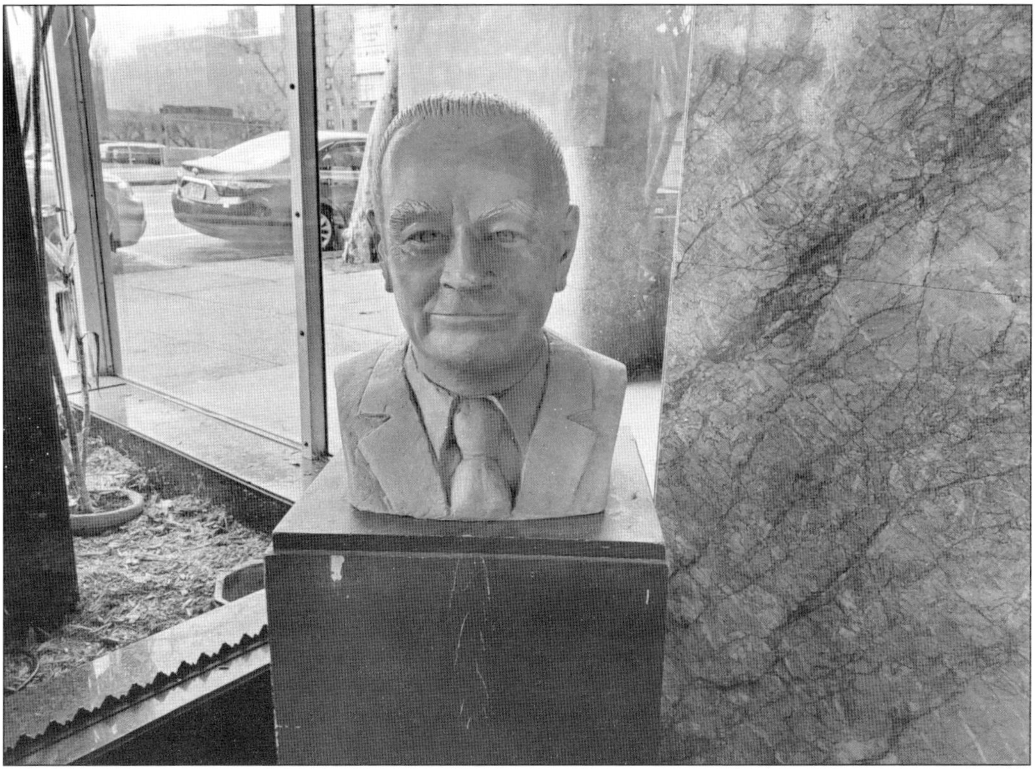

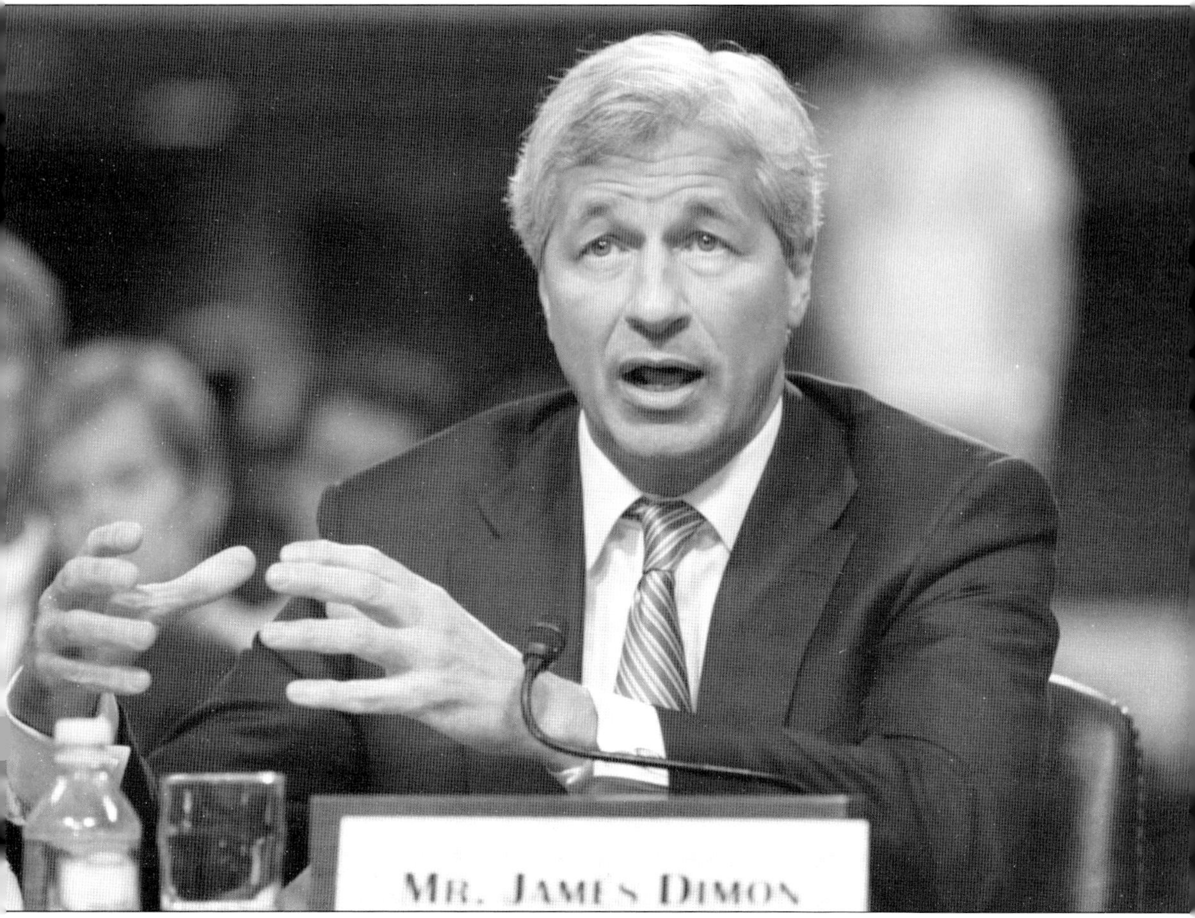


Jamie Dimon is chairman of the board and CEO of JPMorgan Chase & Co. He is worth about $2 billion, and the financial services firm he runs has more than $3.2 billion in assets. The grandson of Greek immigrants, Dimon who was born in 1956 and grew up in Jackson Heights, where he attended PS 69 from kindergarten through the sixth grade before moving to Manhattan. The family name was originally Papademetriou. Dimon graduated summa cum laude from Tufts University and worked at Boston Consulting Group for two years before getting a master of business administration at Harvard Business School. Then he started at American Express with world-famous financier Sandy Weill. Success was quick, and he held high-ranking positions at Commercial Credit, Travelers, Smith Barney, and Citicorp before joining JPMorgan. He was also on the Federal Reserve Bank of New York Board of Directors. (Alamy.)

*Four*

# Drama Queens

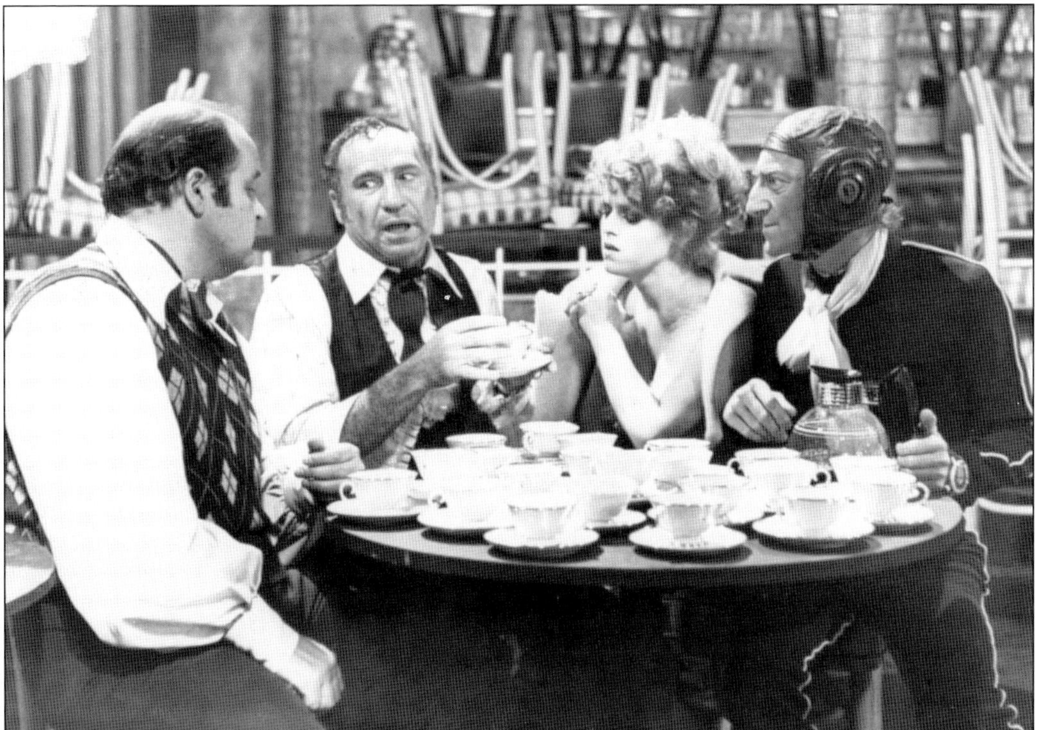

Marguerite Lazzara was a serious stage mom. Her daughter Bernadette, born in 1948, appeared on the game show *Juvenile Jury* at the age of three. Marguerite then decided Lazzara was too Italian and assigned her redheaded girl the last name Peters. The Ozone Park prodigy (in *Silent Movie* above) got her Actors' Equity card at age seven. Since then, the soprano has done it all—acting, dancing, singing, producing, and writing children's books. Her 1987 star on the Hollywood Walk of Fame accompanies an estimated 100 major awards. (Alamy.)

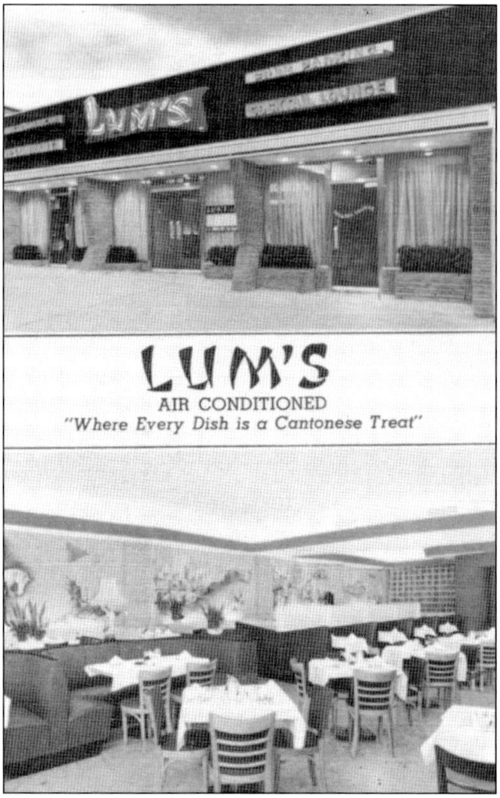


Chinese immigrant Jimmy Lum opened Lum's in Flushing in the 1940s. It was the first Cantonese establishment in the predominantly Jewish neighborhood. Thanks to roast pork turnovers, lobster rolls, and shrimp in black bean sauce, Lum's lasted into the 1980s. His great-granddaughter Nora was born in 1988 and grew up in Forest Hills. She started rapping under the brash alter ego Awkwafina while in high school, rising to fame with "My Vag" in 2011. Her debut album *Yellow Ranger* followed in 2014, the same year she appeared on the MTV comedy series *Girl Code*. Awkwafina became the first Asian American to win a Golden Globe for Best Actress for her role in *The Farewell* in 2019. Then in 2020, she was writer, cocreator, executive producer, and star of Comedy Central's pseudo-biopic *Awkwafina Is Nora from Queens*. (Left, GAHS; below, Alamy.)

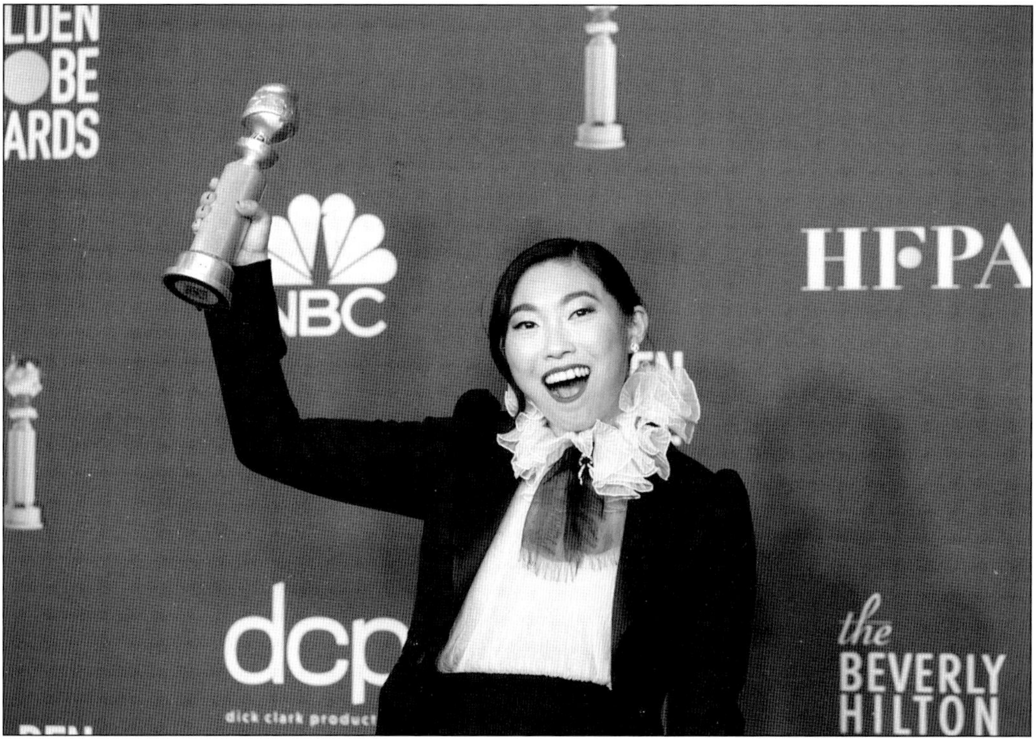

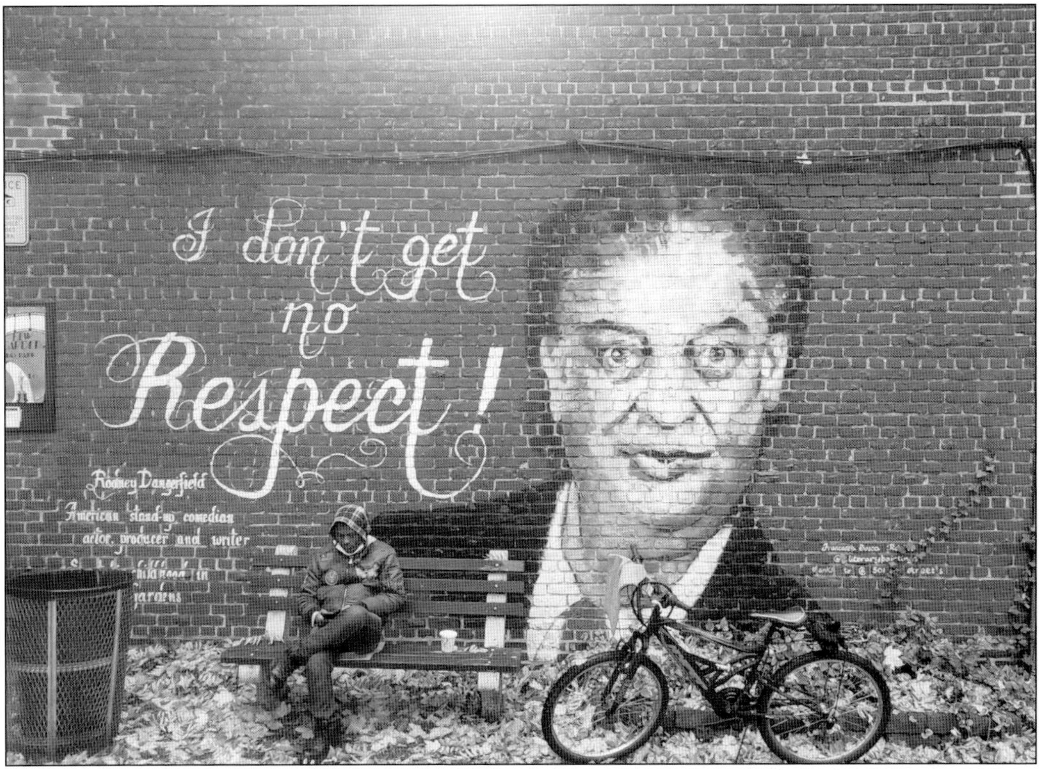


The plaque at right near Austin's Ale House in Kew Gardens has been there since 2017. The mural above by Kew Gardens Cinemas dates to 2016. Located about two blocks from each other, these memorials demonstrate that native son Rodney Dangerfield's "No Respect" comedy routine was pure shtick. Born Jacob Rodney Cohen in 1921, Dangerfield frequently said that his Russian-born father's abandonment led to his self-defacing humor. He graduated from Richmond Hill High School in 1939 and did stand-up while selling aluminum siding before his big break on *The Ed Sullivan Show* in 1968. His monologue killed it. This led to appearances on *The Dean Martin Show* and *The Tonight Show Starring Johnny Carson*, gigs in Las Vegas, and parts in Hollywood films. His best decade was the 1980s with starring roles in *Caddyshack*, *Easy Money*, and *Back to School*. His last act was a serious part in *Natural Born Killers* in 1994. (Both, QTC.)

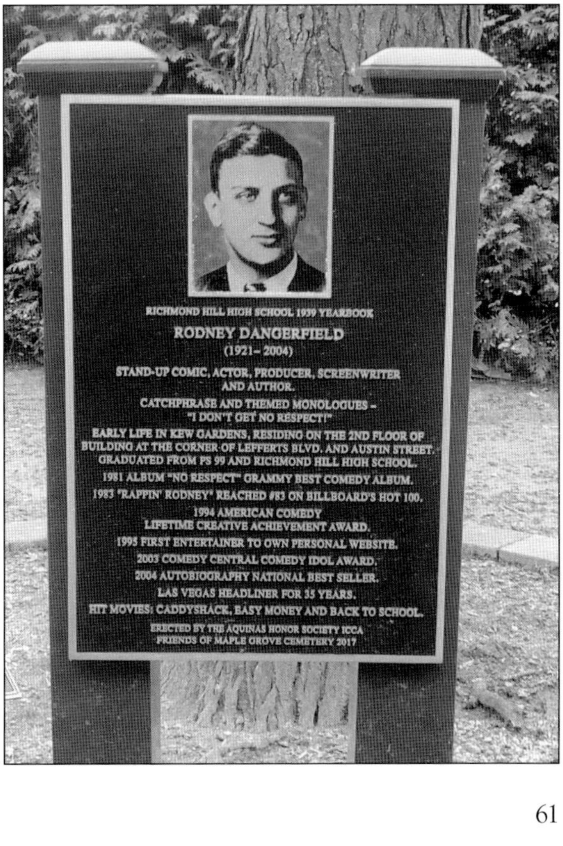

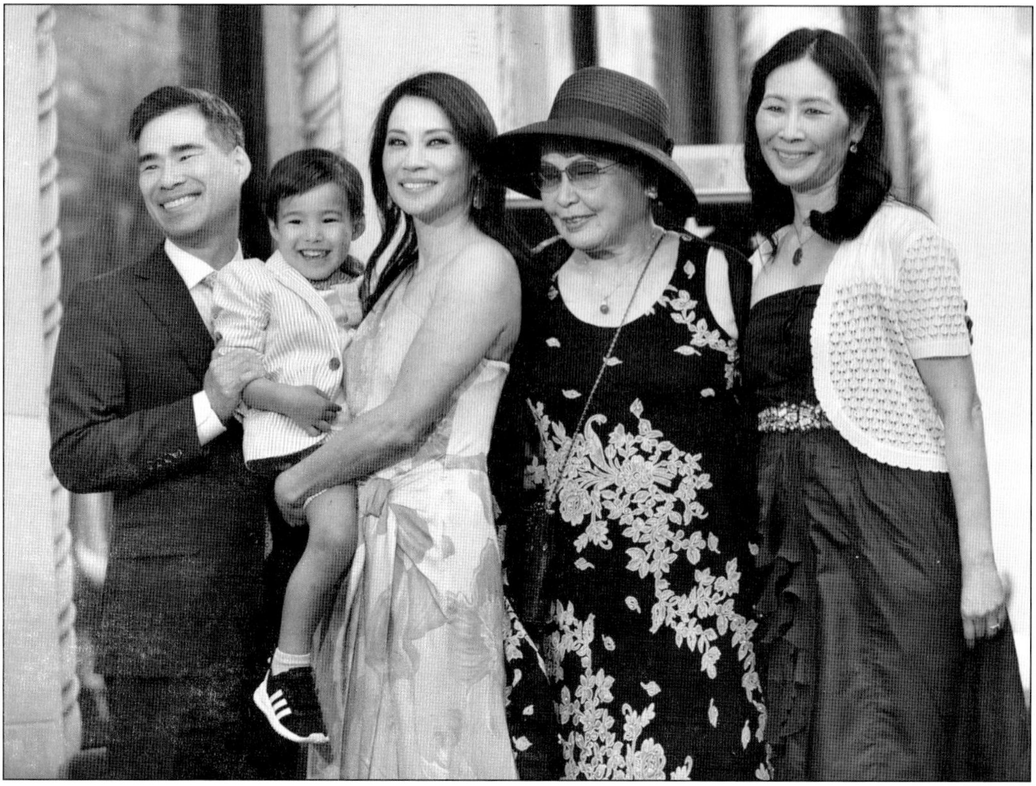

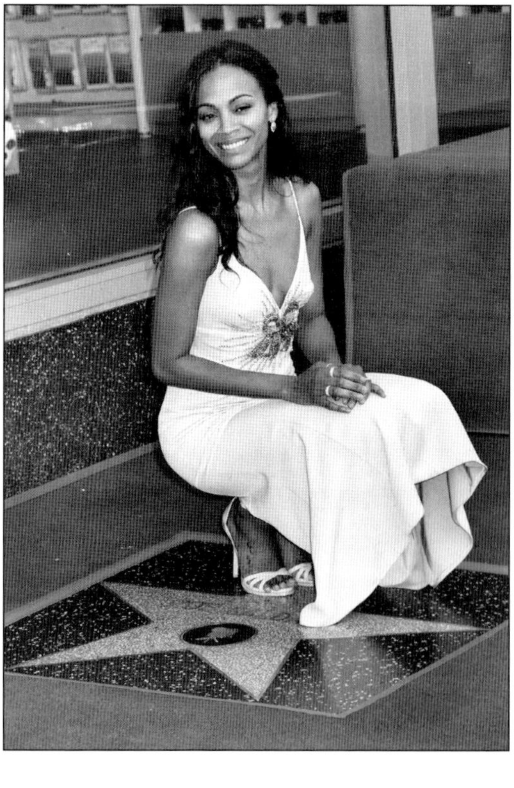

An agent offered Lucy Liu a commercial deal after seeing the 19-year-old on a subway in 1987. Her career skyrocketed after winning a Primetime Emmy Award for playing Ling Woo in Fox's *Ally McBeal*. The Jackson Heights native starred in Quentin Tarantino's *Kill Bill* and two *Charlie's Angels* smashes while making entertainment history as the first Asian to host *Saturday Night Live* (*SNL*) and the second Asian woman to receive a star on the Hollywood Walk of Fame. She is seen above at center with, from left to right, brother Alex, son Rockwell, mother Cecilia, and sister Jenny.) Though born in New Jersey in 1978, Zoe Saldaña grew up in Jackson Heights and lived in Kew Gardens when starting out. She made her television debut on *Law & Order* in 1999, while also working as a dancer. She raised her profile with *Pirates of the Caribbean: The Curse of the Black Pearl* in 2003. Then in 2009 her career beamed up with *Star Trek*, *Avatar*, *Star Trek Into Darkness*, and *Guardians of the Galaxy*. She is pictured at left with her star on the Hollywood Walk of Fame. (Both, Alamy.)

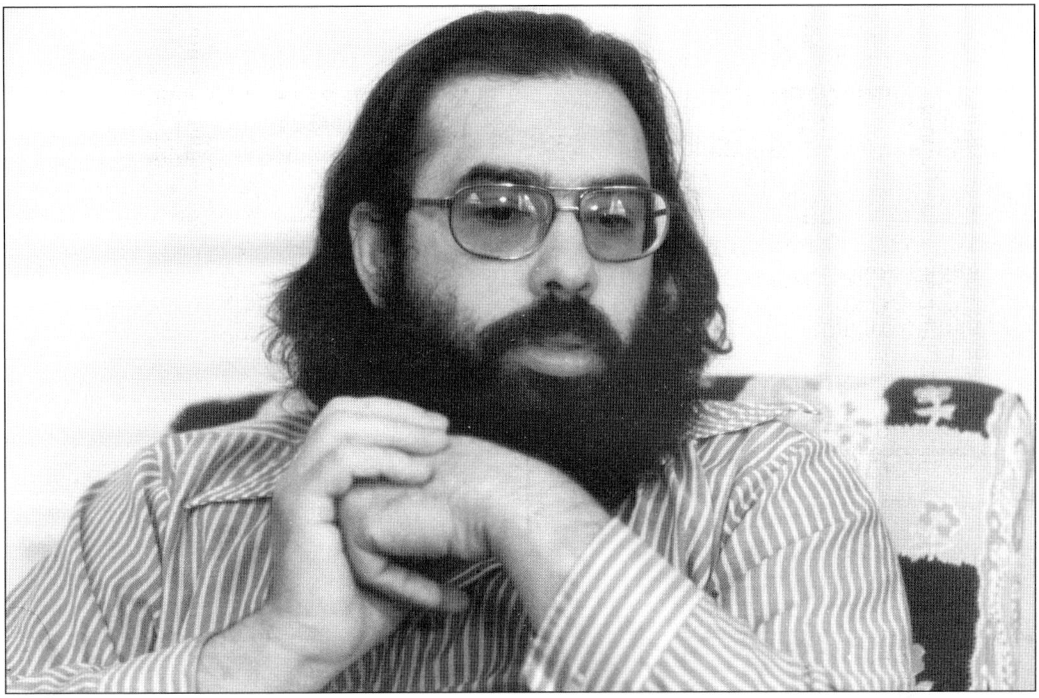

Carmine and Italia Coppola named their second son Francis Ford because he was born in Michigan's Henry Ford Hospital in 1939, but the family moved to Woodside soon thereafter. At nine, Francis was bedridden due to polio, so he amused himself by staging puppet shows. After graduating from Hofstra University, he won his first Oscar for *Patton* in 1970, followed by four more for *Apocalypse Now* and *The Godfather* franchise. He is one of only six people with Oscars as a director, producer, and screenwriter. (LOC.)

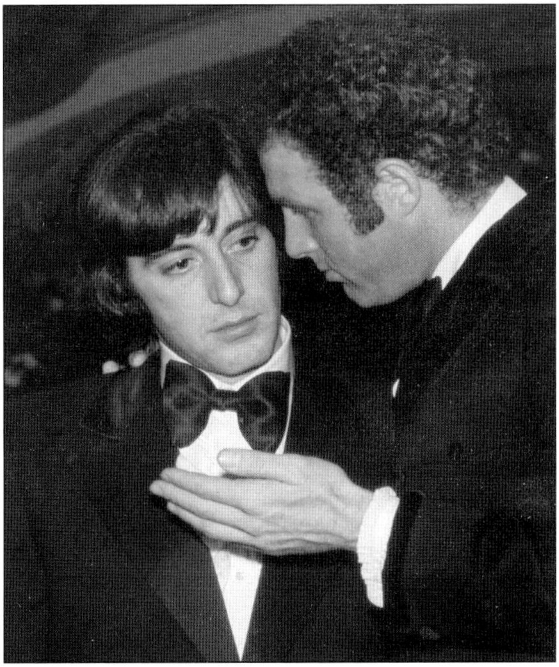

James Caan, who was Jewish, got inspiration for his Italian American Sonny Corleone character in *The Godfather* from his Sunnyside childhood. Born in 1940, he studied the way working-class neighbors walked, talked, and interacted. It's a good thing he was from a diverse neighborhood, because he acted in more than 80 movies over his five-decade career that garnered him eight major awards and a star on the Hollywood Walk of Fame. At right, he chats with his brother Michael (Al Pacino) in *The Godfather* in 1972. (LOC.)

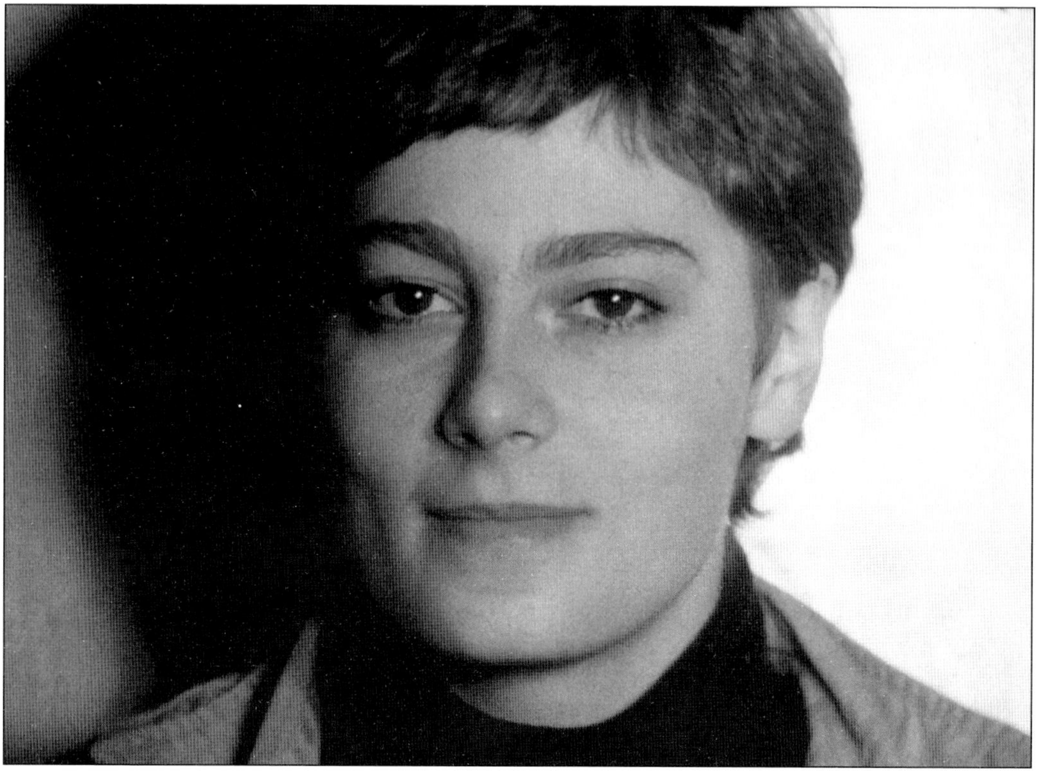

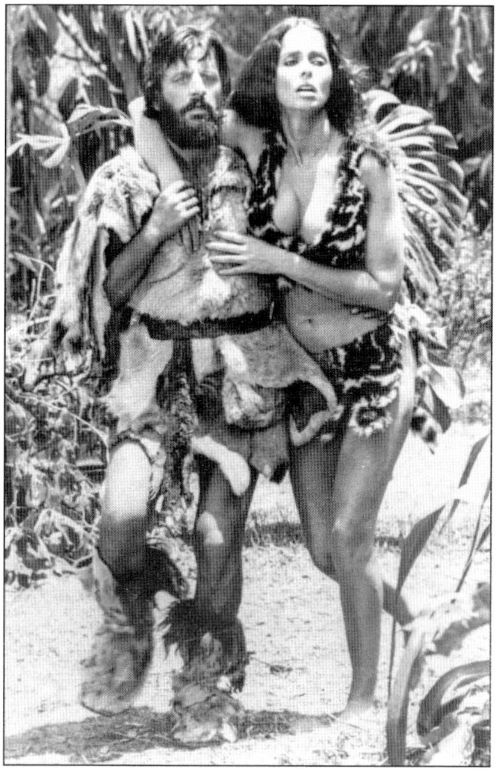

Born in 1945 to middle-class Jewish parents in Cambria Heights, Barbara Rubin epitomized—and promoted—the avant-garde movement of the 1960s and 1970s. She helped Andy Warhol create his Exploding Plastic Inevitable multimedia shows. She organized Allen Ginsberg's beat poetry readings. She nursed Bob Dylan to health after a motorcycle accident. And she was rocker Lou Reed's muse. Then she converted to ultraorthodox Judaism and moved to a religious community in France. (The Andy Warhol Museum.)

Bellerose native Barbara Goldbach had just graduated from Dominican Commercial High School when she attended the famous 1965 Beatles concert in Shea Stadium. Around that time, she was appearing in such magazines as *Seventeen*, *Vogue USA*, and *Playboy*. In 1977, as Barbara Bach, she played sexy Russian spy Anya Amasova in the James Bond thriller *The Spy Who Loved Me*. Later, Bach starred in the 1981 comedy *Caveman* alongside Beatles drummer Ringo Starr (left). By the end of filming, they were dating. In 1981, they got married in London. (Alamy.)

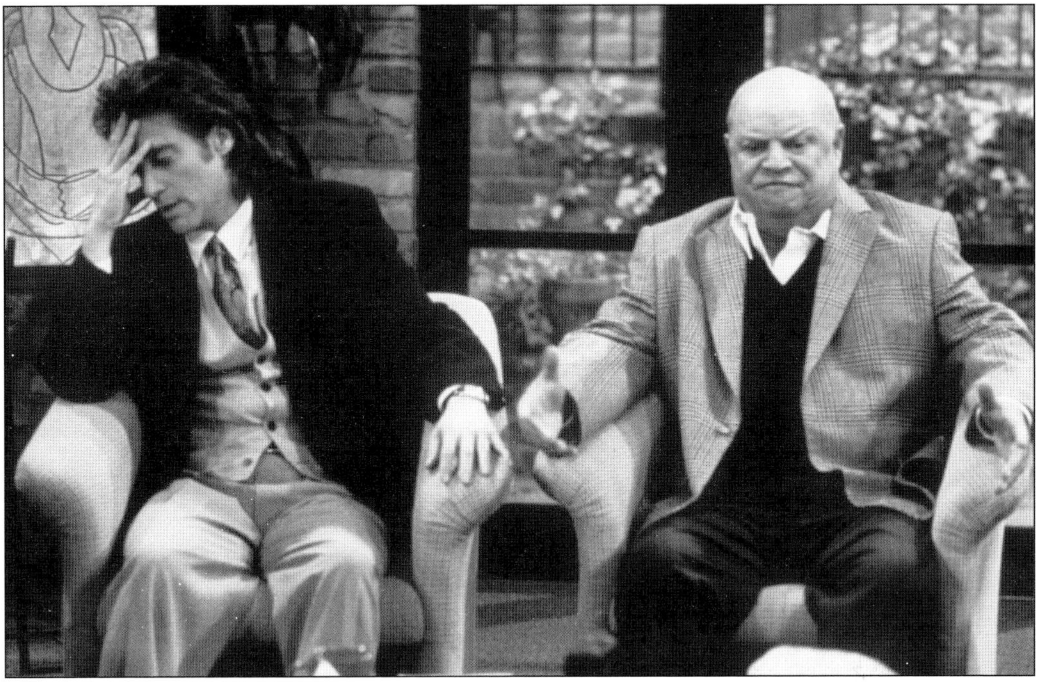

Crowds called him "Mr. Warmth," a compliment compared to what he called them. Born in 1926, Jackson Heights comedian Don Rickles (right) was president of his class and the drama society at Newtown High School. After serving in World War II, he pioneered insult humor, poking fun at everybody, especially hecklers. *Run Silent, Run Deep* with Clark Gable was his movie debut in 1958. Sitcoms, celebrity roasts, beach films, and *The Tonight Show Starring Johnny Carson* followed. He got his Hollywood Walk of Fame star in 2000. (Alamy.)

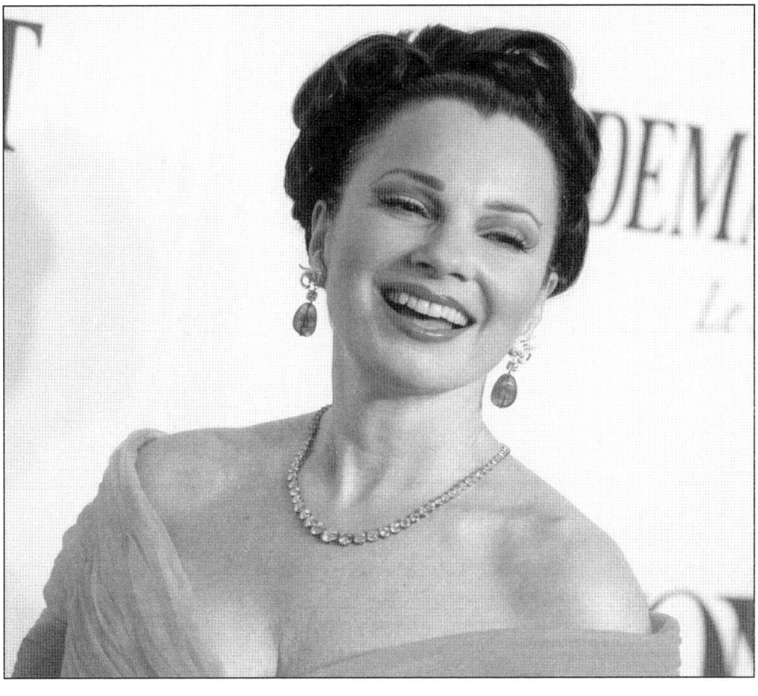

Fran Drescher and Peter Jacobson met at Hillcrest High School and got married at Terrace on the Park in 1978. She struck it big with the CBS sitcom *The Nanny*, which ran from 1993 until 1999, when she divorced Jacobson after he came out as gay. Nevertheless, they starred in the TV Land sitcom *Happily Divorced* (2011–2013), which centered on a couple that divorced after 18 years of marriage after the husband came out as gay. (Alamy.)

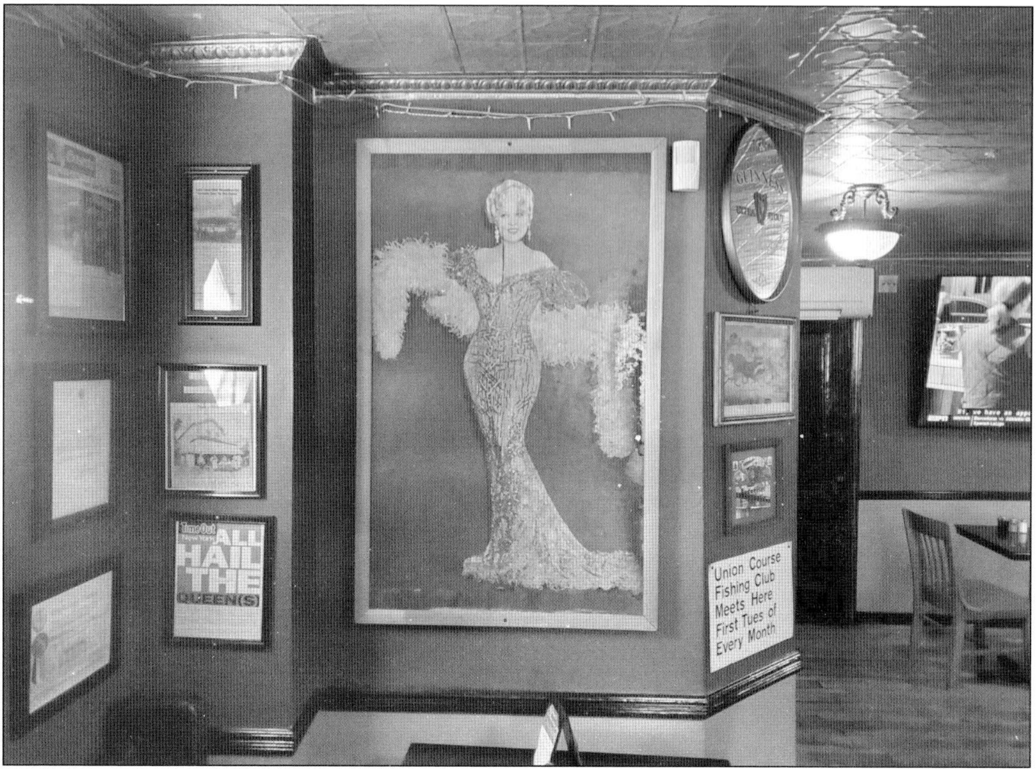


Neir's Tavern has a legendary past. Founded in 1829, the Woodhaven landmark is the oldest pub to operate continuously in the same location in the entire United States. The mahogany bar, where scenes from *Goodfellas* were shot, dates to the Grant administration. It is also where Mae West launched her seven-decade career. Born in 1893 to John Patrick, a boxer who became a private investigator, and Mathilde (née Doelger), a fashion model from Bavaria, Germany, West showed zero interest in school. Luckily, she found Neir's, which featured pin bowling and might have operated a bordello on the second floor at the time. Blessed with a sultry voice and serious acting chops—as well as a voluptuous body and flirty manners—she became a sensation under the stage name "The Baby Vamp." Vaudeville followed, and she got her first Broadway credit in 1911. (Above, QTC; below, LOC.)

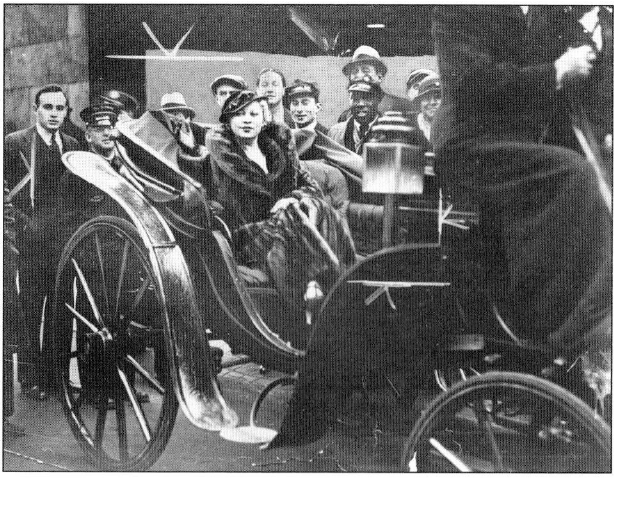

Many groups in the still-puritanical country were repulsed by this big-time sex symbol. In 1927, West spent eight days in jail for acting in the Broadway play *Sex*, which she had written. In 1932, she moved to California, and by 1935, she was the country's highest-paid woman and second-highest-paid person behind newspaper mogul William Randolph Hearst. She never saw action, but she had a profound impact on World War II, as air fighters called their life preservers "Mae Wests," which just happens to rhyme with "breasts." After starring opposite Cary Grant, Randolph Scott, W.C. Fields, and Rock Hudson, she got a star on the Hollywood Walk of Fame in 1960. She is buried in the family mausoleum at Cypress Hills Cemetery about one mile from Neir's. (Both, LOC.)

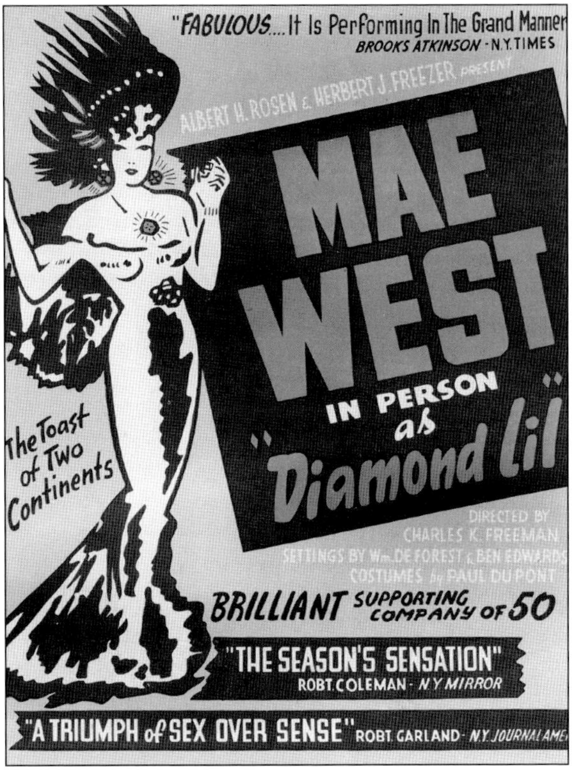


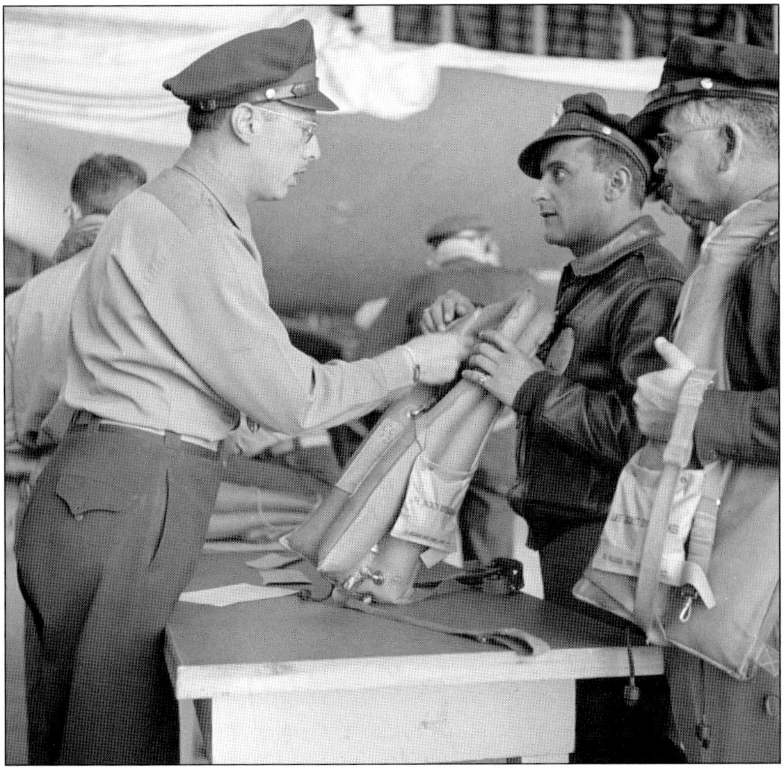

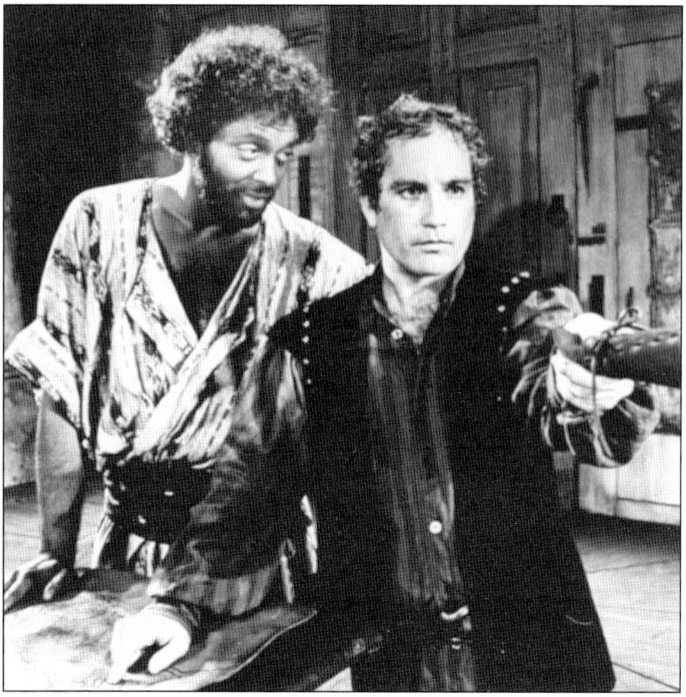

Richard Dreyfuss (right) grew up in Bayside before the family moved to Europe and then Los Angeles. His first credit was a bit part in *The Graduate* before he achieved stardom in *Jaws* in 1975 and *Close Encounters of the Third Kind* in 1977. He was the youngest male to win an Oscar for Best Actor for his 1977 role in *The Goodbye Girl* at 30 years, 4 months, and 5 days, beating Marlon Brando, who got his Oscar for *On the Waterfront* in 1955 at 30 years, 11 months, and 26 days. Here, Dreyfuss's Iago is shown opposite Raul Julia's Othello (left) in the New York Shakespeare Festival's Central Park production of *Othello*. (NYPL.)

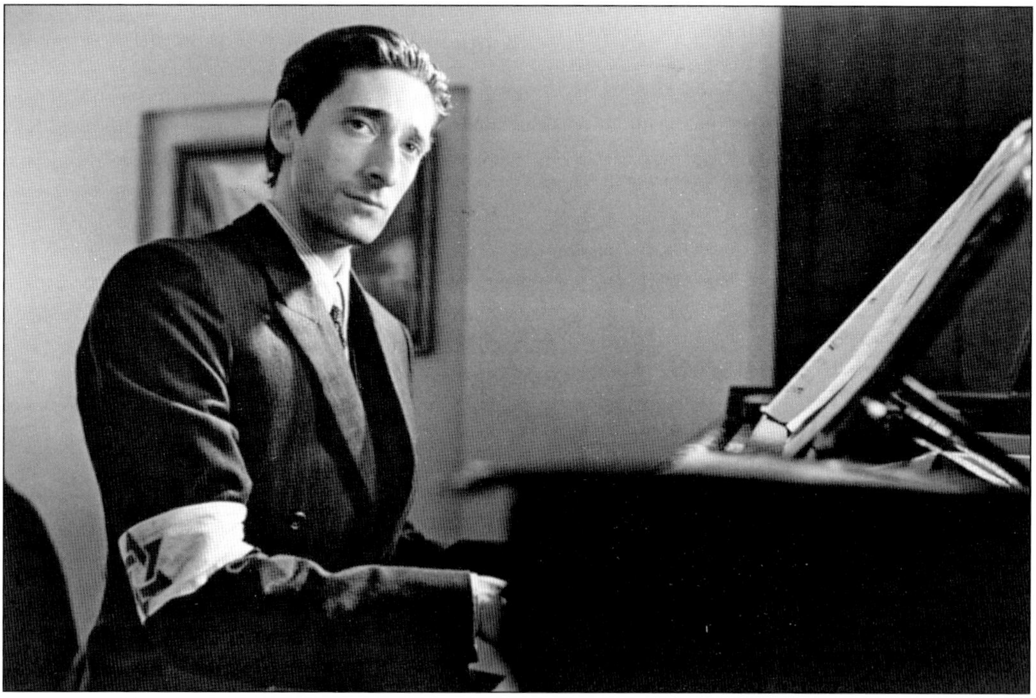

A 29-year-old Adrien Brody broke Dreyfuss's record by taking Best Actor honors for *The Piano* in 2003 (above). He grew up in Woodhaven, so the honor bounced from the borough's northeast to the mid-region. Brody dropped out of Queens College to star alongside Mary Tyler Moore in the CBS television show *Annie McGuire*. That led to so many roles that as this book went to press in 2022, he was one of Hollywood's most coveted actors. (Alamy.)

Anna Marie Duke was eight when her mother surrendered her care to talent managers John and Ethel Ross, who gave her the stage name Patty. They certainly took advantage of the Elmhurst native, a child sensation during amateur nights at the Queens Boulevard Elks Club in the 1950s. But they also led her to a tremendous career, which includes the record as the youngest person to win an Oscar (16), two Golden Globes, three Primetime Emmys, and a star on the Hollywood Walk of Fame. She is pictured here as Helen Keller (see chapter seven) with Anne Bancroft's Annie Sullivan in a late-1960s production of *The Miracle Worker*. (Museum of the City of New York.)

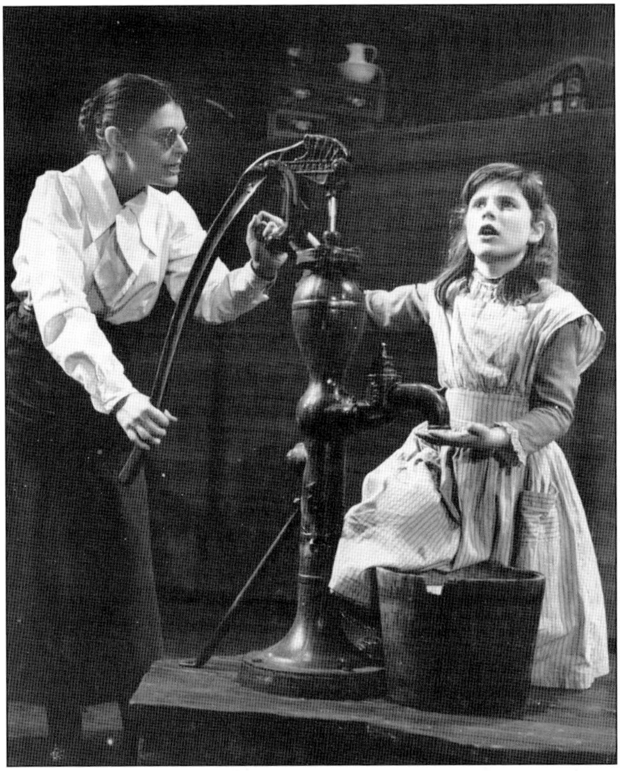

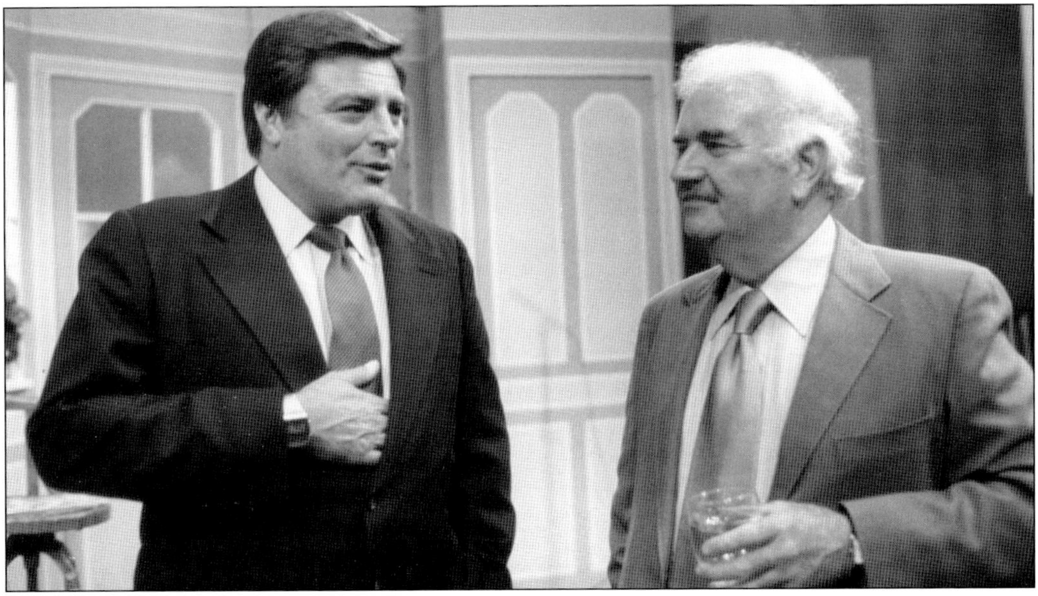

While at Forest Hills High School, Bob Keeshan (right in 1980) would broadcast plays over the loudspeaker. He graduated in 1945 and enlisted to fight in World War II, but it ended before he saw action. Soon thereafter, he appeared as a silent clown on *The Howdy Doody Show*. In 1955, Keeshan's own CBS show, *Captain Kangaroo*, debuted. It ran for almost three decades, and Keeshan won five Emmys, three Peabodys, and one National Education Award and was inducted into the International Clown Hall of Fame and Research Center. (LOC.)

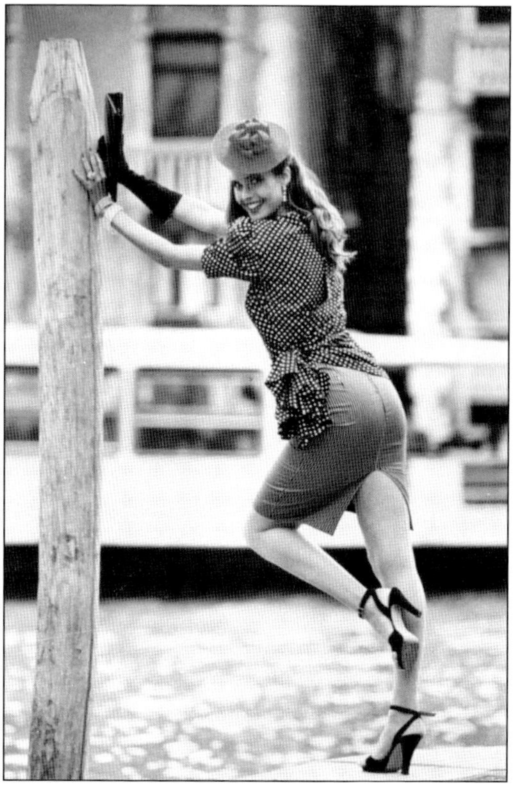

*Life* called her "The Face." *Playboy* described her as the "Most Beautiful Woman in the World." Other media outlets hailed her as the "first supermodel." Flushing native Carol Alt took up modeling to pay her tuition at Hofstra University. In 1979, she rocked the *Harper's Bazaar* cover. Over the 1980s, she appeared on covers of more than 500 magazines, including the 1982 *Sports Illustrated* swimsuit issue. Then came Italian movies (left), television, books, health products, exercise videos, and raw-food advocacy. (Alamy.)

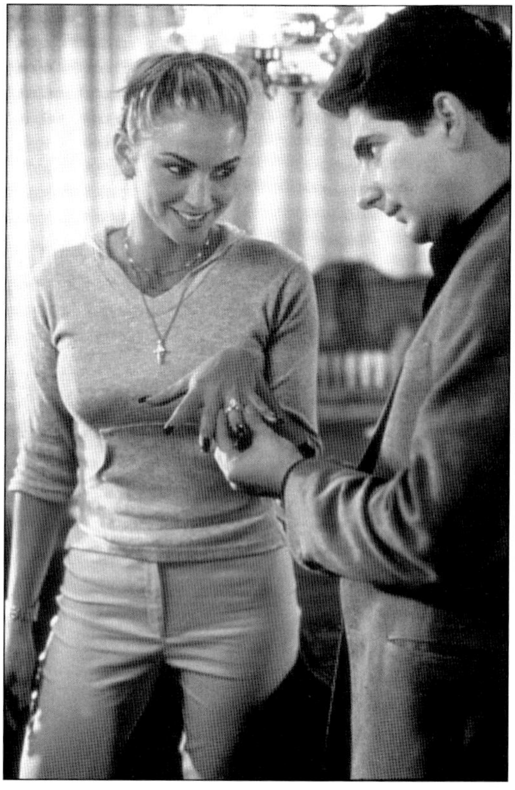

Born in 1972, Drea de Matteo grew up in Malba, not far from the Whitestone Bridge. After graduating from New York University's Tisch School of the Arts, she explored acting while corunning an East Village clothing store. From 1999 to 2004, de Matteo gained millions of fans and won an Emmy and two Primetime Emmys for her portrayal of mob princess Adriana La Cerna in the HBO series *The Sopranos* (right). She then got roles on shows like *Desperate Housewives*, *Joey*, and *Sons of Anarchy*. (Alamy.)

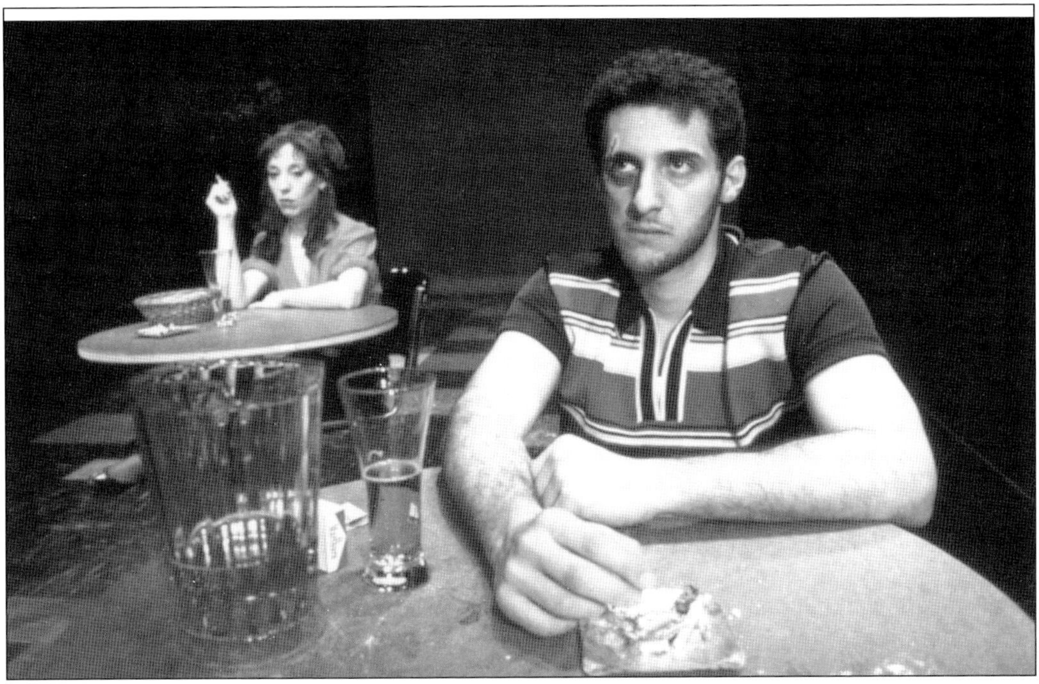

John Turturro, who has an Emmy and an Obie, jokes that he gets along well with director Spike Lee because African American Lee hails from a largely Italian American Brooklyn neighborhood, while his Italian American family is from Rosedale, a largely African American Queens neighborhood. Born in 1957, his first film credit was a nonspeaking part in Martin Scorsese's *Raging Bull* in 1980. This led to an Off-Broadway gig and to a 60-plus film career as an actor, director, producer, and writer. He is shown here with June Stein in a 1984 photograph from the Off-Broadway play *Danny and the Deep Blue Sea*. (NYPL.)

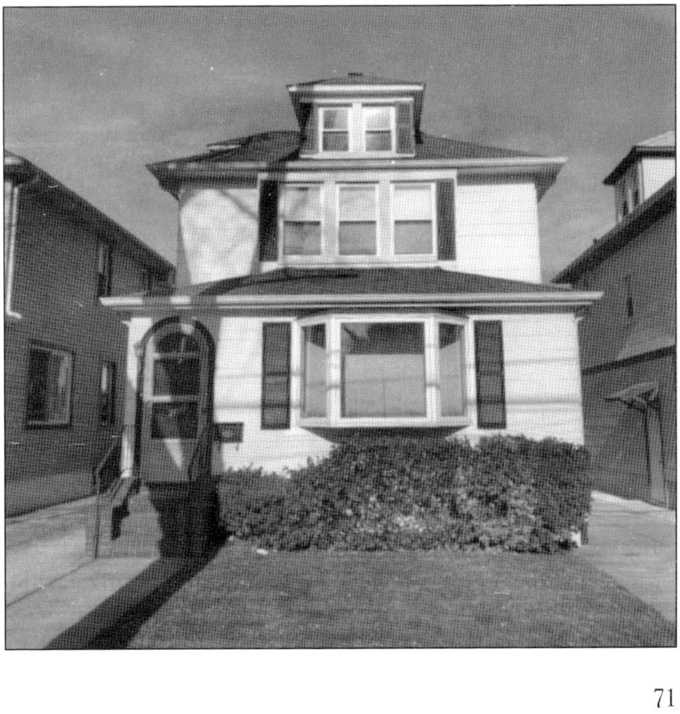

Ray Romano loved his childhood in this Nansen Street house in Forest Hills so much that he wrote the foreword to Nicholas Hirshon's 2013 Arcadia Publishing book on the neighborhood. Born in 1957, the Hillcrest High School graduate dropped out of Queens College to do stand-up. In 1995, his hilarious dialogue on *Late Night with David Letterman* led to his own sitcom, *Everybody Loves Raymond*, which ran from 1996 to 2005 and made him the highest-paid television actor ever and the winner of six Primetime Emmys and two Emmys. (QTC.)

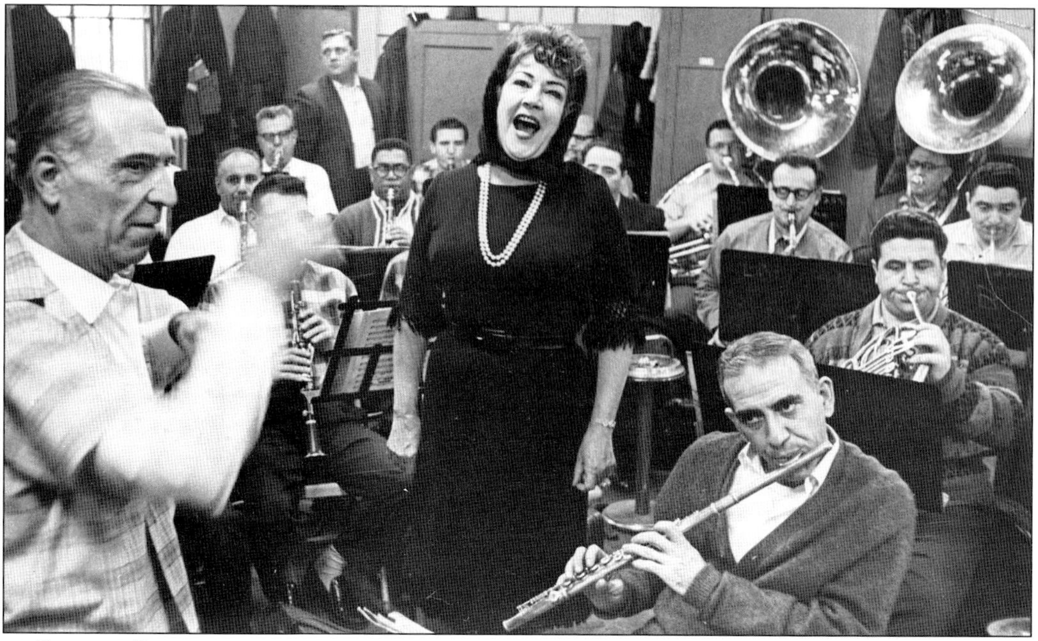

William Cullen Bryant High School's auditorium is named after Ethel Merman, who is easily the Astoria institution's most famous graduate. The actress with the mesmerizing mezzo-soprano voice was born Ethel Agnes Zimmermann in 1908. In 1926, she got a job as a stenographer while performing at nightclubs and private parties. Beautiful, brassy, and funny, she did some Broadway and vaudeville before moving to Hollywood, where she starred in blockbuster films opposite such stars as Bing Crosby, Bob Hope, and Spencer Tracy. She ruled musical comedy, too, especially works by Cole Porter, Irving Berlin, and Ira Gershwin, amassing Grammy, Tony, and Golden Globe Awards and getting a star on the Hollywood Walk of Fame. The lights on Broadway went dim after she died from brain cancer on February 15, 1984. (Both, LOC.)

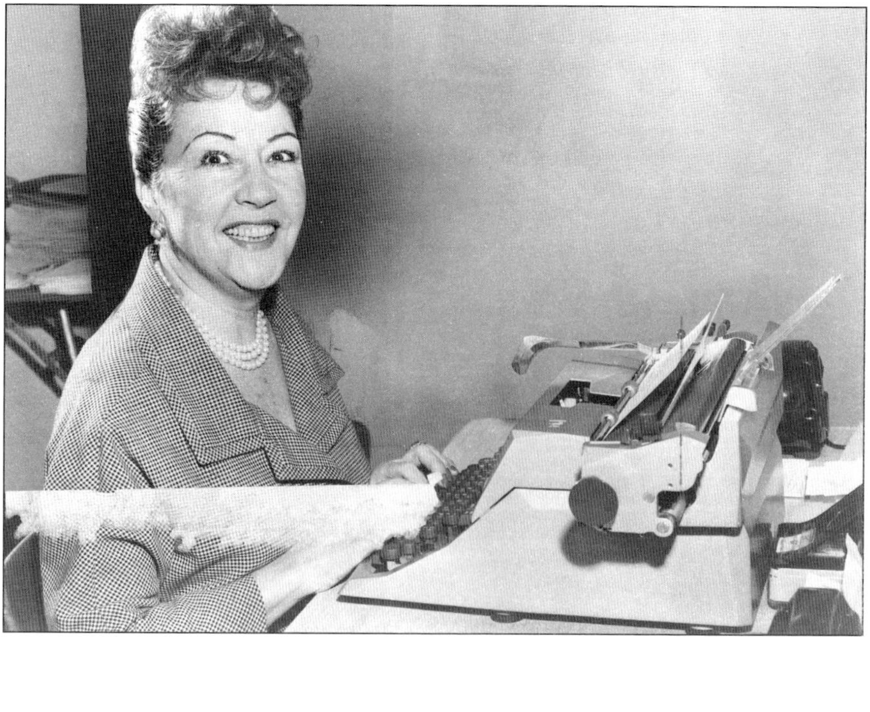

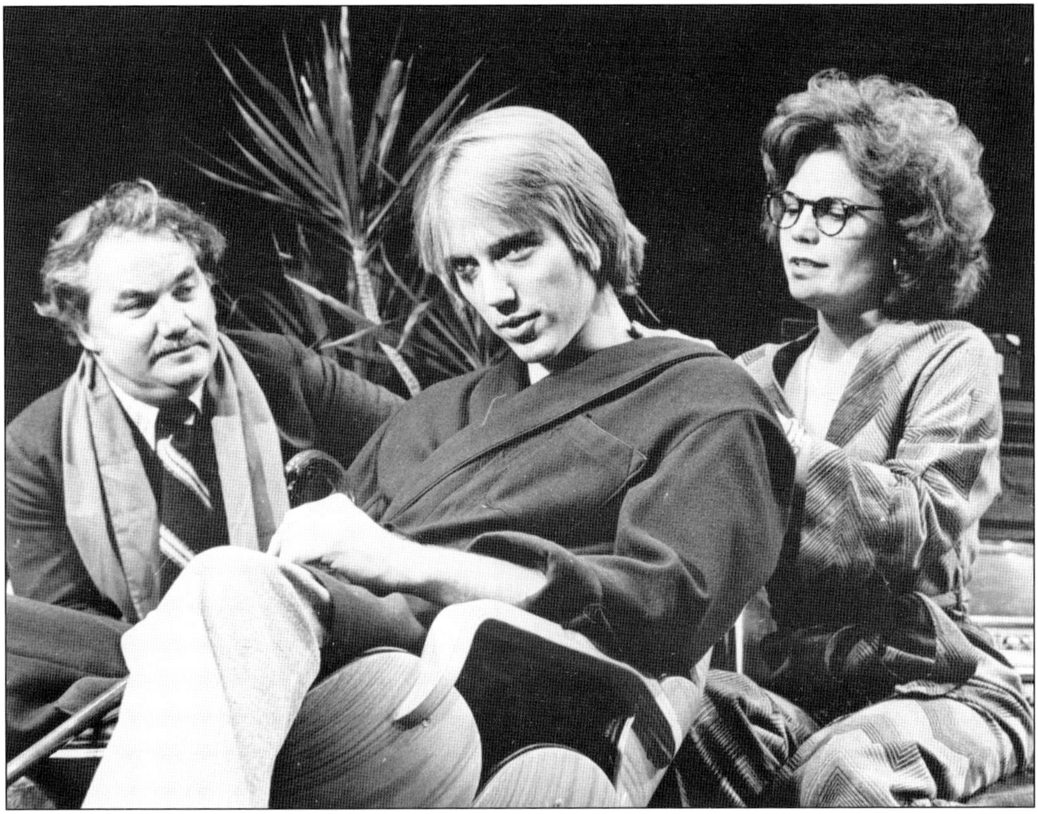

Born in 1943, Ronald Walken grew up in Bayside, spending many hours working at the bakery his German immigrant father established in Astoria in 1931. He and his two brothers were childhood actors, but only he continued, changing his first name to Christopher. Walken, surrounded by Kenneth McMillan and Kathryn Walker in the 1975 play *Kid Champion*, has had roles in more than 100 films, including *Annie Hall* in 1977, *Batman Returns* in 1992, and *Pulp Fiction* in 1994. His effort in *Deer Hunter* won him the 1978 Oscar for Best Supporting Actor. (NYPL.)

Born in 1928, Dick Van Patten grew up with his stage mom in Kew Gardens and Woodhaven. At three, he got his first gig with a modeling agency. He had his first Broadway part at seven. The prodigy, at right with Elaine Shore in a 1969 Off-Broadway production of *Next*, went on to appear in almost 50 feature films, more than 100 television shows, 27 Broadway productions, and dozens of radio novels over an eight-decade-plus career. Though he never won any major awards, he received a star on the Hollywood Walk of Fame in 1985. (NYPL.)

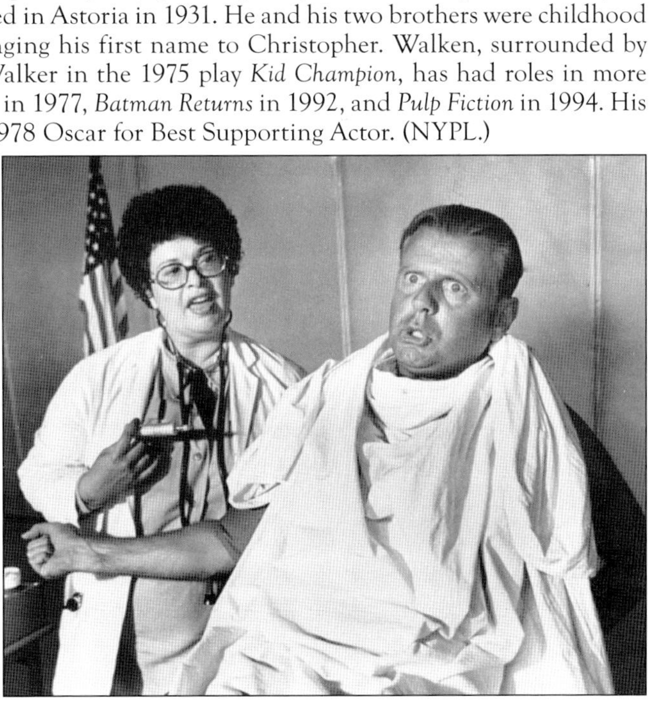

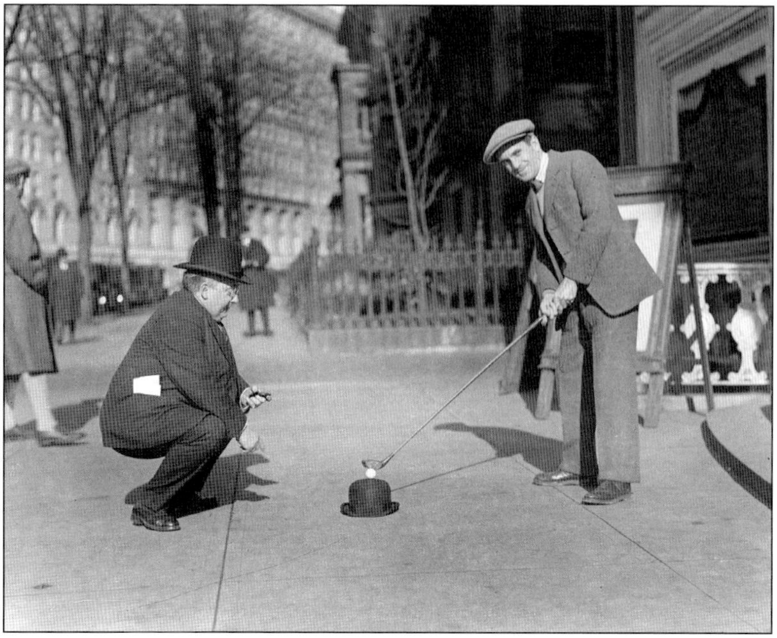

The first openly Jewish movie star in the United States, Asa Yoelson was born in Lithuania in 1886 but rose to fame as Al Jolson in Forest Hills. With uncanny facial expressions and an ear-piercing whistle, the comedian/singer had a long Broadway career before starring in the first-ever talking movie, *The Jazz Singer*, in 1927. Other credits include *The Singing Fool* (1928) and *Big Boy* (1930). (LOC.)

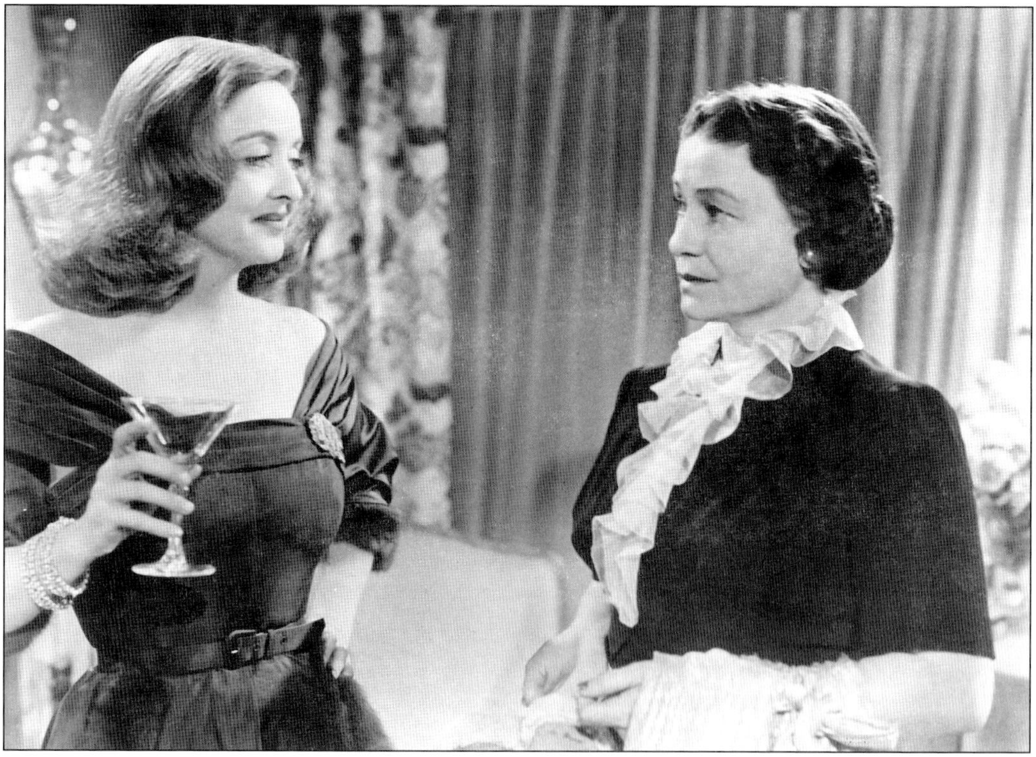

Born in 1902, Thelma Ritter (right) was a shopper in the 1947 classic *Miracle on 34th Street*. The Forest Hills resident with a thick New York accent then got comedic, working-class rolls in major productions. She won a 1958 Tony for Best Actress for the musical *New Girl In Town* and accrued six Oscar nominations for Best Supporting Actress in such box office smashes as *All About Eve* opposite Bette Davis (1950) and *Pillow Talk* (1959). (Alamy.)

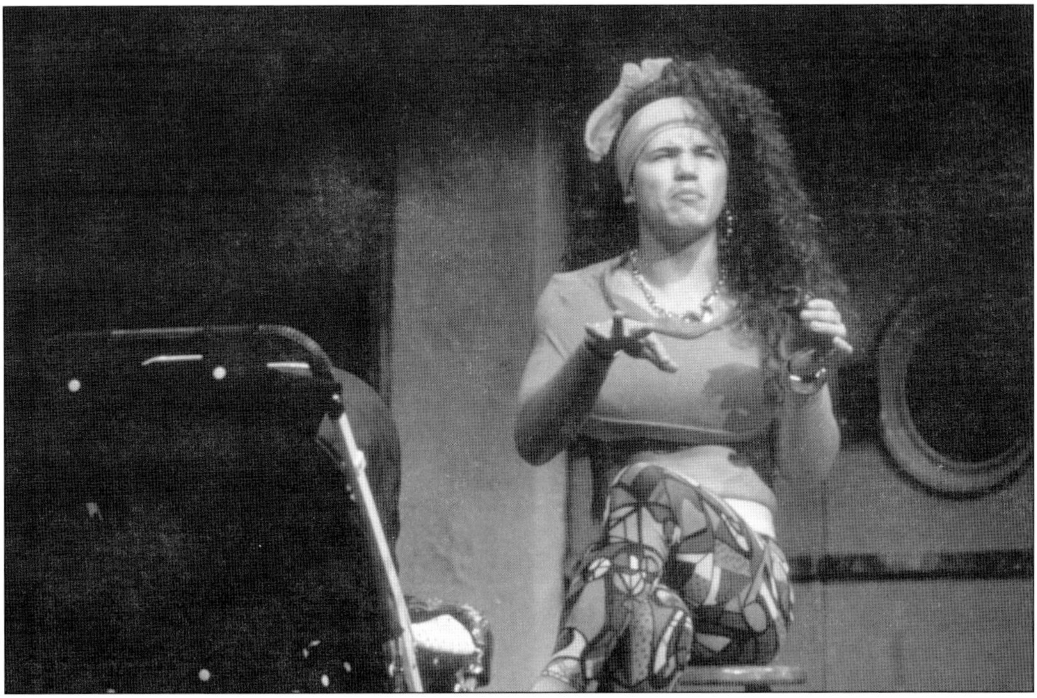

While riding the 7 train during a segment of the 2018 Public Broadcasting Systems (PBS) program *Road to Broadway*, John Leguizamo says his Jackson Heights childhood was key to his self-esteem. "Everybody around me was Latin. . . . We weren't ashamed of ourselves." Born in Colombia in 1964, his career exploded after playing Luigi in *Super Mario Bros.* in 1993. His résumé features a Primetime Emmy, films, Broadway productions, television appearances, a memoir, a graphic book, albums, the one-man Off-Broadway show *Spic-O-Rama* (above in 1992), and voice-overs in movies and video games. (NYPL.)

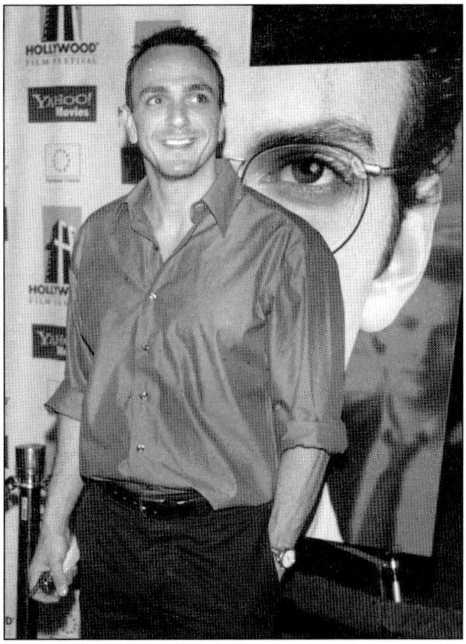


Hank Azaria, who has six Emmys and one Screen Actors Guild Award, is the voice behind many characters in Springfield, where Fox's animated sitcom *The Simpsons* takes place. Moe (the bartender) is one of his most frequently occurring characters, but he is also behind Chief Wiggum, Apu (the convenience store owner), and Bumblebee Man. Azaria fell in love with acting after performing in a play at the Kew-Forest School in Forest Hills. He graduated in 1981. (Alamy.)

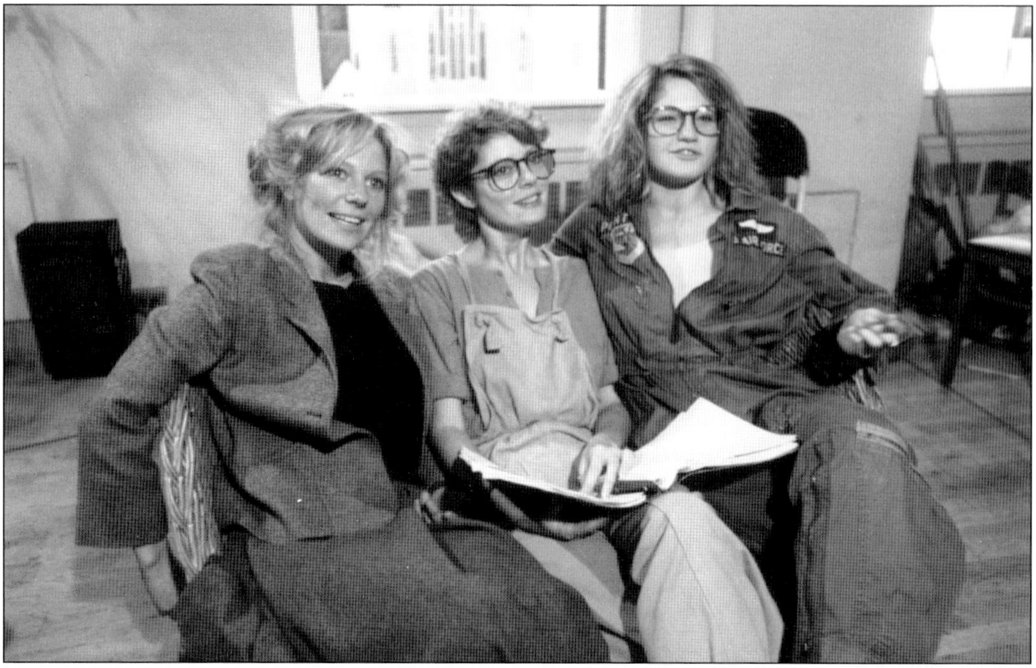

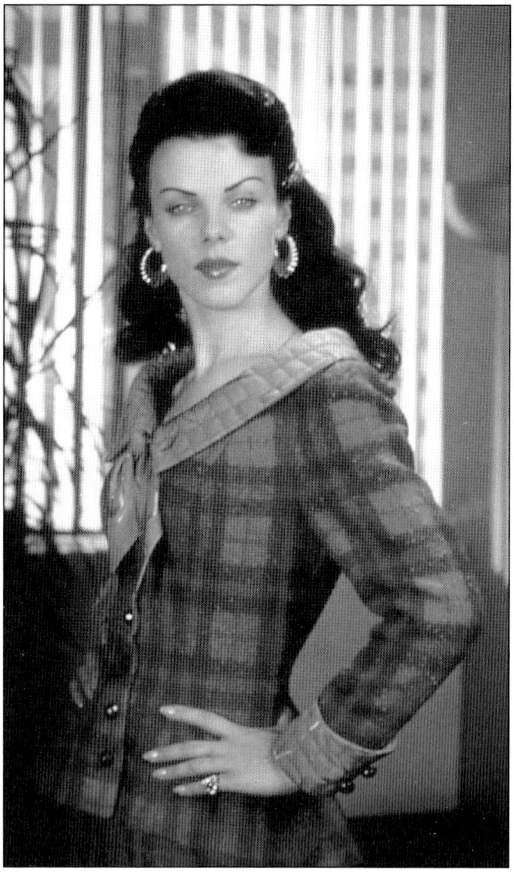

Ellen Barkin's favorite childhood memories include her Kew Garden Hills grandmother's after-school tuna fish sandwich with chopped celery and dill. Born in 1954, she double majored in history and drama at Hunter College while also studying at the Actors Studio. Her first big role was in the 1982 comedy *Diner*, followed by *The Big Easy* in 1987 and *Sea of Love* in 1989. Always combining movies with television and theater, Barkin's award case includes a Primetime Emmy, a Tony, and a Sant Jordi. She is pictured here at right in a rehearsal shot from the 1982 Off-Broadway play *Extremities* with Deborah Hedwall (left) and Susan Sarandon (center). (NYPL.)

Born to a 15-year-old mom in 1964, Jamaica native Debi Mazar eschewed college for the Manhattan disco scene, where she met Madonna. She worked as the Material Girl's makeup artist and appeared in some of her videos. Mazar's first movie role was a small part in Martin Scorsese's 1990 hit *Goodfellas*. Directors as diverse as Spike Lee and Woody Allen took interest, and Mazar appeared in everything from *LA Law* (left) to *Malcolm X* to *Entourage*. (Alamy.)

# *Five*

# Brainy Heads

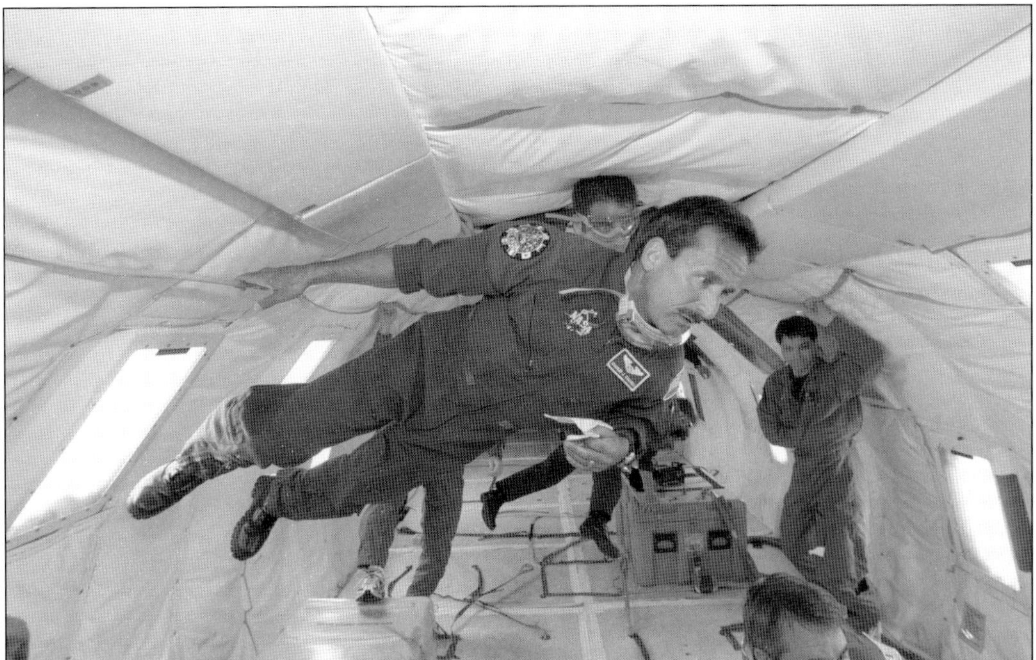

Young Charles Camarda walked around Ozone Park on July 5, picking up dud firecrackers to create rockets. After graduating from Nativity BVM School, where he made the honor roll eight years in a row, and the Polytechnic Institute of New York University in 1974, he got his dream job at NASA. Camarda, floating at center in this photograph, flew on the space shuttle *Discovery* on July 26, 2005. (Alamy.)

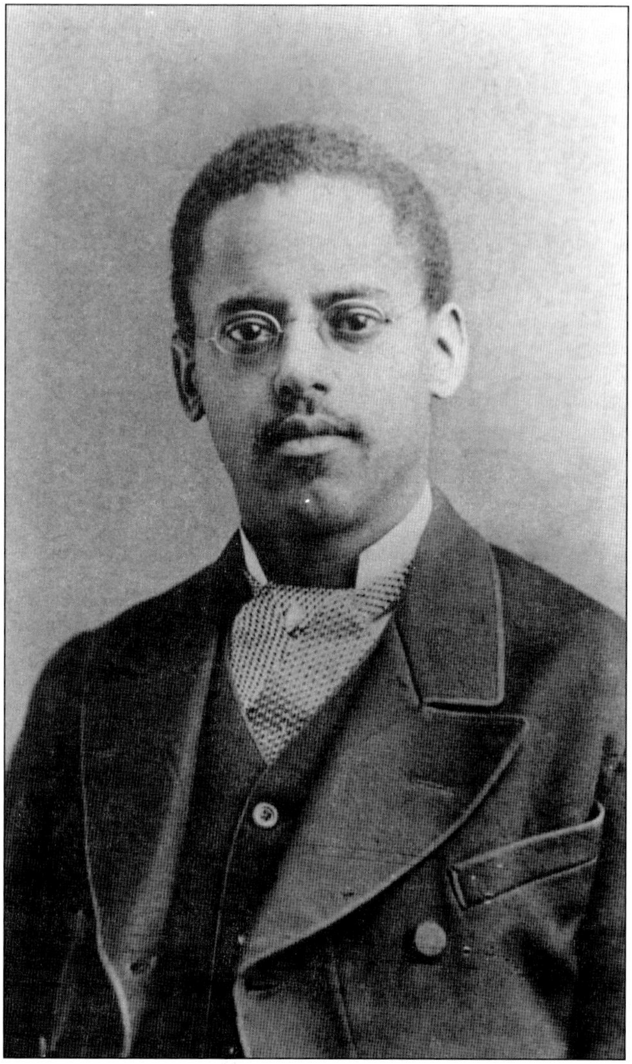

Lewis Latimer (1848–1928), whose father was a fugitive slave, worked with Alexander Graham Bell on the telephone and Thomas Edison on the light bulb. On his own, he got patents for a railroad car toilet, an early air-conditioner, and a socket that allowed light bulbs to screw into fixtures. His biggest invention was durable carbon filament for electric bulbs that made them cheaper and longer lasting. (They soon replaced more dangerous gas lights, changing urban street illumination.) That is only part of the story, though. The Renaissance man also found time to cofound the Unitarian Universalist Congregation of Queens and teach himself mechanical drawing and drafting while mastering patent law, playing the flute, and writing poetry. He lived the last 26 years of his life in a wood-framed, Queen Anne–style house in Flushing, now a museum. (Both, LLHM.)

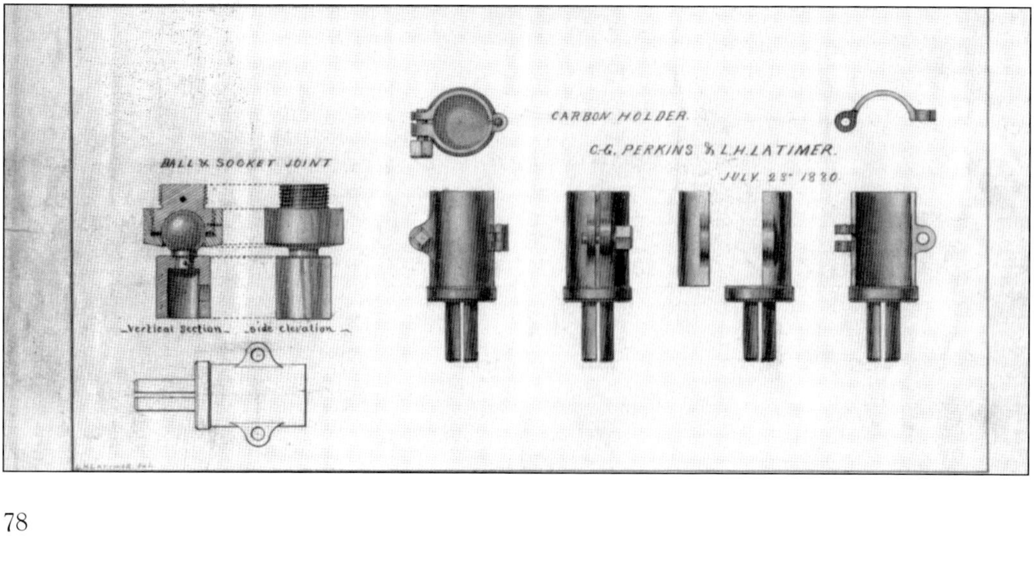

Gerald Edelman trained under legendary music teacher Albert Meiff to become a concert violinist, but at Ozone Park's John Adams High School, he lost interest. At the same time, he was a 1946 Westinghouse Science Talent Search semifinalist. He graduated magna cum laude with a degree in chemistry from Ursinus College in 1950 before joining the Rockefeller Institute for Medical Research. He and his team won a 1972 Nobel Prize in Medicine for discoveries about antibodies that led to reducing organ rejection after transplants. (LOC.)

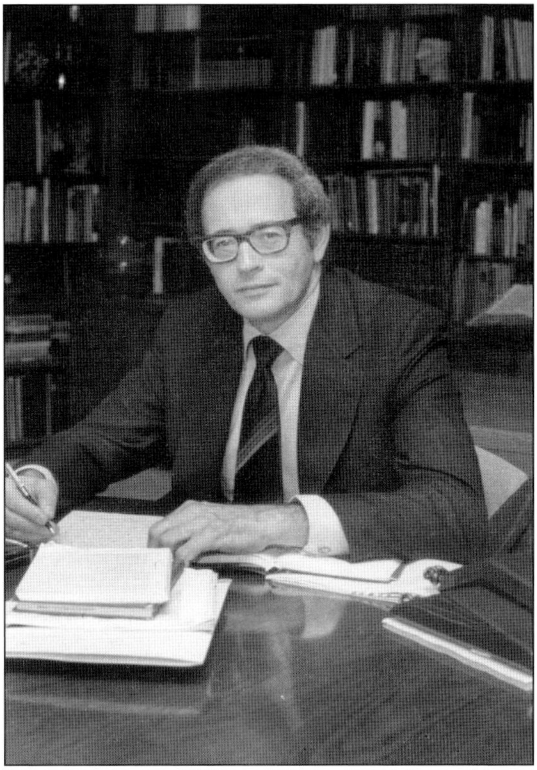

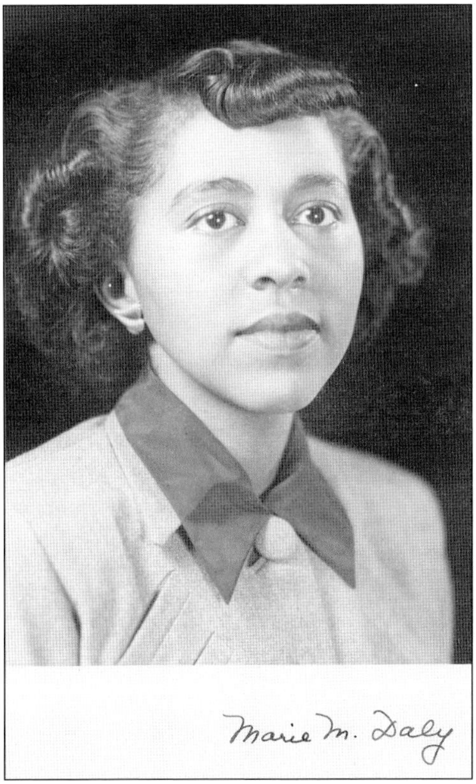


Marie Daly graduated magna cum laude from Queens College with a degree in chemistry in 1942. The next stop was Columbia University, where she made history in 1947 as the first African American woman in the United States to get a doctorate in chemistry. Her career mixed teaching with research on cholesterol, protein synthesis, and smoking at the Rockefeller Institute for Medical Research. In 1988, the Corona native established a scholarship fund for African Americans at Queens College. (Rockefeller University Archive Center.)

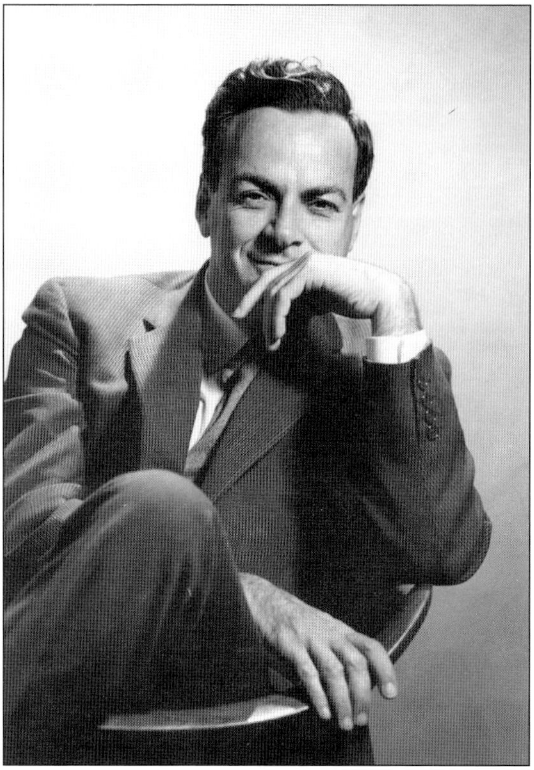

As a child, Richard Feynman created a lab in his Far Rockaway basement and built an alarm system for the house. While at Far Rockaway High School (class of 1935), the Arista Honor Society member taught himself advanced algebra, analytic geometry, calculus, and trigonometry. He also got the highest score in the country on the William Lowell Putnam Mathematical Competition Exam. At the Massachusetts Institute of Technology, he got the highest score ever (a perfect 100) on a math/physics graduate admission exam before receiving a doctorate from Princeton University. After working on the atomic bomb via the Manhattan Project during World War II, he taught theoretical physics at Cornell University before moving to the California Institute of Technology, where he became the de facto father of nanotechnology. He won the 1965 Nobel Prize in Physics. (Left, Caltech Archives; below, NASA.)

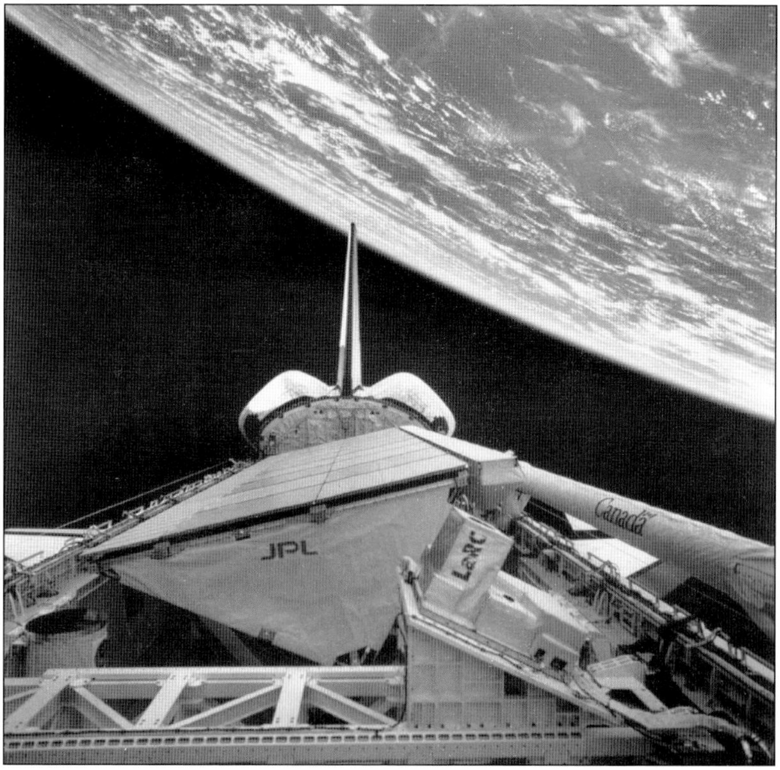

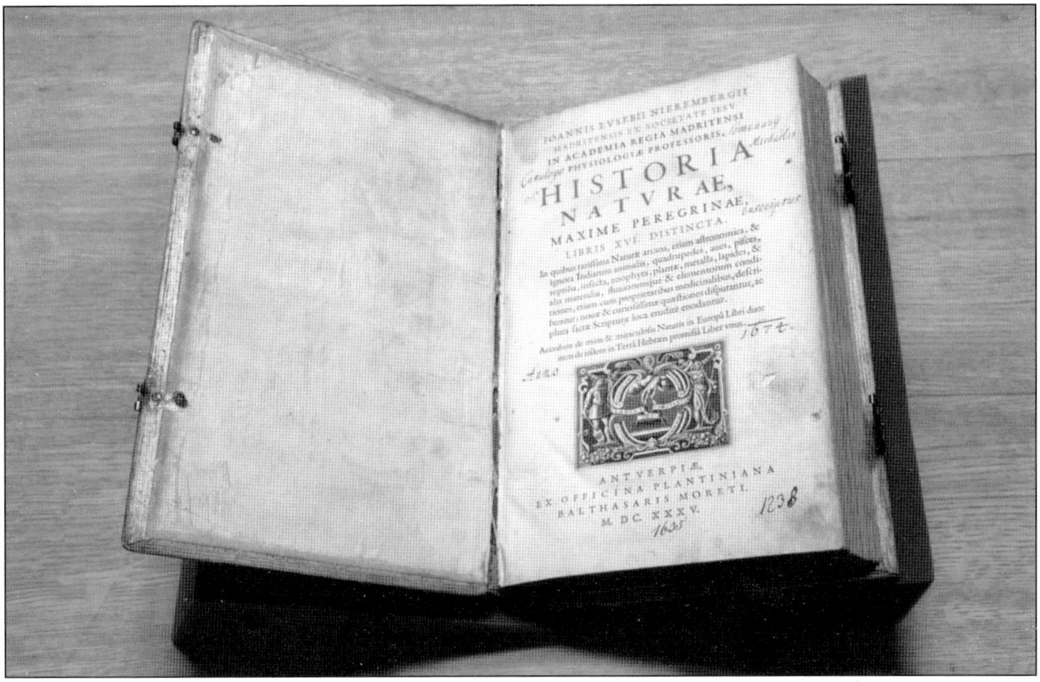


Stephen Gould was five years old in 1946 when he first saw the hulking skeletal display of Tyrannosaurus rex at the American Museum of Natural History. At the age of 11, the Bayside native read Charles Darwin's 1859 book *On the Origin of Species*. After graduating from Jamaica High School at 16, he got a bachelor's degree from Antioch College and a doctorate in paleontology from Columbia University before joining Harvard University's faculty. Within four years, Harvard granted him tenure. He and Niles Eldredge developed the theory of punctuated equilibrium, which purports that species do not evolve at the same pace but experience periods of stasis mixed with periods of rapid change. He went on to write 22 books, amass more than 40 honorary degrees, and win a 1981 MacArthur Fellowship and a 2000 Library of Congress Living Legend Award. (Both, Stanford University Libraries.)

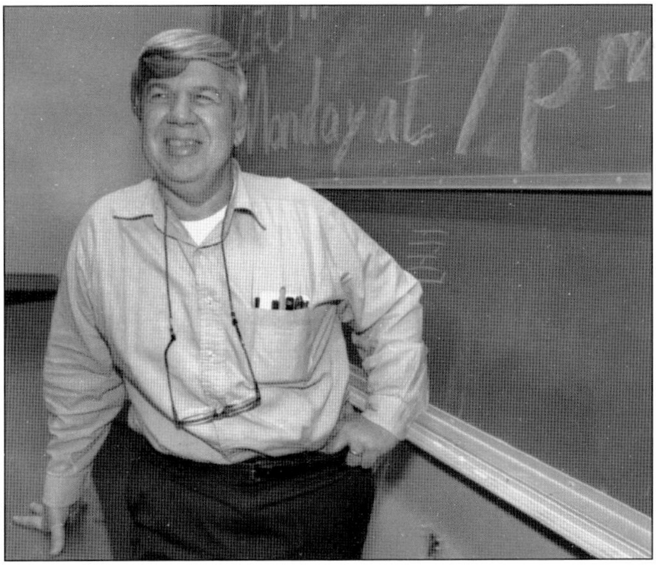

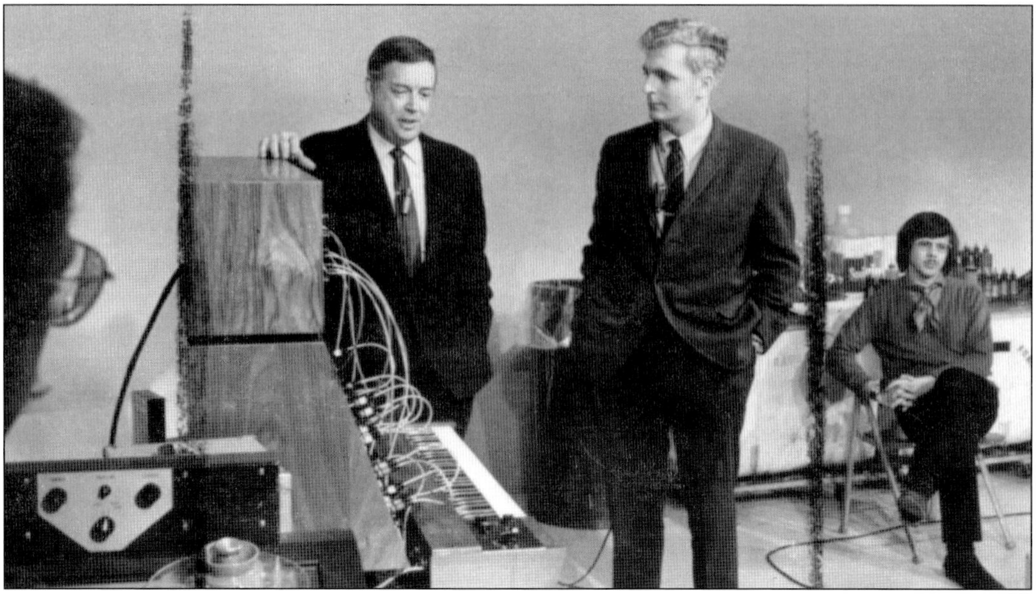

He is popular in North Carolina, where a museum and a music festival honor his life, but he grew up in Flushing. Born in 1934, Robert Moog spent countless hours in his childhood basement creating small instruments. While at the Bronx High School of Science, he read an article about the theremin, an eerie-sounding electronic instrument played by waving hands in the vicinity of metal rods to control pitch and volume. He built one. Then he built more and started selling them. In 1964, he invented the Moog synthesizer, whose knobs control the sound's fade, intensity, and onset. In 1968, Walter Carlos won a Grammy with *Switched-On Bach*, a compilation of the German composer's songs with a Moog-induced sound. The Beatles used a Moog on the 1969 *Abbey Road* album. These photographs are from the 1960 and 1970s. (Both, Cornell University Library.)

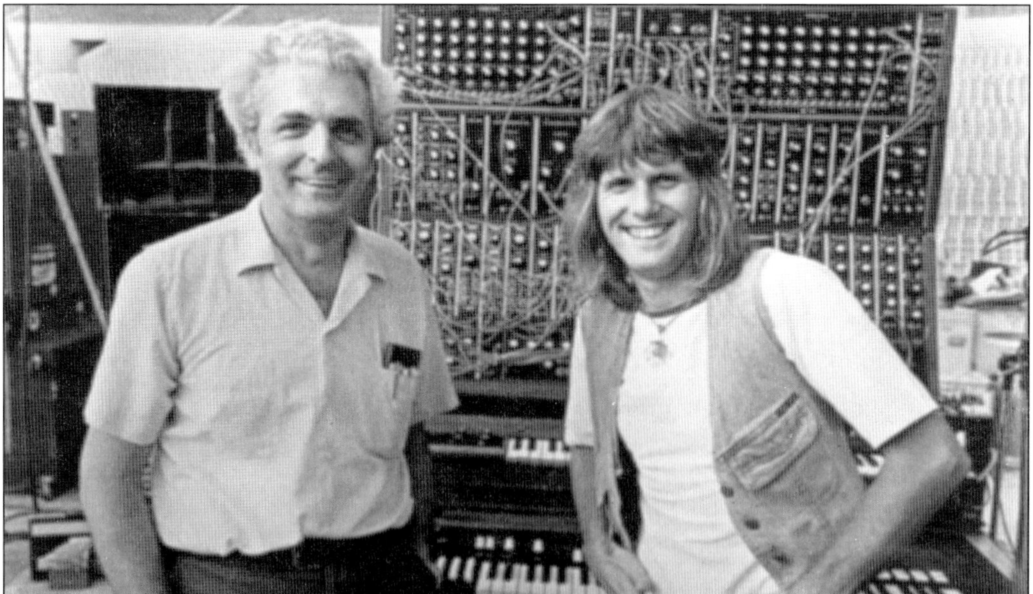

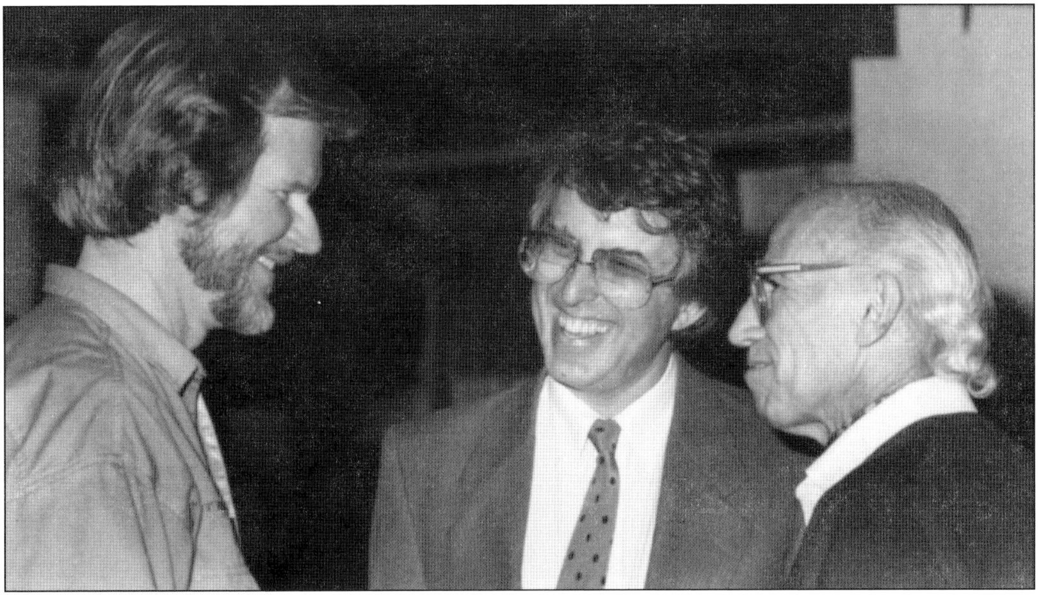

Jonas Salk (center), who grew up during the 1918 Spanish influenza pandemic, was so intent on saving the world that his brothers called him "Little Jesus." At the age of 12, he entered Flushing's Townsend Harris High School, where he graduated in three years before heading to the City College of New York. After graduating from New York University's School of Medicine, the perfectionist became a doctor at the age of 25. Fascinated by virology, he developed the vaccine for polio, which causes nerve damage, paralysis, and even death. (LOC.)

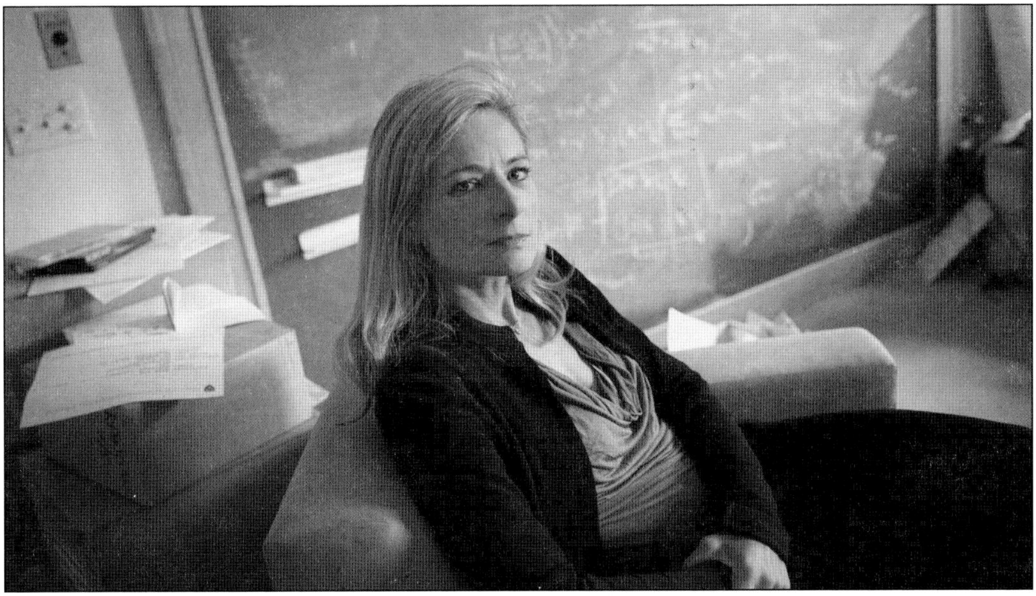

Fresh Meadows native Lisa Randall was the first female captain of Stuyvesant High School's math team. She graduated in 1980, the same year that she won first place in the Westinghouse Science Talent Search and a National Merit Scholarship. After earning a bachelor of arts in physics and a doctorate in theoretical particle physics from Harvard University, Randall was the first woman in Princeton University's Department of Physics to get tenure. She has taught at Harvard since 2001. (Harvard University.)

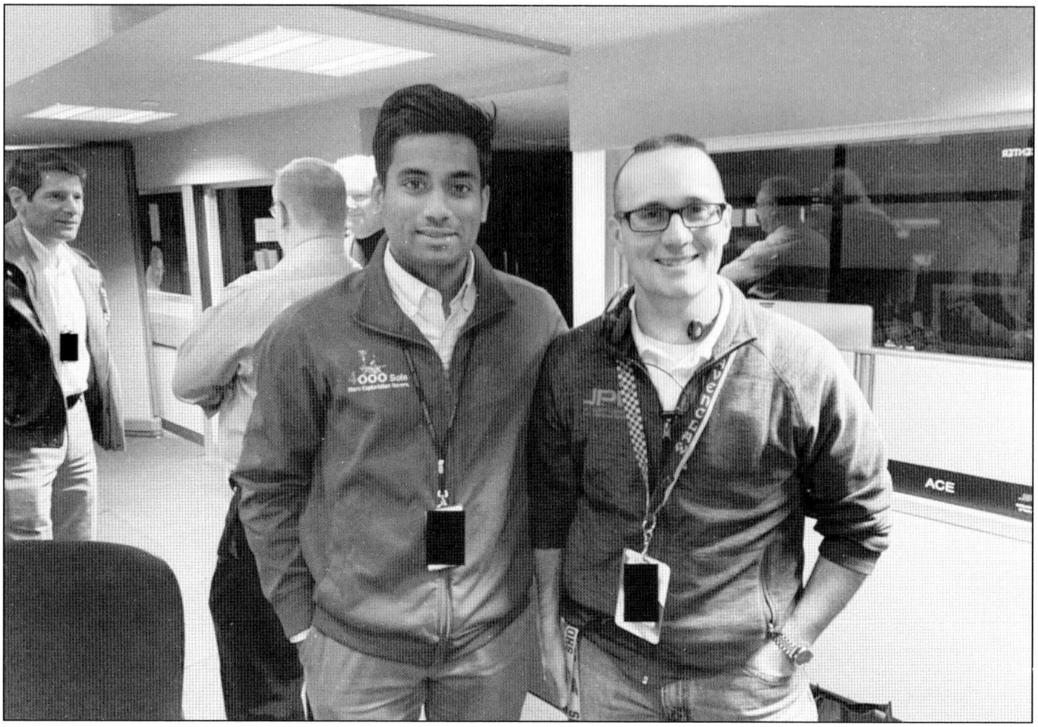


Vishnu Sridhar (left) was the lead systems engineer for NASA's mechanical rover *Perseverance*, which landed on Mars in 2021. He ran the SuperCam, which scans rocks from as far away as 20 feet; determines their chemical makeup; and takes high-resolution images. Sridhar, whose grandfather helped build India's second-largest dam, developed his interest in space while watching planes above his Rego Park apartment as they landed and took off from LaGuardia Airport. For a project at Aviation High School, he sent a weather balloon about 100,000 feet in the air. He installed an altitude pressure sensor and a camera in the balloon to marvel at space's vastness and Earth's curvature. He got an aerospace engineering degree from the Georgia Institute of Technology in 2015 before eventually landing at NASA's Jet Propulsion Laboratory. (Above, Georgia Institute of Technology; below, NASA.)

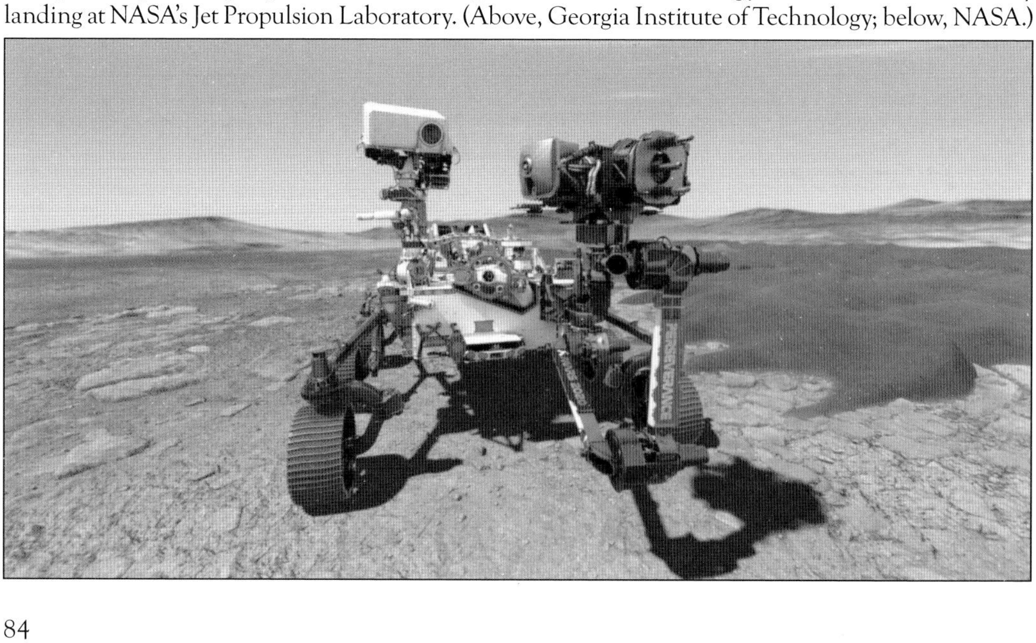

# *Six*

# Towers of Power

Japan's current prime minister says his love of diversity and his desire for social justice come from his childhood in Elmhurst. Fumio Kishida was six years old in 1963 when his father got a job as a trade official in New York City and moved the family to Queens. The Tokyo native attended PS 13. Years later, he entered Japanese politics with the Liberal Democratic Party, rising steadily until succeeding Prime Minister Shinzo Abe in 2021. (Official website of the prime minister of Japan and his cabinet.)

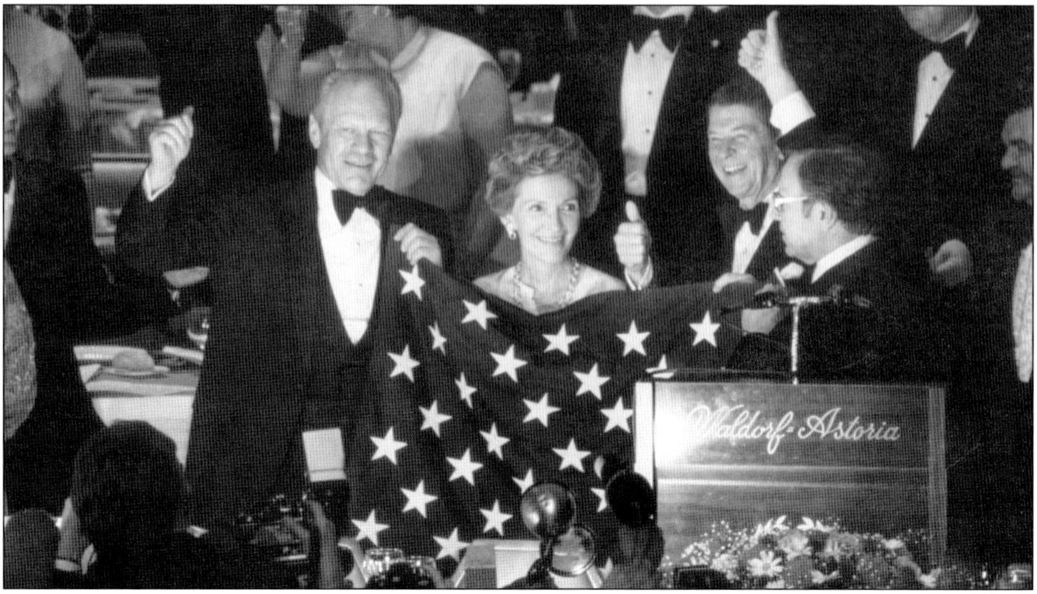


As a two-time First Lady, movie actress, and drug prevention advocate, Nancy Reagan lived in front of cameras. Nevertheless, few people know that she was born Ann Frances Robbins in 1921, and her first residence was a three-story frame house in Murray Hill. Nancy (center), who married Ronald Reagan (right) in 1952 before he was governor of California and president of the United States, is seen with Pres. Gerald Ford (left) at the Waldorf-Astoria New York in this 1980 photograph. (LOC.)

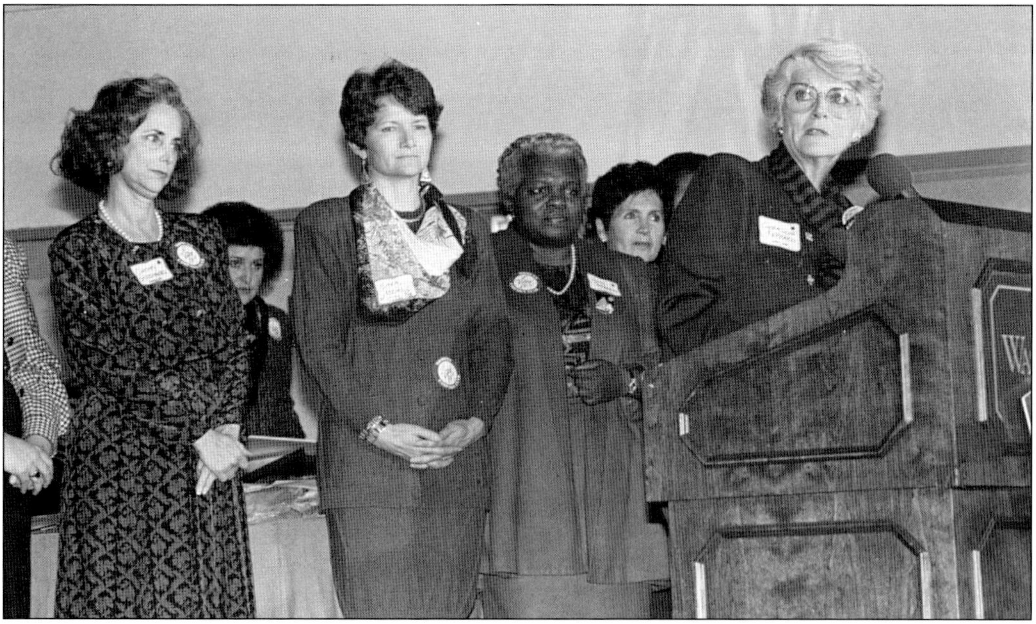

In 1984, presidential candidate Walter Mondale tried to breathe life into his campaign by choosing Congresswoman Geraldine Ferraro (right), a 48-year-old Democrat, as his vice presidential candidate. They lost to Pres. Ronald Reagan and Vice Pres. George H.W. Bush in a landslide, but the Forest Hills Gardens resident made history as the first woman to represent a major party in a national election. Ferraro started her career as a prosecutor with the Queens District Attorney's Office. She then won a seat in Congress with the slogan "Finally, A Tough Democrat." (LOC.)

Eric Holder was attorney general of the United States during Pres. Barack Obama's first term and deputy attorney general during Pres. Bill Clinton's administration. He was the first African American to be named to both posts. The East Elmhurst native attended a gifted and talented program in elementary school before heading to Manhattan for Stuyvesant High School, Columbia University, and Columbia Law School. He then began his 40-year Washington, DC, career in the Department of Justice under six presidents. This family portrait includes his wife, Dr. Sharon (Malone) Holder. (LOC.)

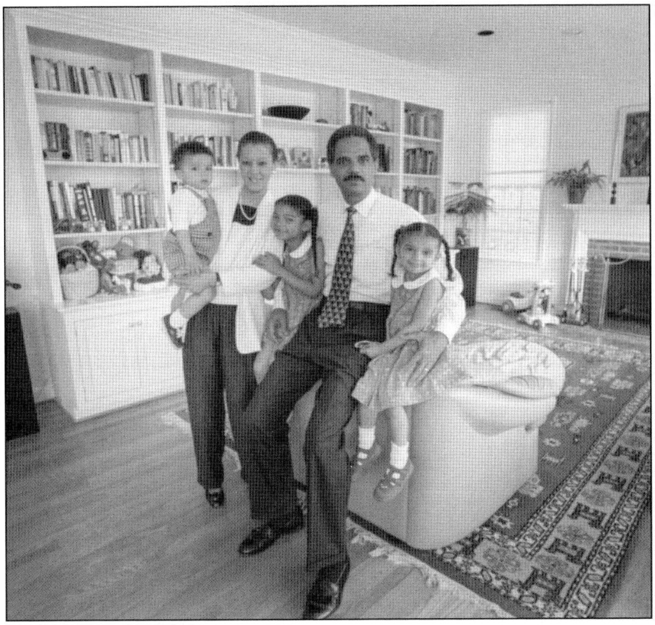

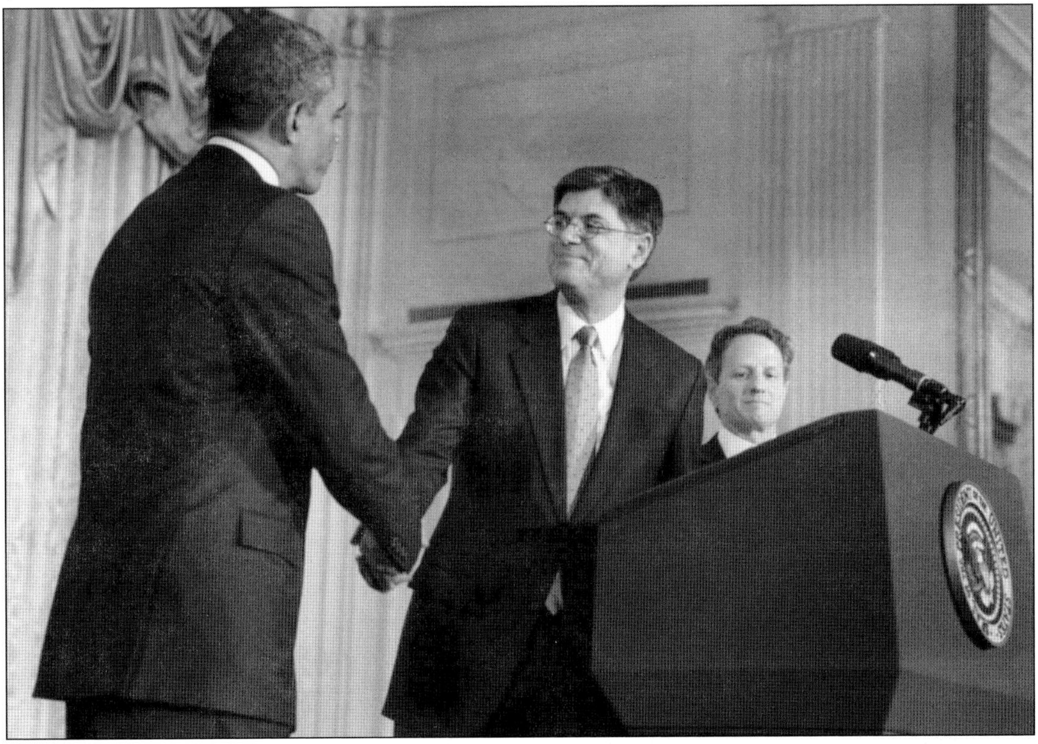

Jacob Lew's (center) résumé includes treasury secretary, Office of Management and Budget director, Pres. Barack Obama's chief of staff, AmeriCorps cofounder, and deputy secretary of state. These titles would not surprise anyone who knew the ambitious Democrat when he was growing up on Yellowstone Boulevard in Forest Hills. His career was definitely influenced by his time at the Forest Hills Jewish Center, a conservative synagogue led by Rabbi Ben Zion Bosker, a passionate social justice advocate. (White House.)

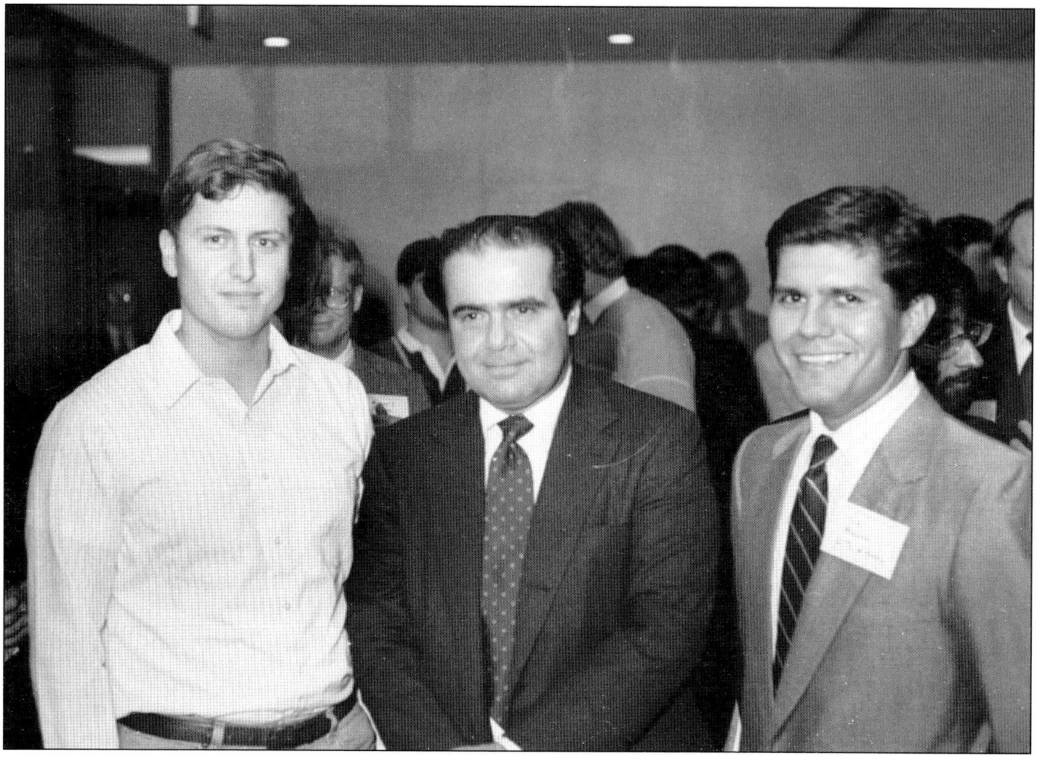

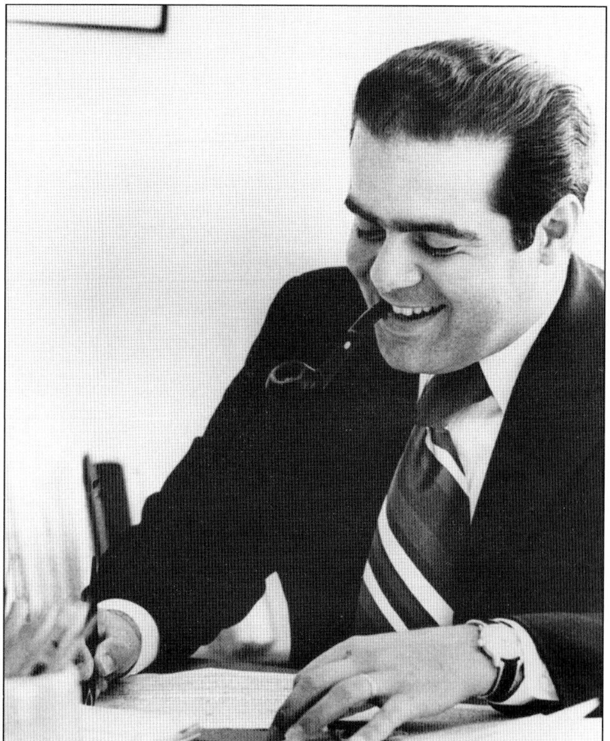

Opinionated. Funny. Conservative. Justice Antonin Scalia (center) had a tremendous career after Pres. Ronald Reagan nominated him to be the first Roman Catholic on the Supreme Court in 1986. But through all the cases, speeches, and dissents, he always maintained that he was just an Elmhurst kid who learned life's major lessons while playing street hockey in the PS 13 schoolyard. Born in 1936 to a Sicilian immigrant father and first-generation Italian American mother, Justice Scalia was first in his class at Manhattan's Xavier High School and valedictorian at Georgetown University. He then graduated magna cum laude from Harvard Law School, where he was editor of *Harvard Law Review*. He died at the age of 79 in 2016. Pres. Donald Trump, a Republican, awarded him a posthumous Presidential Medal of Freedom in 2018. (Above, University of Virginia Law; left, Antonin Scalia Papers, Harvard Law School.)

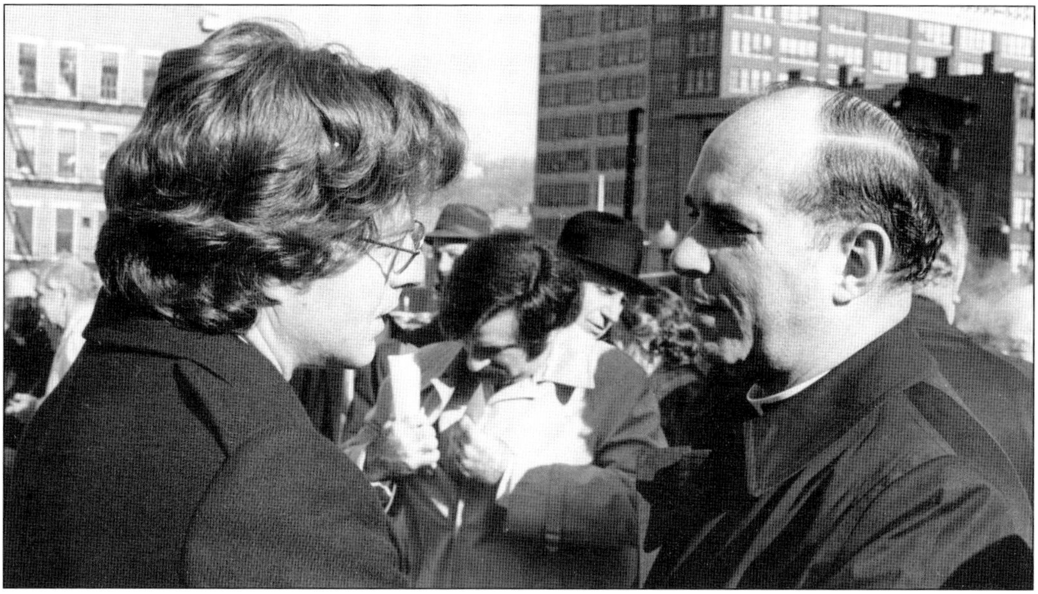

In the 1940s and 1950s, some Jews fled Nazi Germany and settled in Kew Gardens. Their children went to PS 99, where they learned English while speaking German at home. The community produced several overachievers, including Penguin Books CEO Peter Mayer; Cornell University physics professor Robert Lieberman; and Jerry Springer, who was mayor of Cincinnati before starring in NBC's *The Jerry Springer Show* from 1991 to 2018. Mayor Springer (left) talks to Archbishop Joseph Bernardin (right) in this 1977 photograph. (Cincinnati & Hamilton County Public Library.)

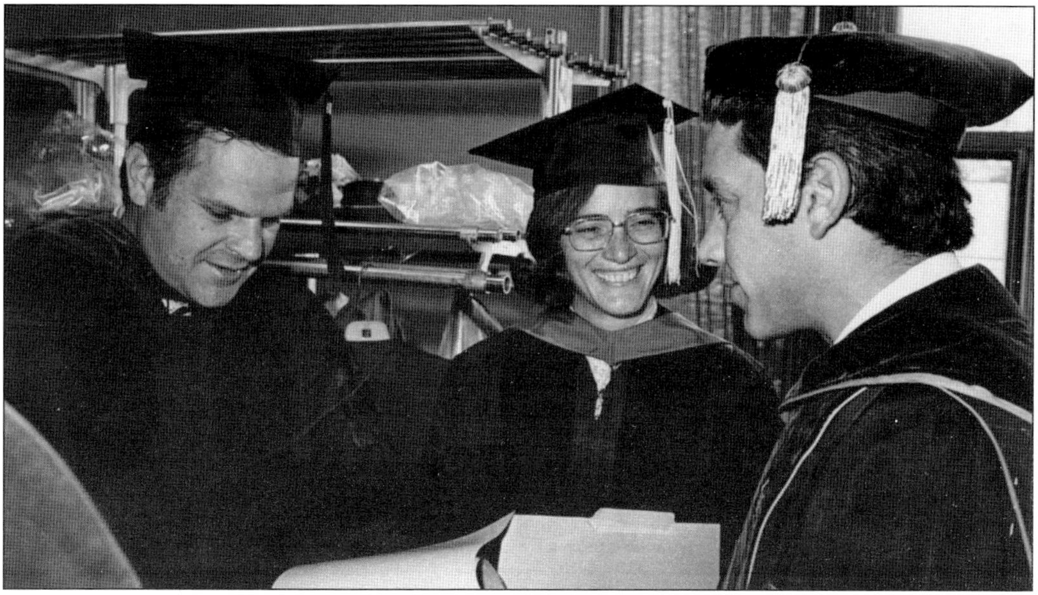

Queens has had dozens of borough presidents but none as colorful—and controversial—as Donald Manes (left). The youngest borough president ever when he ascended at 37 in 1971, the Democrat was popular, winning reelection four times and serving as a delegate to the 1980 Democratic National Convention. Soon thereafter, his career spun out of control due to allegations of corruption, drugs, and orgies. Manes fatally stabbed himself with a knife in his Jamaica Estates house in 1986. (LaGuardia Community College Institutional Archives.)

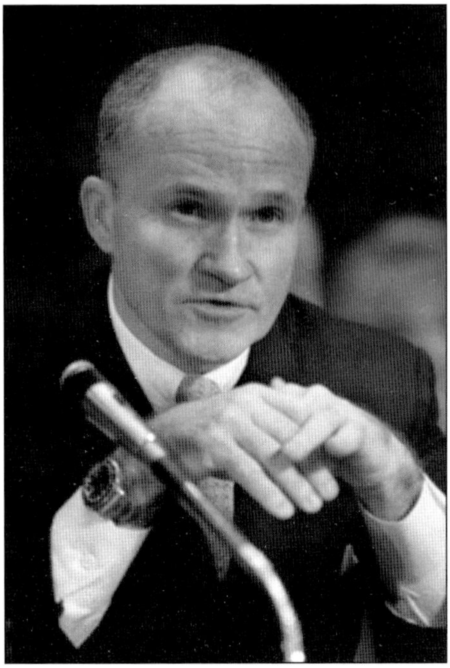

Ray Kelly is the longest-serving New York City Police Department commissioner and the first to hold nonconsecutive terms (1992–1994 under Mayor David Dinkins and 2002–2013 under Mayor Michael Bloomberg). In 43 years on the force, he held 25 ranks, starting as a cadet. Outside the Big Apple, the Marine Corps veteran directed policing during the United Nations mission in Haiti under Pres. Bill Clinton. The Archbishop Molloy High School grad, who mostly grew up in Sunnyside, testifies before the Senate Finance Committee in this photograph. (LOC.)

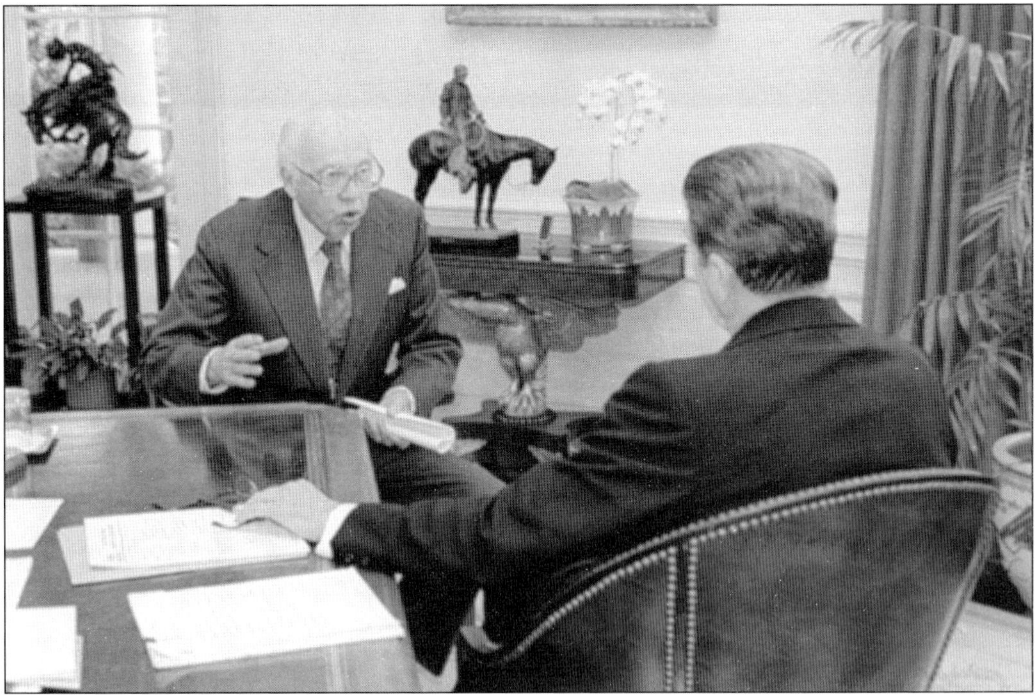

Born in 1913, William Casey grew up as a huge Horatio Alger and Buffalo Bill fan. During World War II, the Elmhurst native joined the Office of Strategic Services, which later became the Central Intelligence Agency (CIA), directing Nazi spies from London. After holding various positions in Pres. Richard Nixon's administration, he led Ronald Reagan's successful 1980 presidential campaign. His reward was to be named CIA director, although he later resigned due to the Iran-Contra Affair. (Central Intelligence Agency.)

New York state has had two Governor Cuomos (Nos. 52 and 56), and both grew up in Queens. Mario (right, 1981) was born in Briarwood in 1932. He won the gubernatorial campaign in 1982 and served three terms before losing to George Pataki in 1994. Andrew was born in 1957 and grew up in Holliswood. He became state attorney general in 2006 and governor in 2010. Though reelected twice, he resigned due to corruption and sexual harassment allegations in 2021. (LOC.)

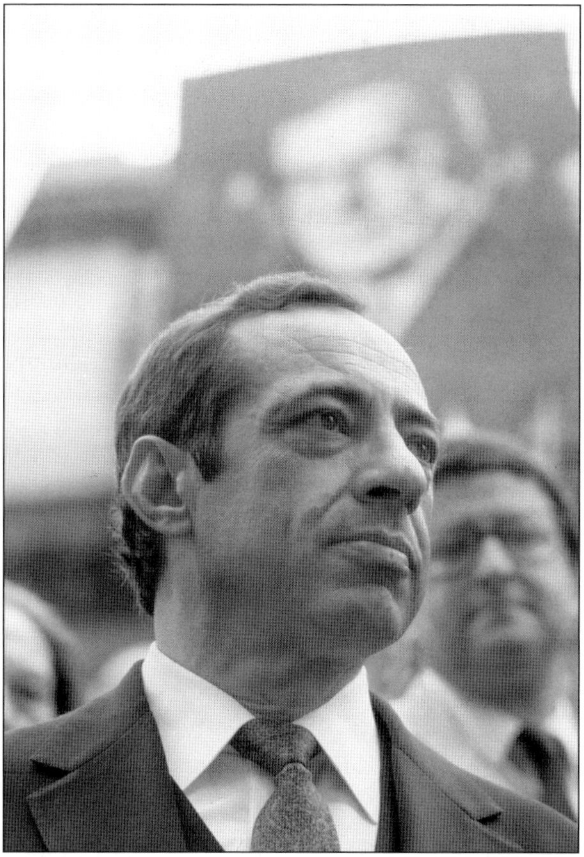

Eleven-term Congresswoman Sheila Jackson Lee (right) is a senior member of the House Judiciary, Homeland Security, and Budget Committees, among other honors. The Democrat sat on the Houston City Council and served as a municipal judge before joining Congress in 1995. Though she made her political career in Texas, she was born in Queens and graduated from Jamaica High School in 1968. Here, she talks to Sen. Joe Lieberman (left) of Connecticut during the Enron hearings in 2002. (LOC.)

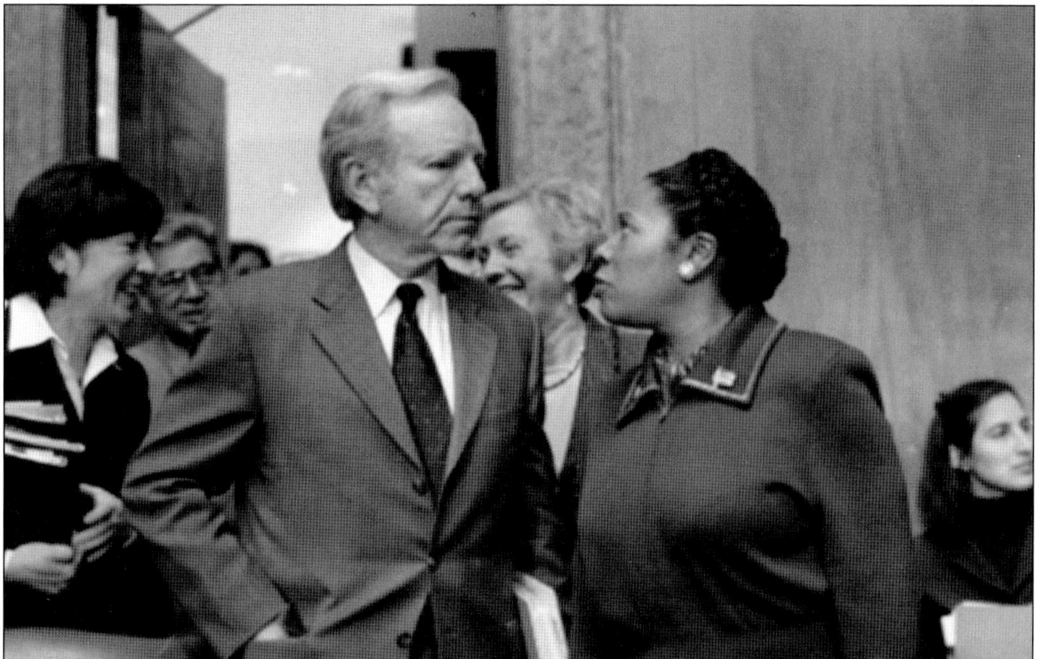

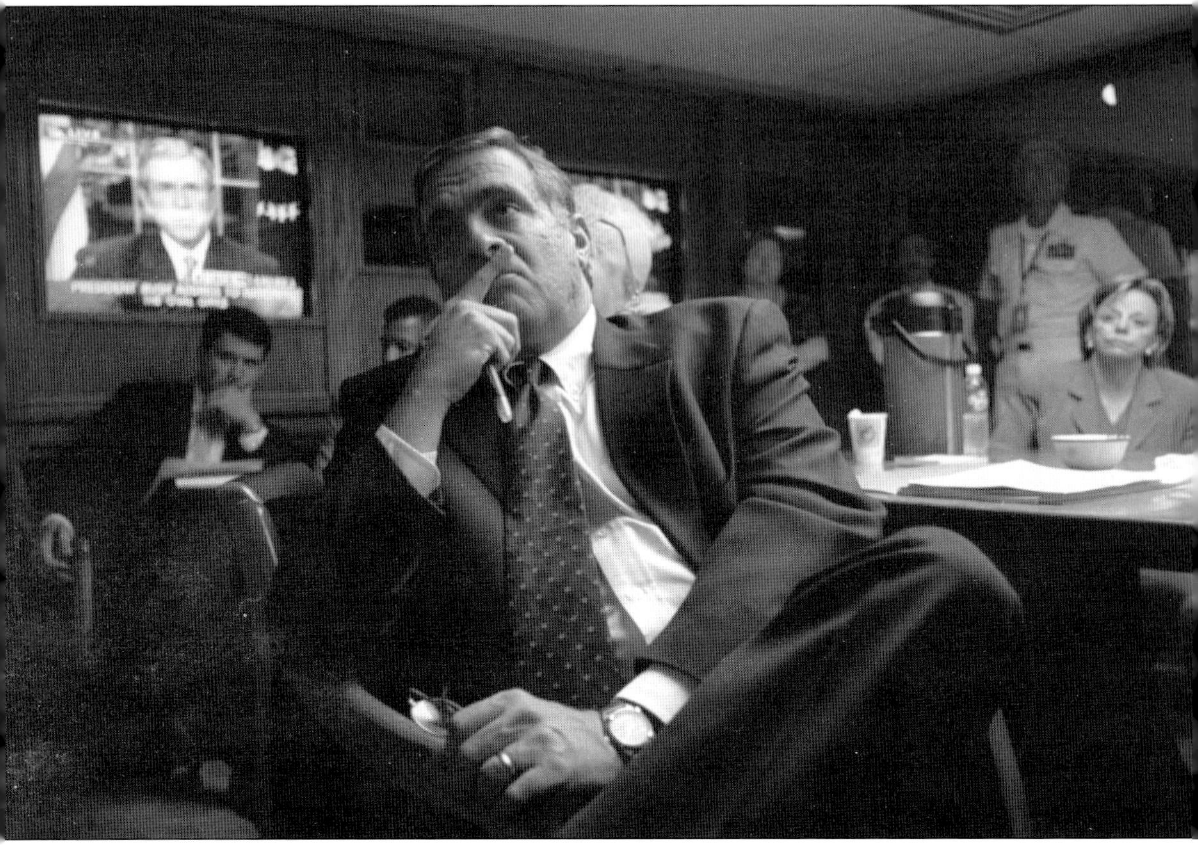

Born on January 5, 1953, George Tenet grew up at 42–28 Marathon Parkway, only a few blocks from the Twentieth Century Diner, which delighted patrons with late-night pizza burgers, Sunday morning brunches, and addictive milkshakes. His Greek immigrant parents, John and Evangelia, owned the Little Neck establishment, where he worked as a busboy. The graduate of Bayside's Benjamin N. Cardozo High School had a long career in international affairs that included serving as CIA director from 1997 to 2004, a time marked by the 9/11 terrorist attacks and the Iraq War build-up. One of very few CIA directors to serve a Democrat (Pres. Bill Clinton) and a Republican (Pres. George W. Bush), Tenet received a Presidential Medal of Freedom in 2004. (National Archives.)

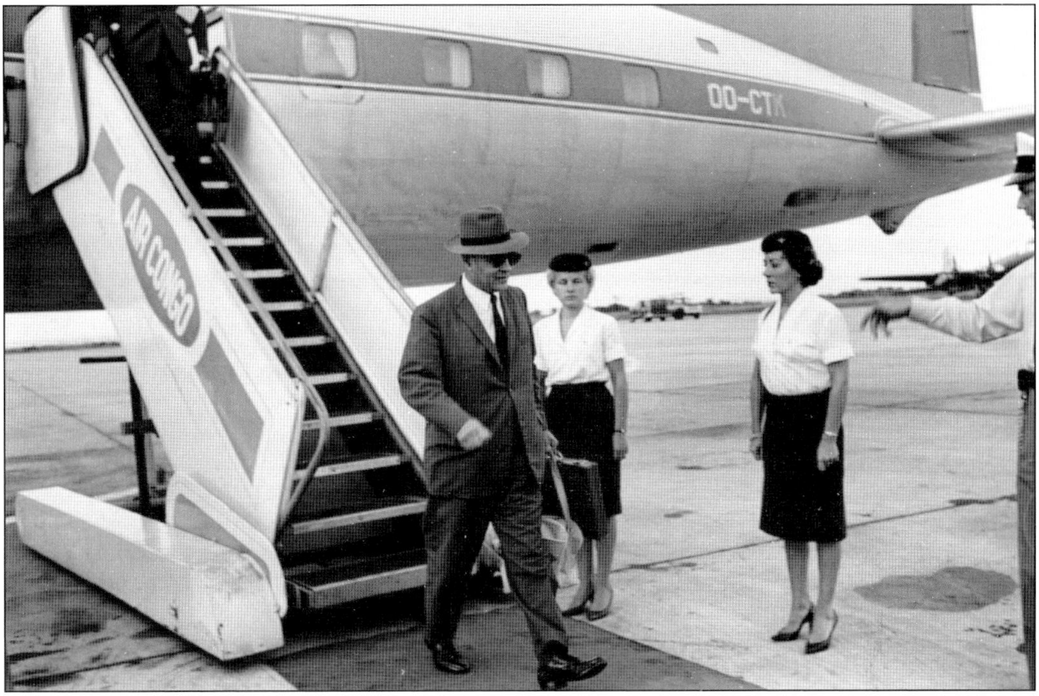


For negotiating with Palestine after Israel became a nation in 1948, Ralph Bunche was the first African American to win a Nobel Prize in 1950. The United Nations undersecretary-general also received a Presidential Medal of Freedom from Pres. Lyndon B. Johnson (he was selected by Pres. John F. Kennedy, who was assassinated before the medal was awarded). He lived in a Neo-Tudor house in Kew Gardens that was declared a national historic landmark in 1976. Above, Bunche arrives in Belgian Congo in 1960. (Both, LOC.)

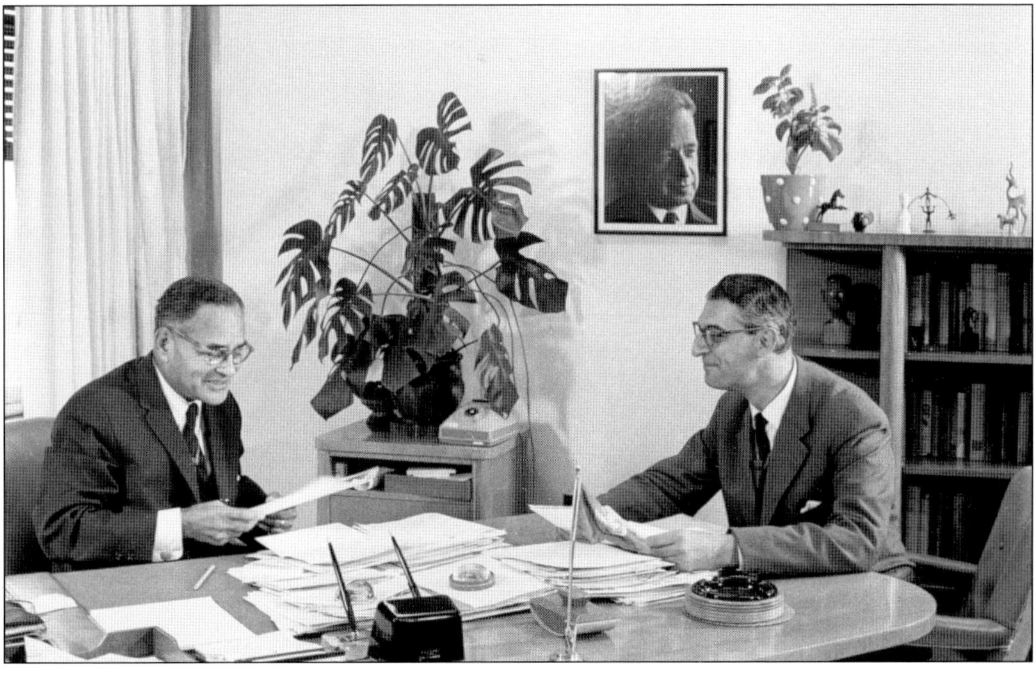

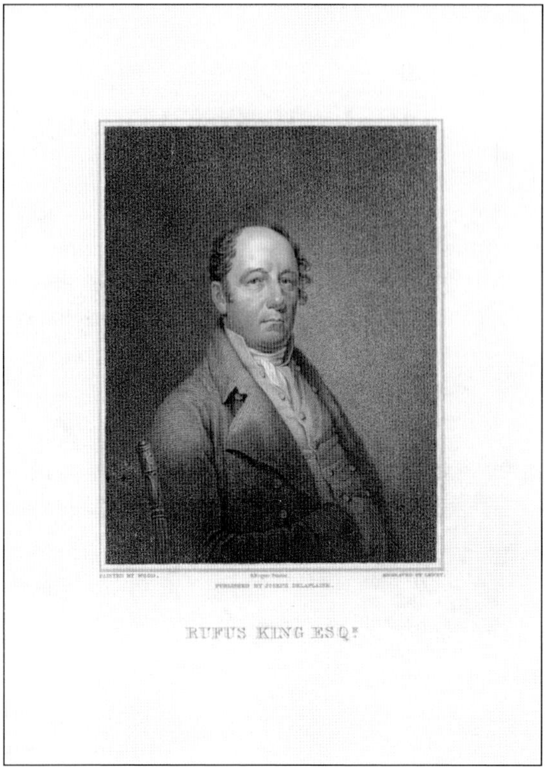


Rufus King was a senator for almost 18 years and ambassador to Great Britain. Though he did not win, he was twice selected as the Federalist Party candidate for vice president and once for president. From 1805 to 1896, King and his descendants lived in King Manor, a three-story, three-chimney mansion with clapboard windows that was built in 1730 and is now a landmarked museum. They raised livestock and grew apples, barley, corn, peaches, potatoes, strawberries, and wheat on about 150 acres in Jamaica. (Both, King Manor Museum.)

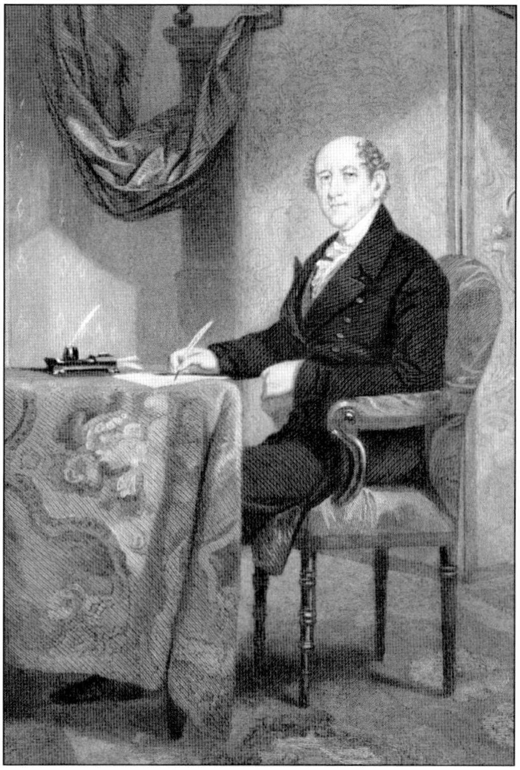

# *Seven*

# Local Heroes

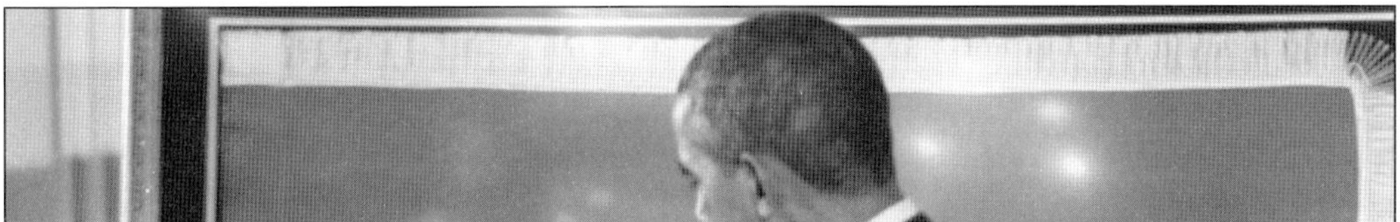

Alfred Nietzel enlisted in 1940. The Jamaica native survived action in North Africa and Europe while rising to the rank of sergeant. On November 18, 1944, German forces attacked his unit during the Battle of Hürtgen. Nietzel covered squad members by firing a machine gun on the Nazi advance before a grenade killed him. Above, his cousin Robert Nietzel accepts a Congressional Medal of Honor on his behalf from Pres. Barack Obama on March 18, 2014. (US Department of Defense.)

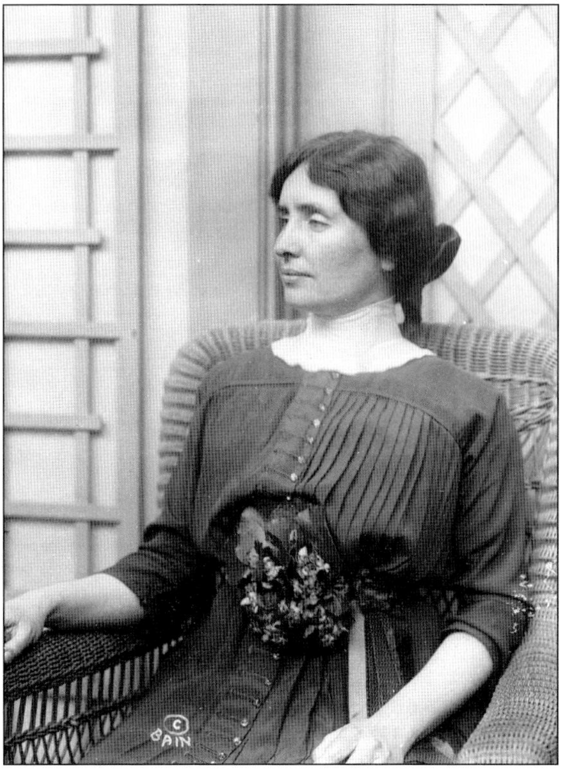

Helen Keller graduated from Radcliffe College, cofounded the American Civil Liberties Union (ACLU), and fought for women's suffrage and other causes despite being blind and deaf due to scarlet fever. The overachiever, seen with her tutor Anne "Miracle Worker" Sullivan, grew up in Forest Hills, and her house, which she called Castle on the Marsh, was a hotbed of activism. Keller's family had a de facto open-door policy for friends, colleagues, and community groups, especially the 42nd Infantry Division of the US Army, which Gen. Douglas MacArthur called the "Rainbow Division." She held fundraisers for charities at the brick house at 112th Street and Seventy-First Road and organized birthday parties for the blind on her front lawn. Castle on the Marsh burned down after the family had moved out. The Reform Temple of Forest Hills currently operates on the site. (Both, LOC.)

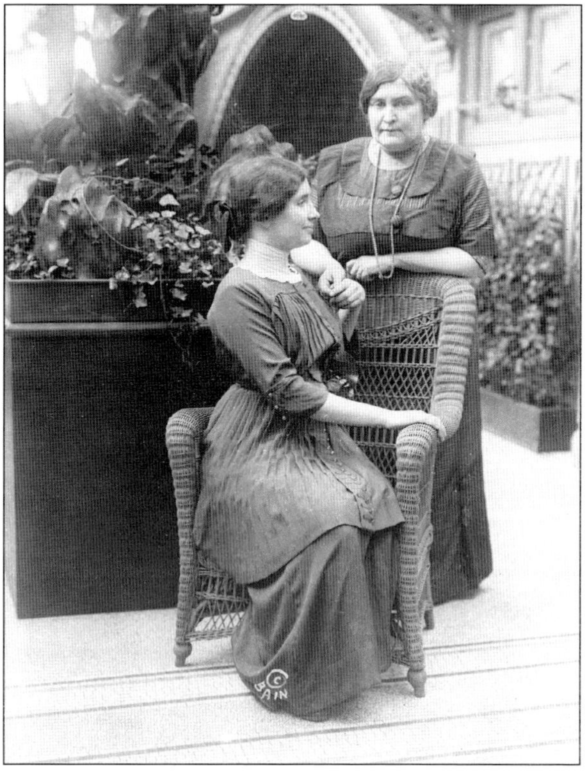

Richmond Hill's Louis Willet was drafted into the Vietnam War with the rank of US Army private first class and a specialty in light weapons infantry in 1966. In Kontum Province on February 15, 1967, he was killed while protecting squad members from heavy enemy fire. He was the first Archbishop Molloy High School graduate (class of 1963) to receive a Congressional Medal of Honor. He also received a Purple Heart and National Defense Service Medal. (CMHS.)

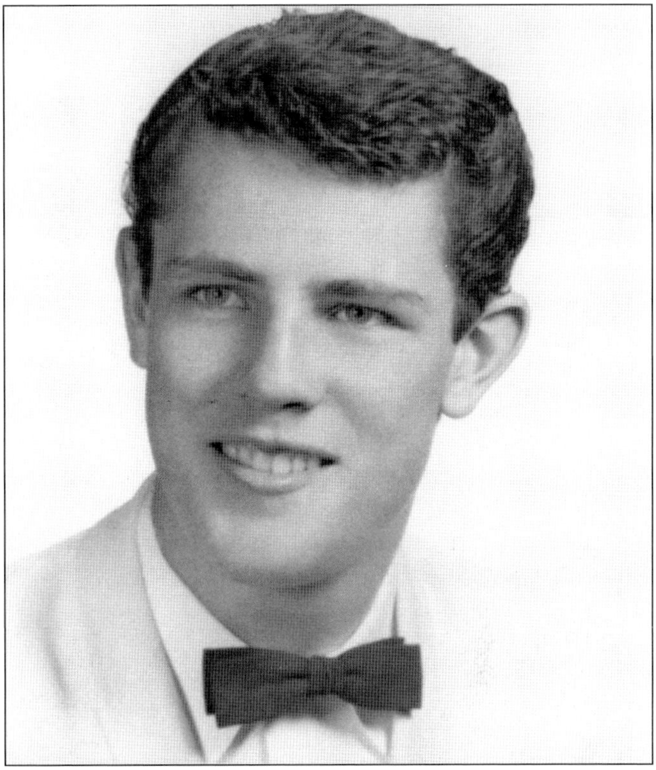

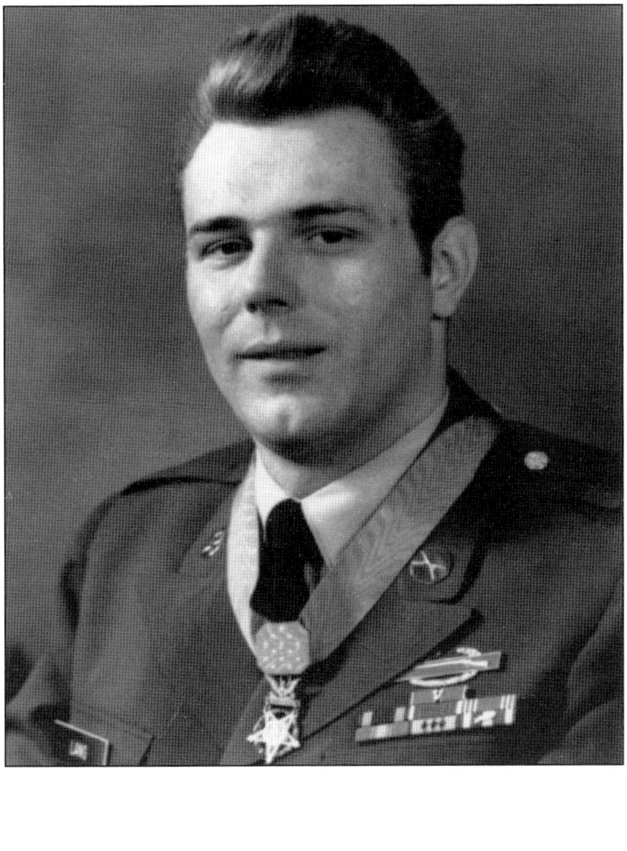

Sp4c. George Charles Lang went on a reconnaissance mission in Vietnam's Kien Hoa Province on February 22, 1969. Under attack, the 21-year-old Flushing native and his squad destroyed a bunker with grenades and rifles before jumping across a canal and moving through heavy fire to attack more bunkers. A rocket cut his spinal cord, leading to paraplegia. Pres. Richard Nixon presented wheelchair-bound Lang with the Congressional Medal of Honor on March 2, 1971. (CMHS.)

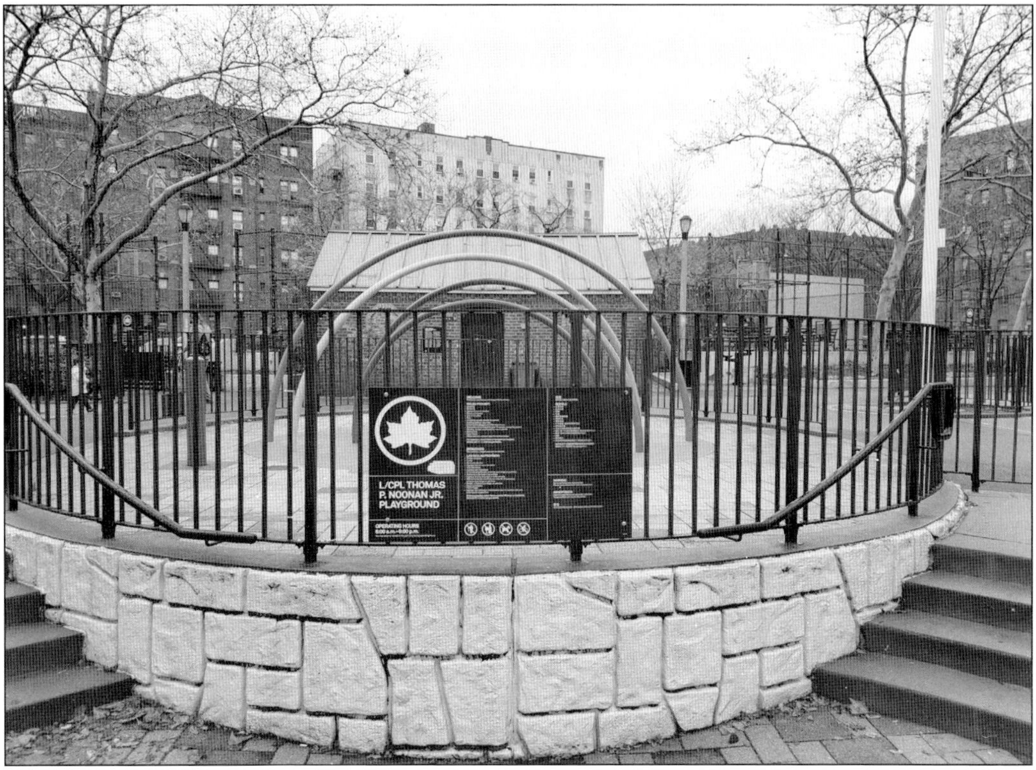


Thomas Noonan enlisted in the US Marine Corps Reserve in 1967. A few months later, the Sunnyside native was sent to the Vietnam War, where he served as a motorman and rifleman. On February 5, 1969, in the A Sầu Valley, he was killed by an enemy round while dragging wounded soldiers to safety. His posthumous awards include a Congressional Medal of Honor, a Purple Heart, two Bronze Stars, and a Sunnyside playground named in his honor. (QTC.)

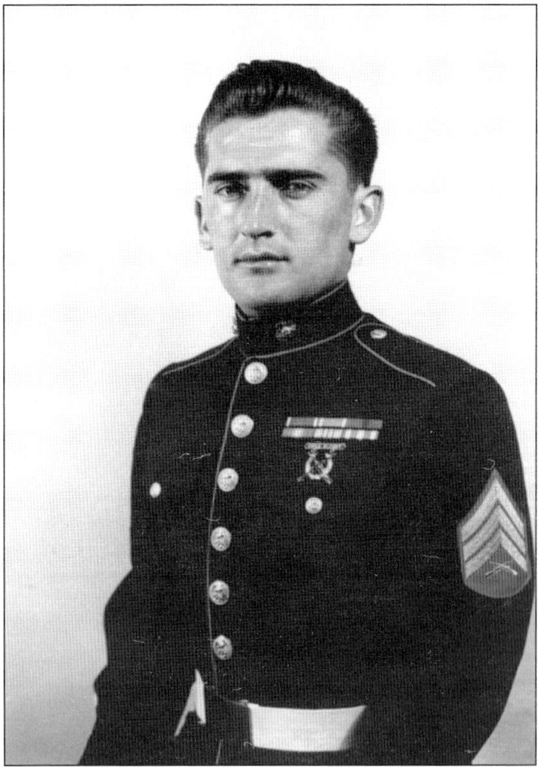

Robert O'Malley grew up near Thomas Noonan in Woodside, and they knew each other as children. O'Malley was a US Marines Corps sergeant in the Vietnam War. On August 18, 1965, he ran across a rice paddy, jumped into a trench line, and killed eight enemy soldiers with a rifle and grenades. Though wounded, he helped evacuate others. O'Malley received a Congressional Medal of Honor, Purple Heart, Bronze Star, and National Defense Service Medal. (CMHS.)

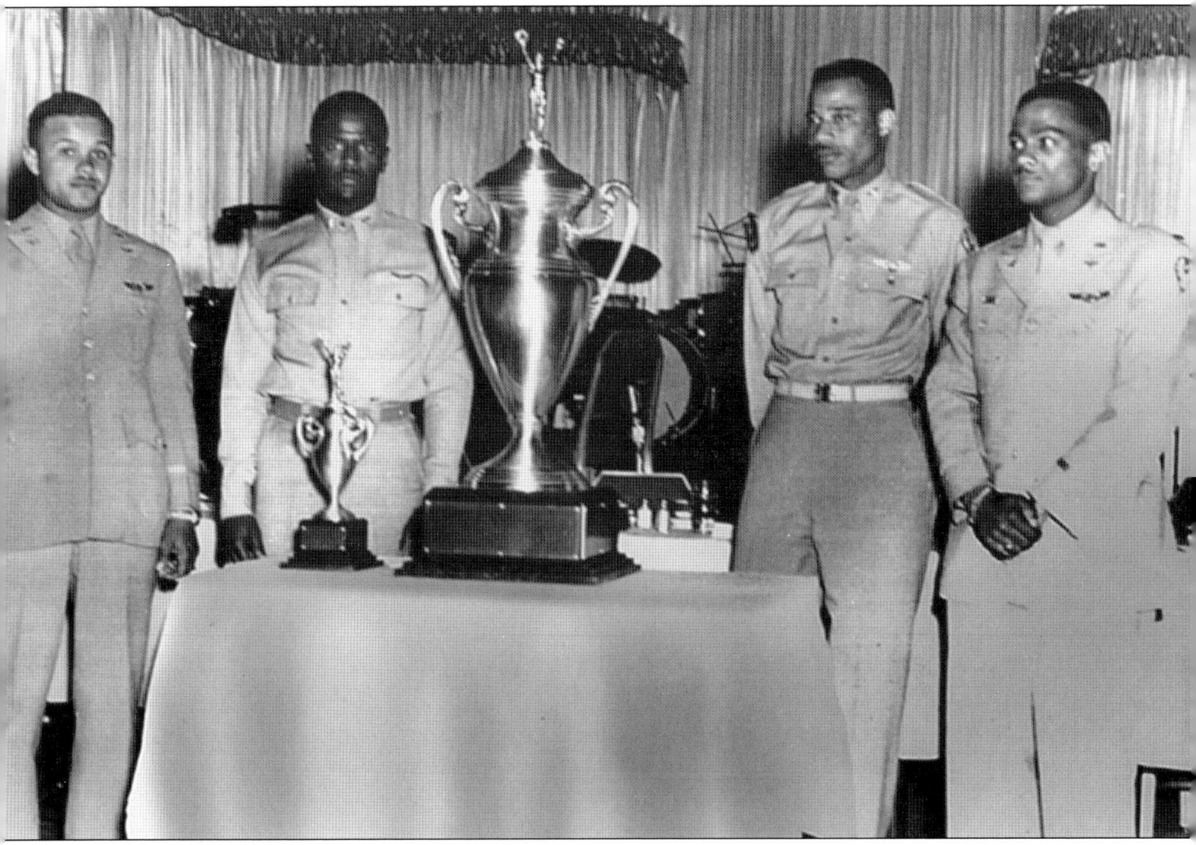

The Tuskegee Airmen were 992 African American pilots who flew and maintained planes in a segregated Army during World War II. Many achieved combat successes with tremendous demonstrations of ability and fearless acts of heroism. Harry T. Stewart Jr. (right), who grew up in East Elmhurst, was one of the most decorated. Born in 1924, he enlisted in the Army Air Corps as an aviation cadet at 17 and was still a teenager when he got his wings and commission. In Italy in 1944, he flew 43 combat missions in a P-51 Mustang with the 332nd Fighter Group's 301st Fighter Squadron. During a battle against Nazis in Austrian skies in 1945, Stewart shot down three Focke-Wulf 190s, earning him a Distinguished Flying Cross. He is one of four Tuskegee Airmen to win three aerial dogfights in one day. (US Air Force.)

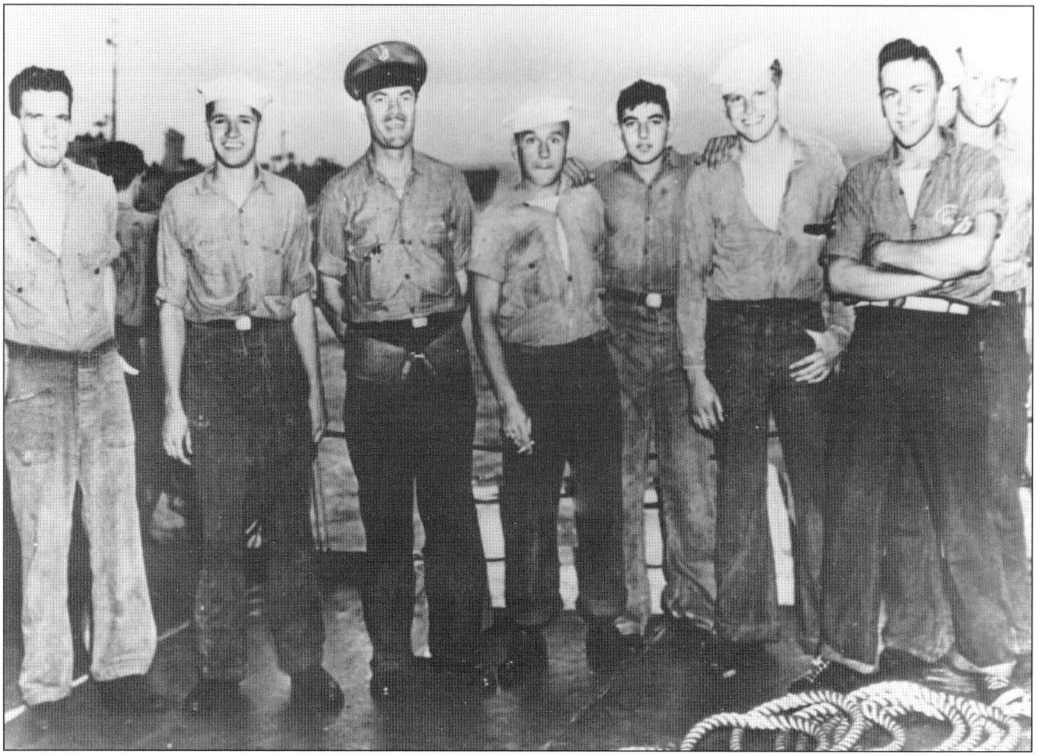

Maspeth native Stanley Wdowiak was 17 when he joined the Navy to fight in World War II. Off the northwestern coast of Africa on June 4, 1944, he and another sailor attacked a German submarine using rifles and grenades. They controlled the crew, allowing others to enter the craft and decode German military communications. The armed forces used the intelligence to save hundreds of lives during the D-Day invasion. Wdowiak, second from the right, earned a Navy Cross. (US Navy.)

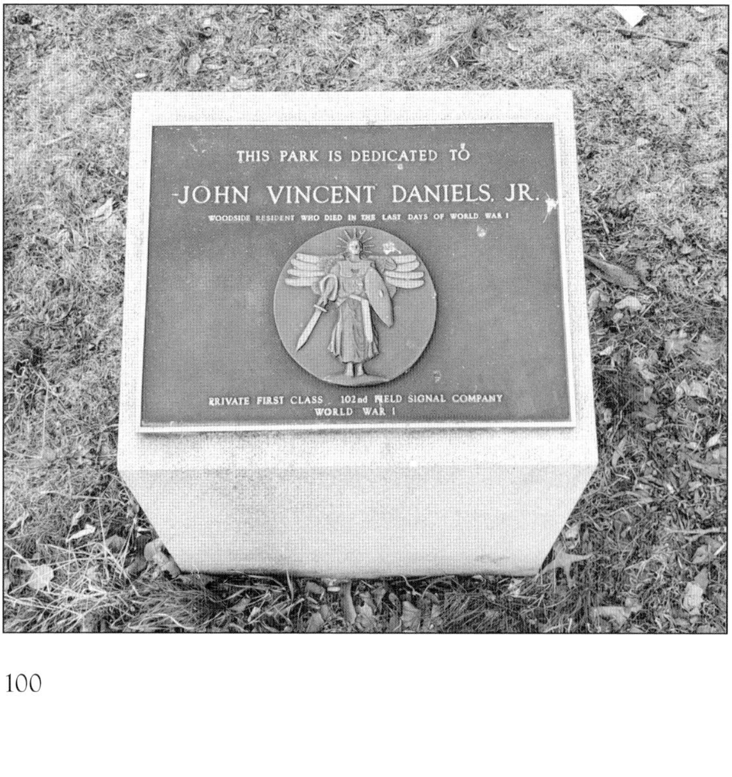


There are two tragedies related to John Vincent Daniels Jr. A private first class with the 102nd Field Signal Company, he was killed in action in France in 1918 during the final days of World War I. A few years later, the Veterans of Foreign Wars established Post 2813 in his honor near where his parents lived in Sunnyside. Though busy during the 1960s, the post closed at the height of the COVID pandemic in 2020. Most members had died or passed away. (QTC.)

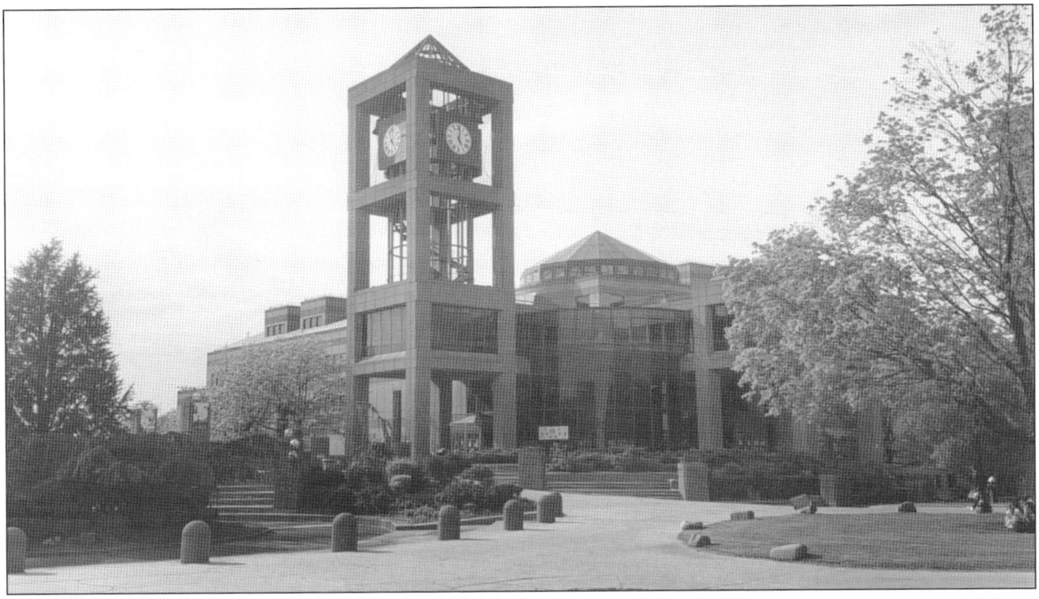

Queens College student Andrew Goodman decided to spend the 1964 summer registering African Americans to vote in Mississippi with the Congress for Racial Equality's Freedom Summer Project. On June 21, Ku Klux Klan members abducted and fatally shot the 20-year-old student and two others, James Chaney and Michael Schwerner. The murders caused public outrage and sparked efforts to pass the 1965 Voting Rights Act. Simon & Garfunkel's song "He Was My Brother" is dedicated to Goodman, who was Paul Simon's friend at Queens College, and the other two men who were killed. In 1989, Queens College dedicated the Chaney-Goodman-Schwerner library clock shown in the above photograph. Below, civil rights leader Martin Luther King Jr. shows photographs of the three martyrs during a speech. In 2014, Pres. Barack Obama awarded posthumous Presidential Medals of Freedom to all three. (Above, QTC; below, The Andrew Goodman Foundation.)

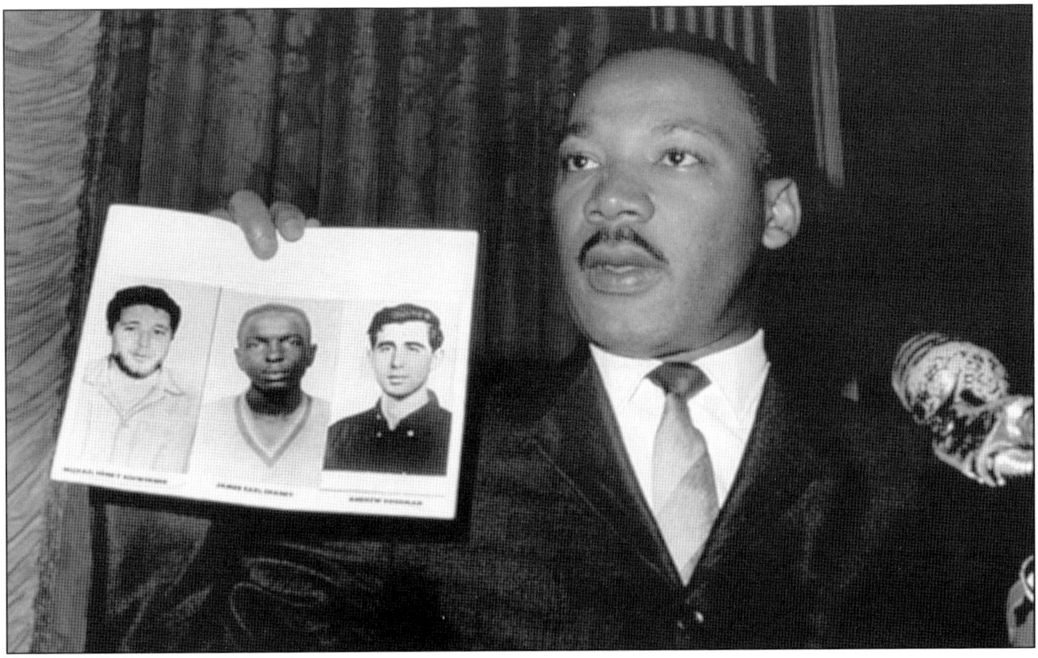

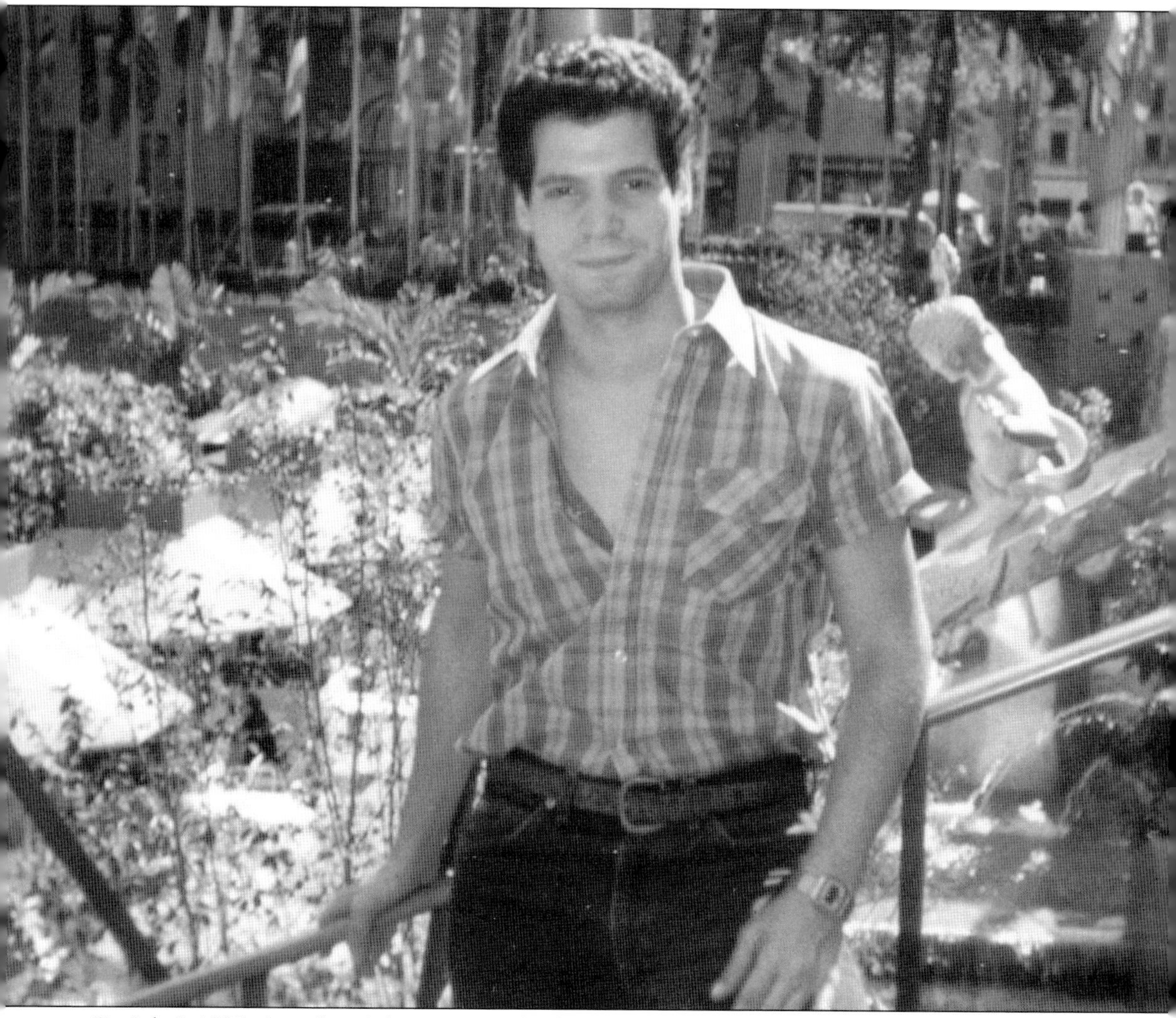

On July 2, 1990, thugs beat Julio Rivera with a hammer and wrench and stabbed the 29-year-old with a knife near Seventy-Eighth Street and Thirty-Seventh Avenue in Jackson Heights. The community responded with outrage, activism, and candlelight vigils, sparking the creation of several local LGBT organizations and the documentary *Julio of Jackson Heights*, directed by Richard Shpuntoff. The murder was reclassified as a bias crime, and the perpetrators were convicted. The intersection where Rivera collapsed was conamed Julio Rivera Corner. (Richard Shpuntoff and Alex Florez.)

*Eight*

# Media Moguls

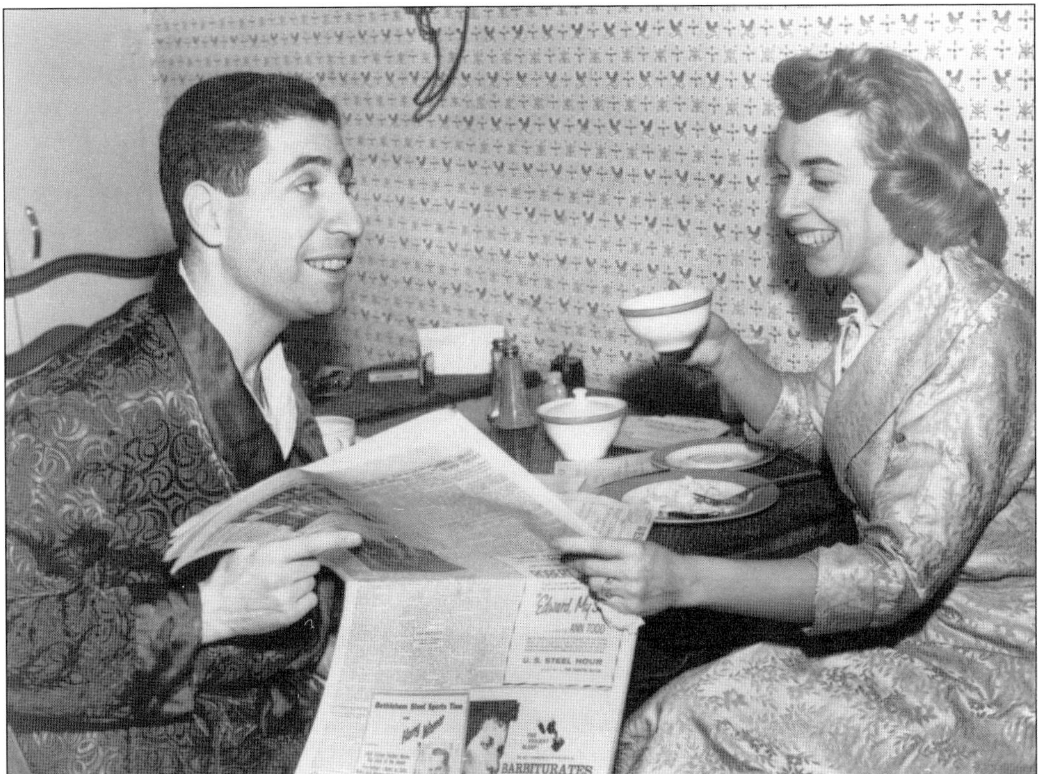


Laurelton native Joyce Bauer married Milton Brothers in 1949. (They are seen eating breakfast in this 1955 photograph.) Finances were tough, so she appeared on *The $64,000 Question*. The Far Rockaway High School graduate lasted for seven weeks and became the first woman to win the top prize. She parlayed the hype into a boxing commentator gig, which led to the talk show *Living Easy with Dr. Joyce Brothers* and appearances on *The Tonight Show Starring Johnny Carson* and *Good Morning America*. (Alamy.)

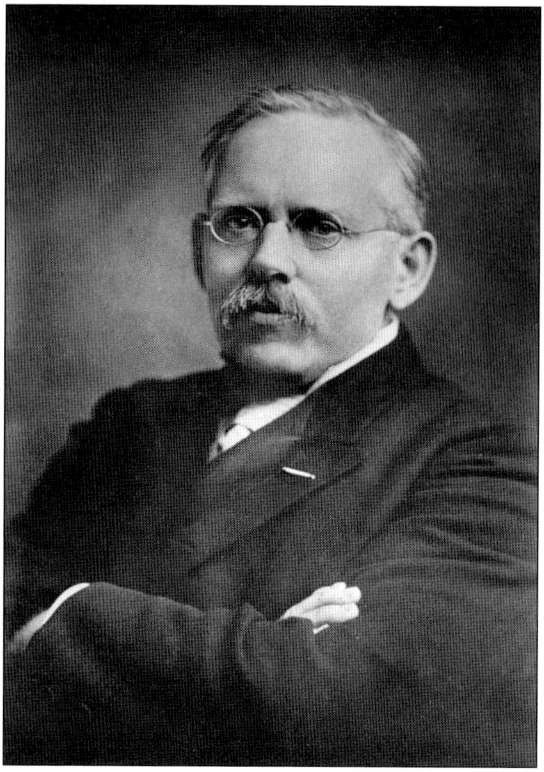

Jacob Riis (left) was 21 when he immigrated to the United States from Denmark in 1870. He traveled the country, working as a brickmaker, coal miner, farmer, and peddler before getting a steady job as a police reporter for the *New-York Tribune* in 1887. That led to a widely read column in the *Evening Sun* and various books, such as *How the Other Half Lives* in 1890 and *Children of the Tenements* in 1903. His pioneering use of photographs to depict poverty and horrid social conditions led to international fame and sparked many reforms aimed at improving conditions in poor neighborhoods, including the 1895 New York Tenement House Act, which increased fire safety regulations, ventilation rules, and room space requirements, among other dictates. He is pictured below in 1905 with Pres. Theodore Roosevelt (center) and Bishop John Vincent (right). (Both, LOC.)

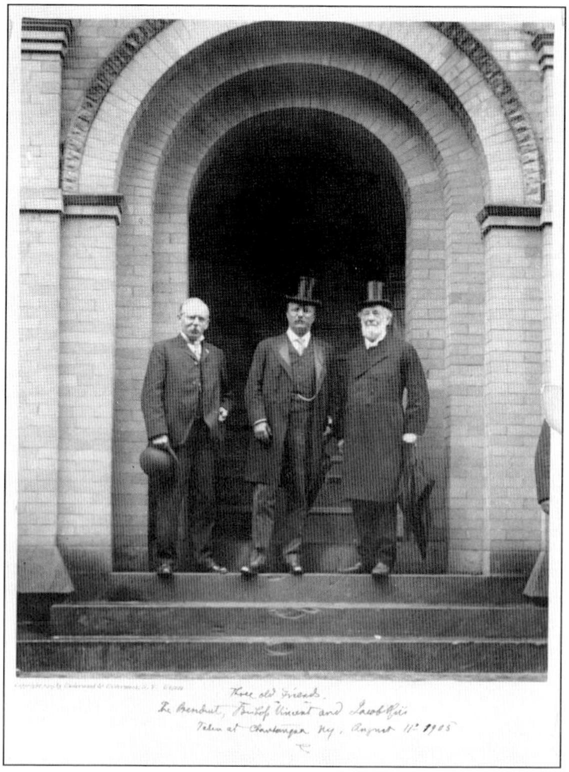

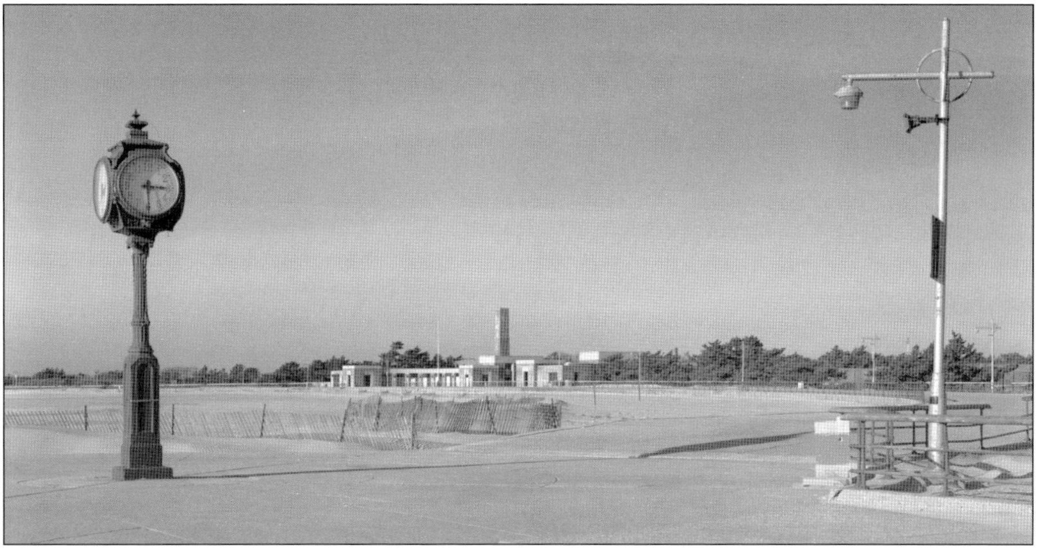

A beach in the Rockaways and a community center in Queensbridge bear Jacob Riis's name, as does a public housing project in Manhattan. Riis and his wife, Elisabeth, lived at 84-41 120th Street in Richmond Hill, and they would frequently bring groups of poor children from tenements to their farm for a day with sheep, chickens, and plenty of nature. The photograph below depicts the house where Riis wrote *How the Other Half Lives.* It had landmark status, but the designation was revoked after damage to the facility's integrity was found. A large apartment building is there now. (Above, LOC; below, Carl Ballenas.)

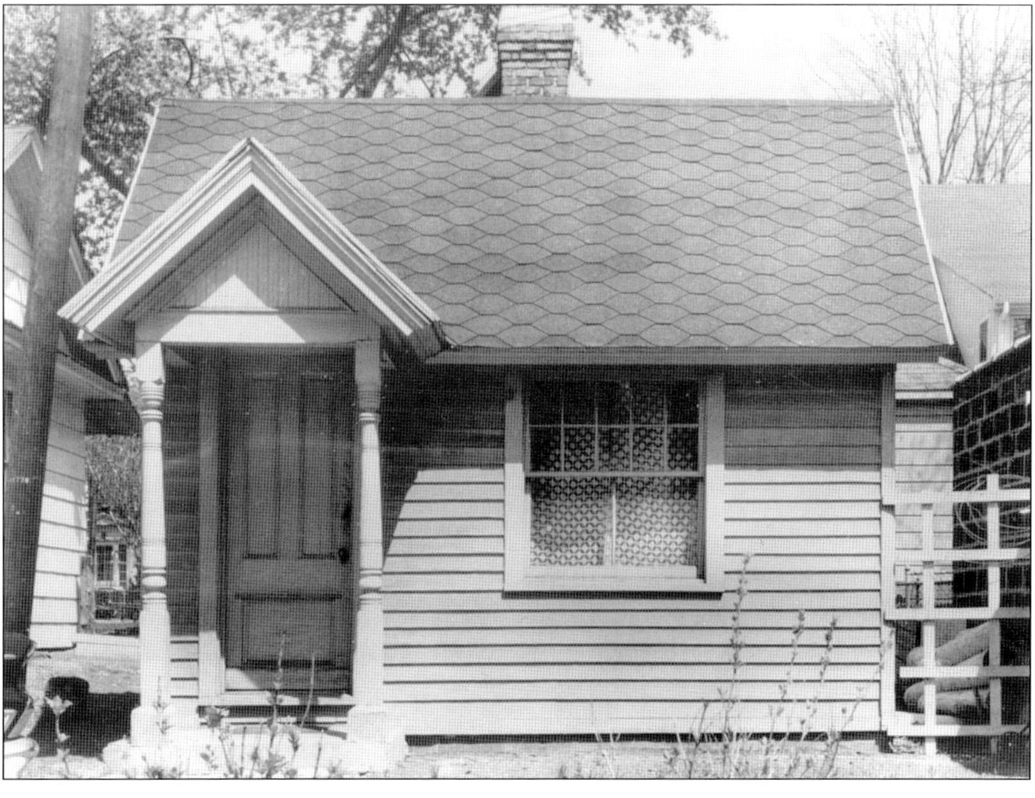

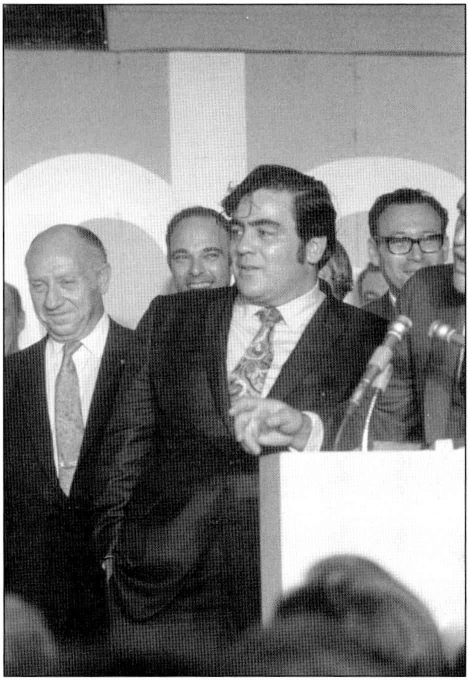

Jimmy Breslin lived in Queens, and Queens lived in him. He walked the streets, frequented the bars, and wrote about the people. Born in 1928, the Richmond Hill native studied at John Adams High School, where a teacher said he was good with words but bad with attendance. After dropping out of college, he got into the newspaper business as a copy boy. This led to columns in the *New York Herald Tribune*, *New York Daily News*, *New York Post*, and *Newsday* and to a 1986 Pulitzer Prize. (LOC.)

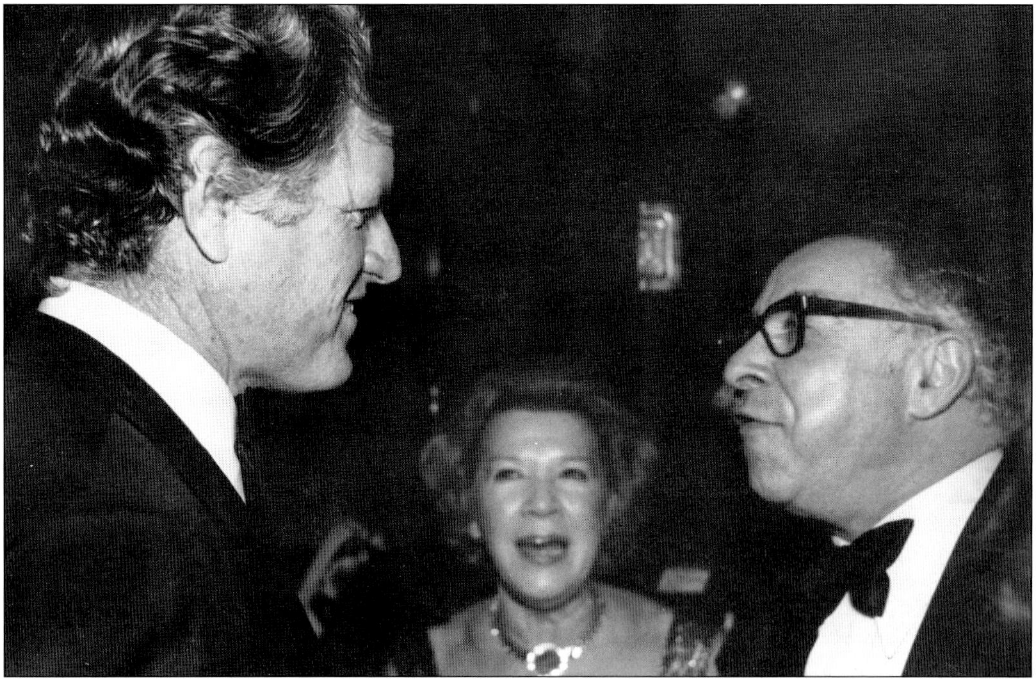

Art Buchwald's mother went to an asylum due to depression shortly after his 1925 birth, and he grew up in an orphanage and a foster home in Hollis. The class clown at PS 35 then dropped out of Forest Hills High School. Luckily, he could write, especially about politics. Buchwald (right), above with Massachusetts senator Ted Kennedy (left), wrote more than 30 books and had a syndicated column that appeared in more than 500 newspapers. He won a 1981 Pulitzer Prize. (LOC.)

While visiting a next-door cousin in South Ozone Park, Charles Casillo started leafing through a copy of *Cosmopolitan*. His 11-year-old eyes stopped on a photograph of Marilyn Monroe. The blonde bombshell was so glamorous and her career was on fire, but the article contained sad details about her personal life. From then on, family and friends knew what to buy Casillo for Christmas or his birthday: anything related to Marilyn Monroe! Fast forward to the present, and Casillo is author of the 2018 biography *Marilyn Monroe: The Private Life of a Public Icon* and *The Marilyn Diaries*, a fictional biography based on a purportedly lost diary. The expert on tragic Hollywood figures also penned *Elizabeth and Monty: The Untold Story of Their Intimate Friendship*, which dives deep into Elizabeth Taylor's relationship with Montgomery Clift. (Both, Charles Casillo.)

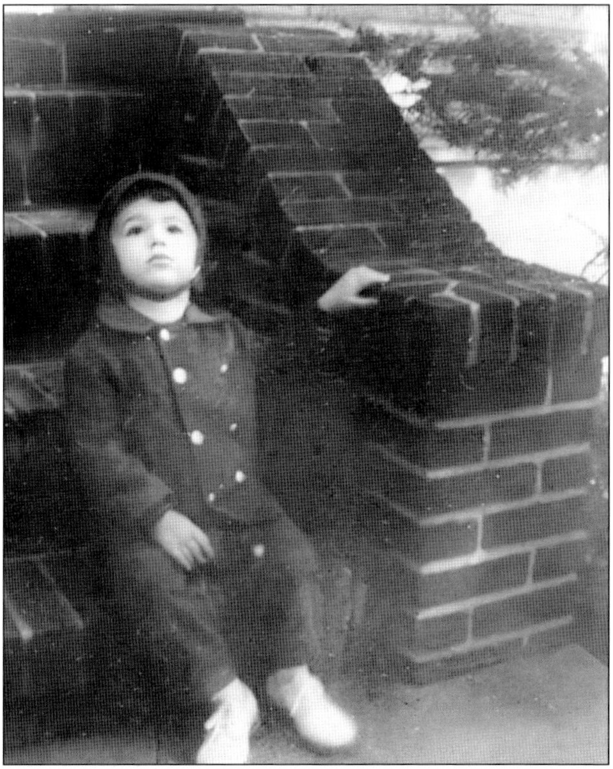

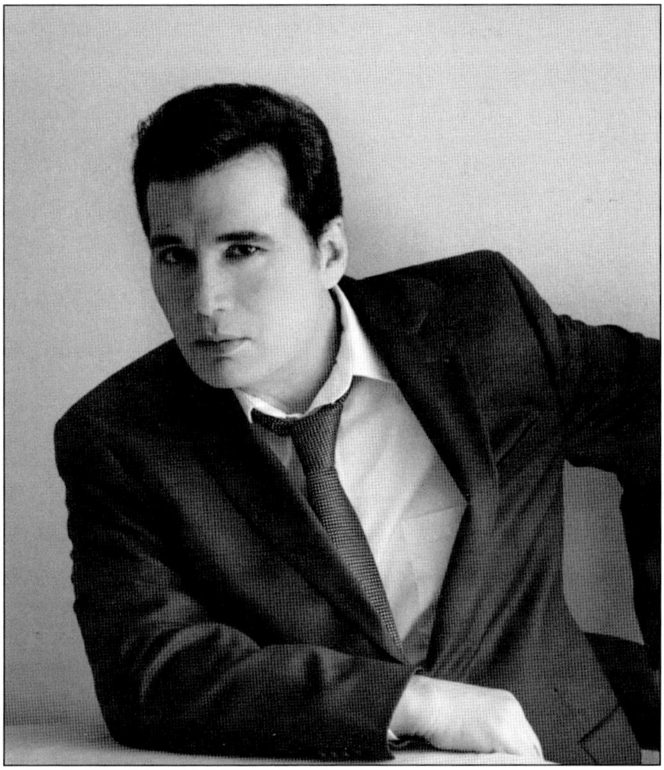

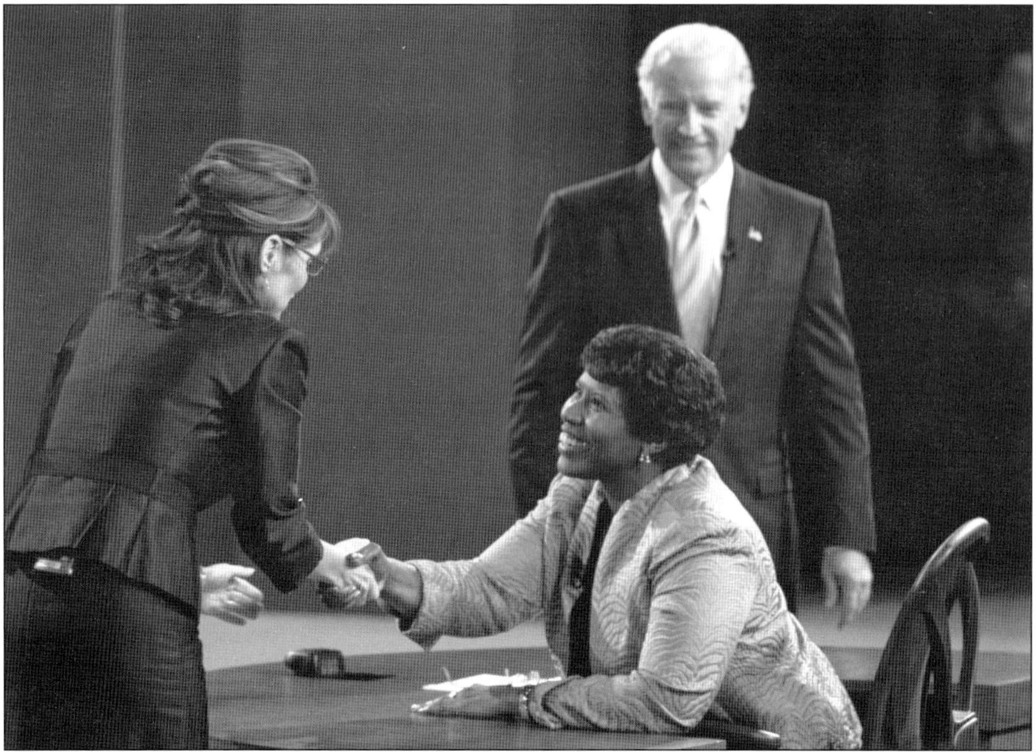

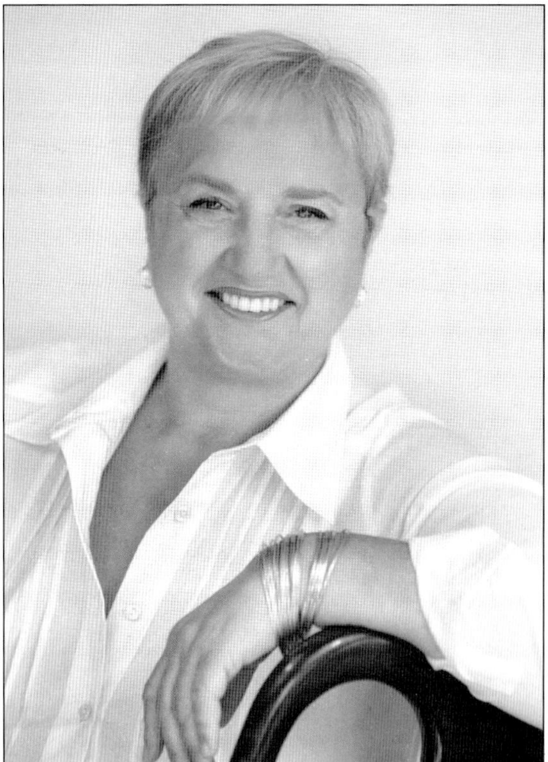

Gwen Ifill is the first African American woman to host a national political talk show. Born in Jamaica in 1955, she got a reporting job at the *Boston Herald* after graduating from Simmons College. She then worked at the *Baltimore Sun*, *Washington Post*, and *New York Times*. She became the moderator of PBS's *Washington Week* in October 1999 and then a senior correspondent for the *PBS NewsHour* while also appearing on such news shows at *Meet the Press*, *Face the Nation*, and *Inside Washington*. (Alamy.)

After fleeing Yugoslavia's Communist dictatorship in 1956, Lidia Bastianich worked odd food jobs before opening Buonovia restaurant in Forest Hills with her husband, Felice, in 1971. Next up were Villa Secondo in Fresh Meadows and Felidia in Manhattan, which blew up after getting a three-star review in the *New York Times*. Bastianich, who lives in Douglaston, blew up with it. The Emmy-winning cooking show host has also written 14 cookbooks. (Lidia Bastianich.)

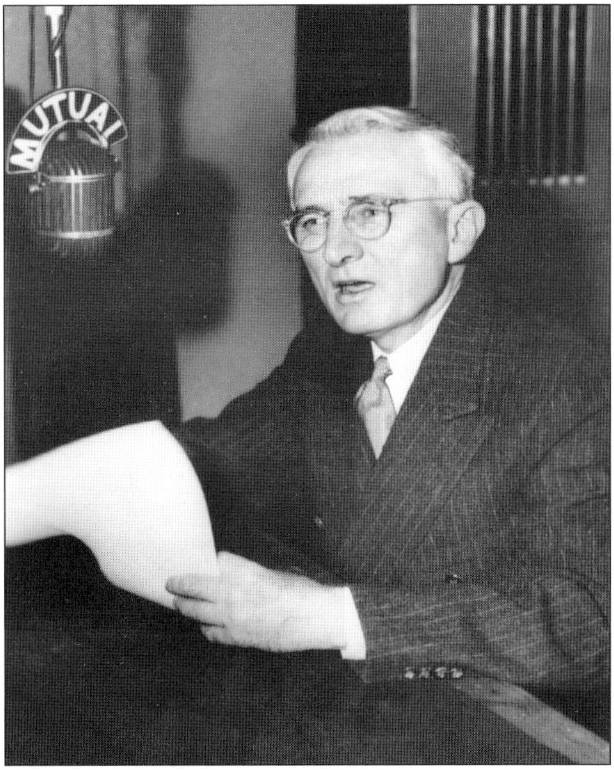


Dale Carnegie's 1939 *How to Win Friends and Influence People* stressed the importance of being considerate, listening to other viewpoints, showing interest in others, and thinking positively. The instantly successful book had a 17th print run a few months after hitting the market and remained on best-seller lists for almost a decade. After more books and television appearances, the Forest Hills Gardens resident founded the Dale Carnegie Institute, which offered courses on corporate training, interpersonal skills, public speaking, and salesmanship. (Right, Alamy; below, QTC.)

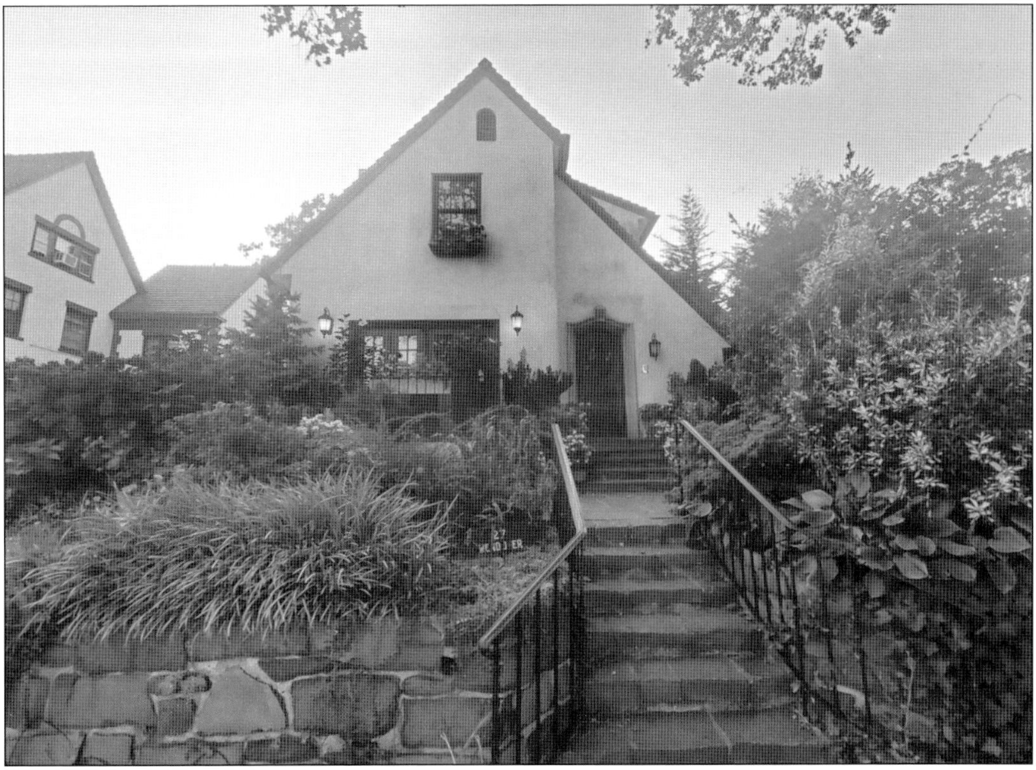

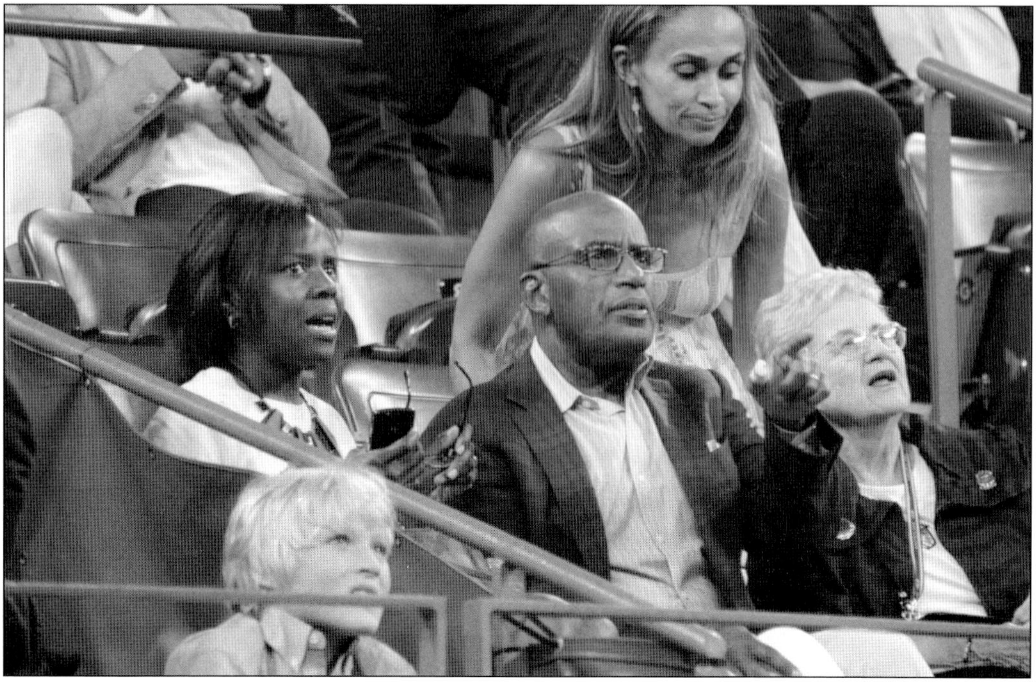

Al Roker has 14 Emmys and the Guinness World Record for most hours of uninterrupted weather coverage with 34 in early November 2014. He has also written 13 books, including a mystery novel called *The Morning Show Murders*. The St. Albans native, who is best known as the long-standing weatherman on NBC's *Today* show, has also hosted Macy's Thanksgiving Day Parade in Manhattan since 1995. Here he is watching the US Open with his wife, Deborah Roberts, only a few miles from his childhood home. (Alamy.)

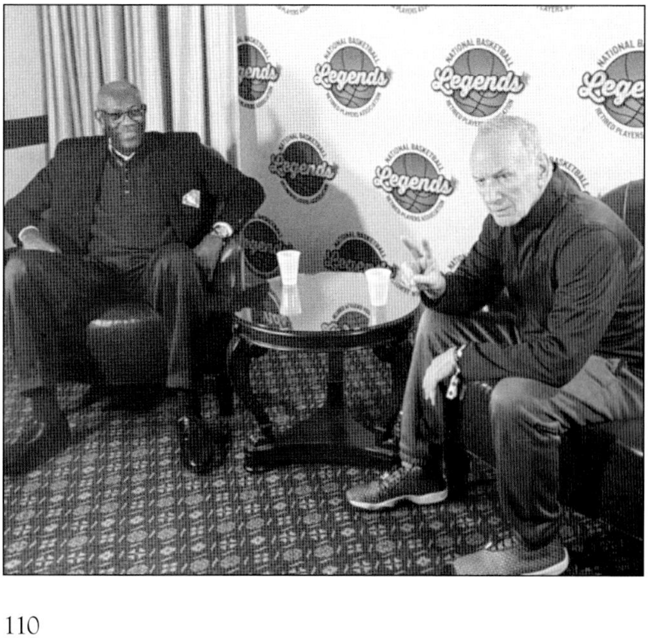


Peter Vecsey's father, George, was the sports editor for *Long Island Press*. His mother, May Spencer, was the same newspaper's society editor. So he grew up analyzing, telling stories, and speaking his mind at the kitchen table. The Hollis native revolutionized basketball journalism by adding gossip, humor, and confrontation. For 36 years, Vecsey (right) worked for the *New York Post*, where he launched his Hoop Du Jour column before jumping to television. He was inducted into the Naismith Memorial Basketball Hall of Fame in 2009. (Naismith Memorial Basketball Hall of Fame.)

The 1939–1940 World's Fair in Flushing Meadows Corona Park inspired Joseph Cornell, who lived within walking distance in a small wooden-frame house at 37–08 Utopia Parkway. Seen at home with an unidentified woman, he started creating wooden boxes filled with found objects, such as buttons, corks, and photographs. Many pieces were from the World's Fair, but others were from vintage shops, garage sales, and flea markets. He named the boxes, which he fronted with glass panels, after faraway places and famous artists. Surreal and a bit unnerving, the boxes gained international fame. He exhibited at the Metropolitan Museum of Art, the Solomon R. Guggenheim Museum, Cooper Union, and other places around the United States as well as in London and Vienna posthumously. Cornell, who is with family around 1915 below, also made 12 mini movies, mostly from found footage. The most famous, *Flushing Meadows: A Work of Art and Mourning* (1965), is an ode to a waitress who was a crush of his before her brutal murder in 1964. (She stole some of his boxes, but he refused to press charges.) Eight minutes long, the silent film features shots of Flushing Cemetery. (Both, Smithsonian Institution.)

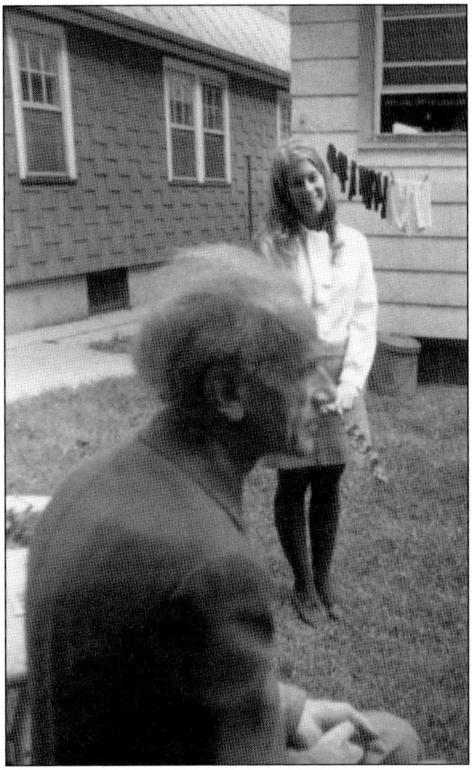

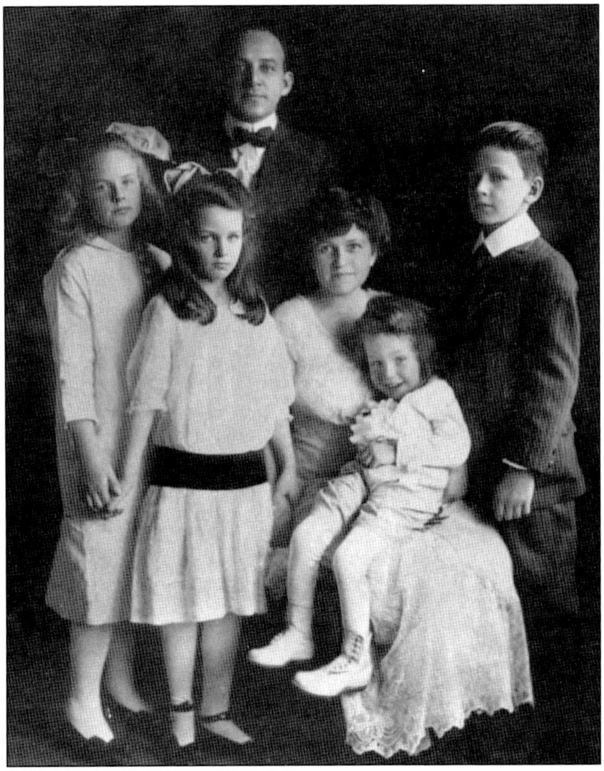

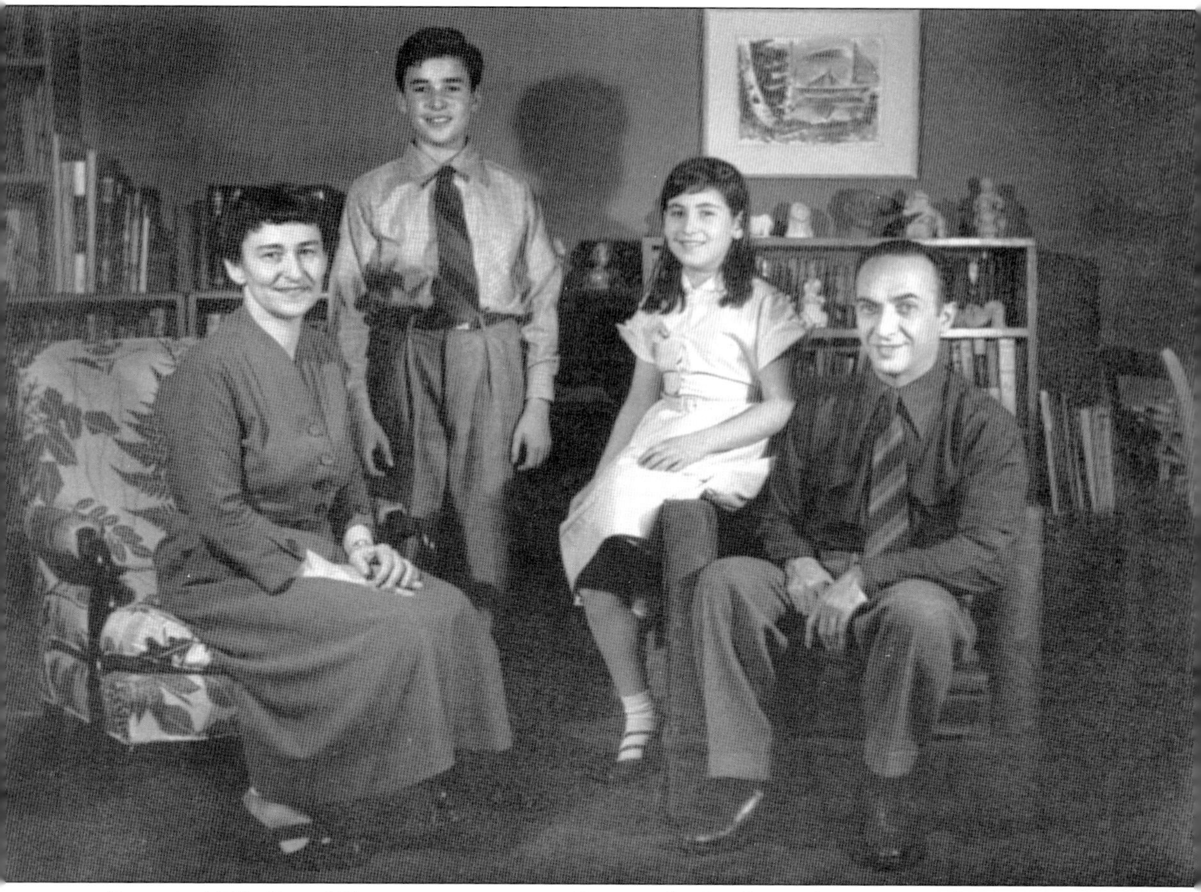

Born in 1939, David Horowitz grew up in Sunnyside Gardens when it was a hotbed of Soviet sympathizers. His parents, Communist Party USA members Blanche and Phil, were public school teachers and union organizers. David, with his parents and sister Ruth in this 1952 photograph, spent his childhood attending Vietnam War protests, railing against capitalism, and reading the *Daily Worker*. As an adult, the red diaper baby moved to the Bay Area, where he edited *Ramparts*, a radical 1960s magazine. But then came utter disillusionment with liberalism. (He describes his conversion to conservatism in his 1997 memoir *Radical Son: A Generational Odyssey*.) While maintaining his characteristic fast pace, he founded various right wing think tanks and legal entities, including the Center for the Study of Popular Culture, the Individual Rights Foundation, the David Horowitz Freedom Center, and the Students for Academic Freedom. (Nancy Brown.)

# Nine

# Spiritual Leaders

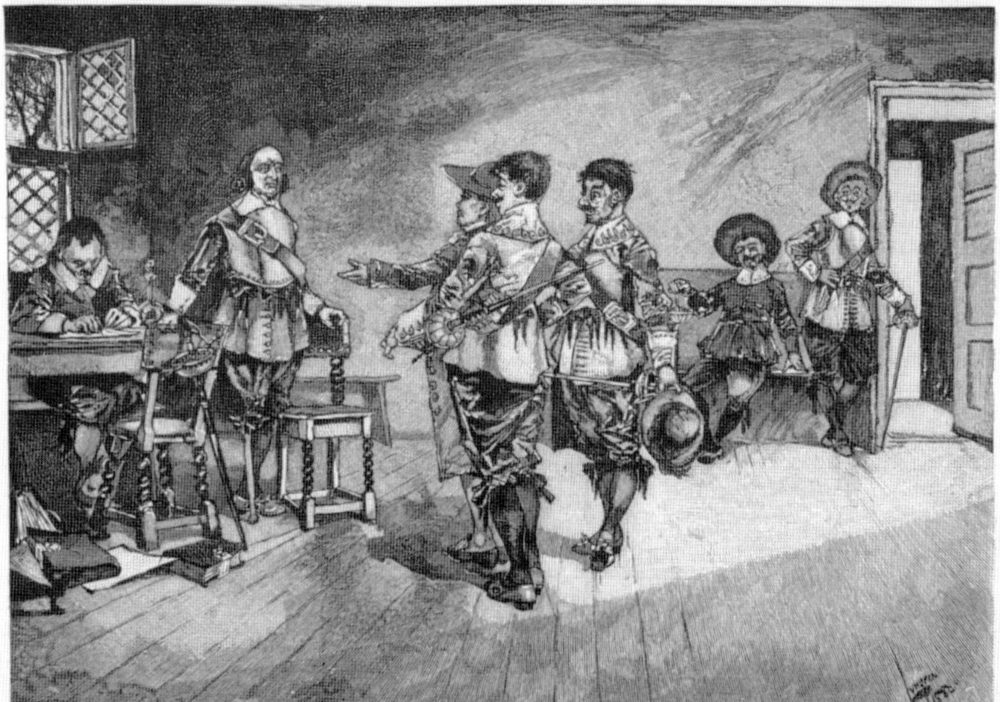

JOHN BOWNE BEFORE GOVERNOR STUYVESANT.

In 1657, Dutch Reformed Protestantism was the only permitted religion in New Netherlands, which is now New York. John Bowne, who had moved from England to Flushing, hosted town meetings that led to the Flushing Remonstrance, a document demanding Quakers' freedom to practice their faith. Historians regard it as the model for parts of the Bill of Rights. Bowne, arguing for his freedom in this image, was exiled to Holland in 1662 but later returned a hero. (*Scribner's Monthly*, Bowne House Archives.)

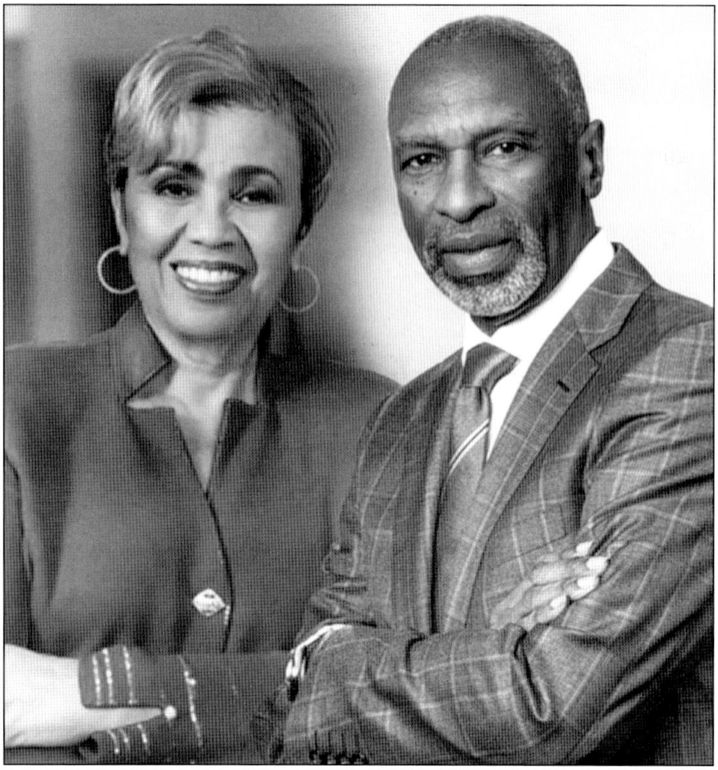

Founded in 1834, the Greater Allen AME Cathedral of New York combines serving a 25,000-plus-member congregation with providing social services, running commercial enterprises, and educating students. Rev. Dr. Floyd Flake (above, right), a former six-term congressman, led the Jamaica-based organization, which donated this photograph, for more than 40 years before retiring in 2020. He handed the reins to his longtime copastor, Rev. Dr. Margaret Elaine (McCollins) Flake (above, left), who is also his wife. At right, Rev. Dr. W. Sterling Cary was in his Hollis home in 1972 when he got the call. The 45-year-old had been unanimously chosen as the first African American to lead the National Council of Churches, the country's largest coalition of Christian organizations. As the civil rights movement was at its height, it was major news, leading *Ebony* magazine to describe Reverend Cary as one of the most influential African Americans ever. (Above, Greater Allen AME Cathedral of New York; right, National Council of Churches.)

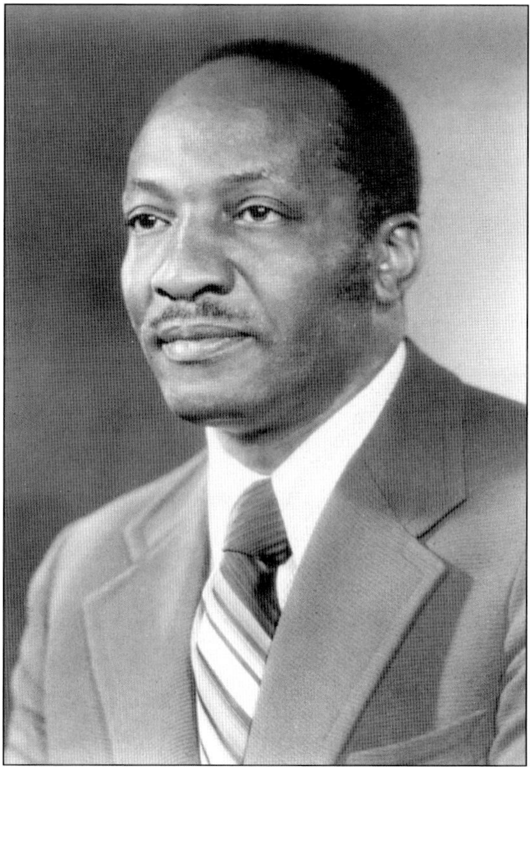

Malcolm X is known as a civil rights leader, but his Muslim religion was the base of his career and character. While ministering the Nation of Islam's Mosque No. 7 in Harlem, he lived in a brick house on Ninety-Seventh Street in East Elmhurst. His wife, Betty Shabazz, gave birth to four of their daughters—Attallah, Qubilah, Ilyasah, and Gamilan—in Queens. Problems arose after the Nation of Islam stripped Malcolm X of his job in 1965. The group demanded the residence, but he contended that he had received it as a gift. Molotov cocktails shattered the house's windows before a fire engulfed its walls on February 14, 1965, at about 2:45 a.m. Malcolm X and his family escaped, but the structure sustained severe smoke and water damage, as seen below. Malcolm X was assassinated in Harlem seven days later. (Both, LOC.)

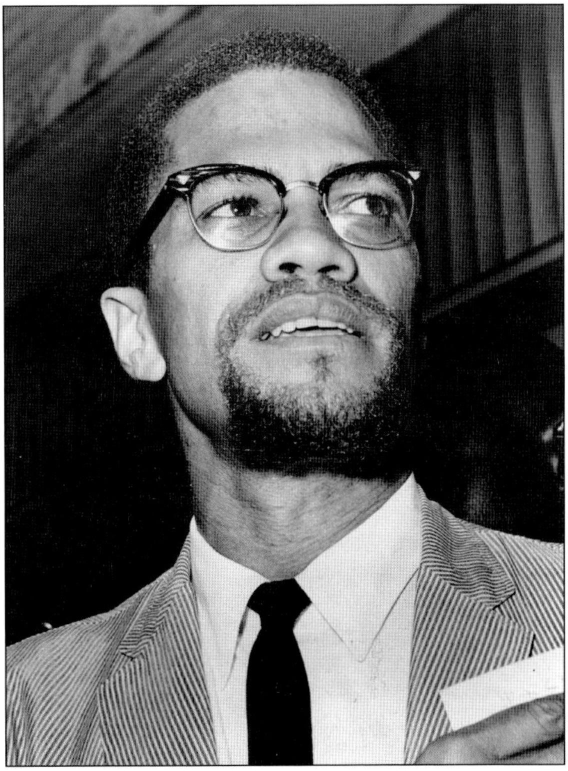

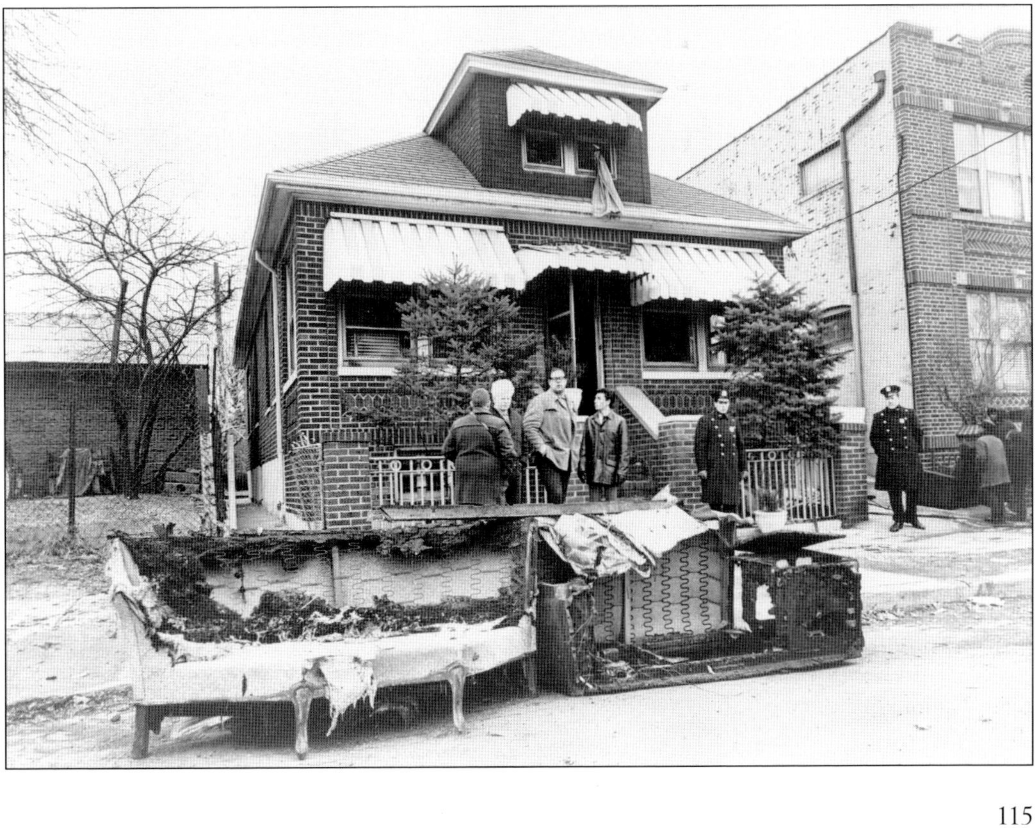

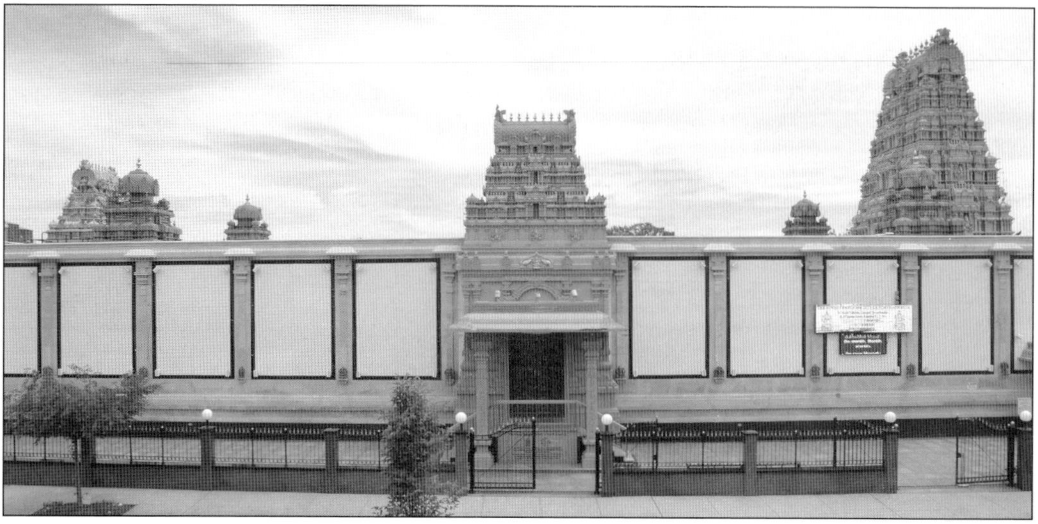

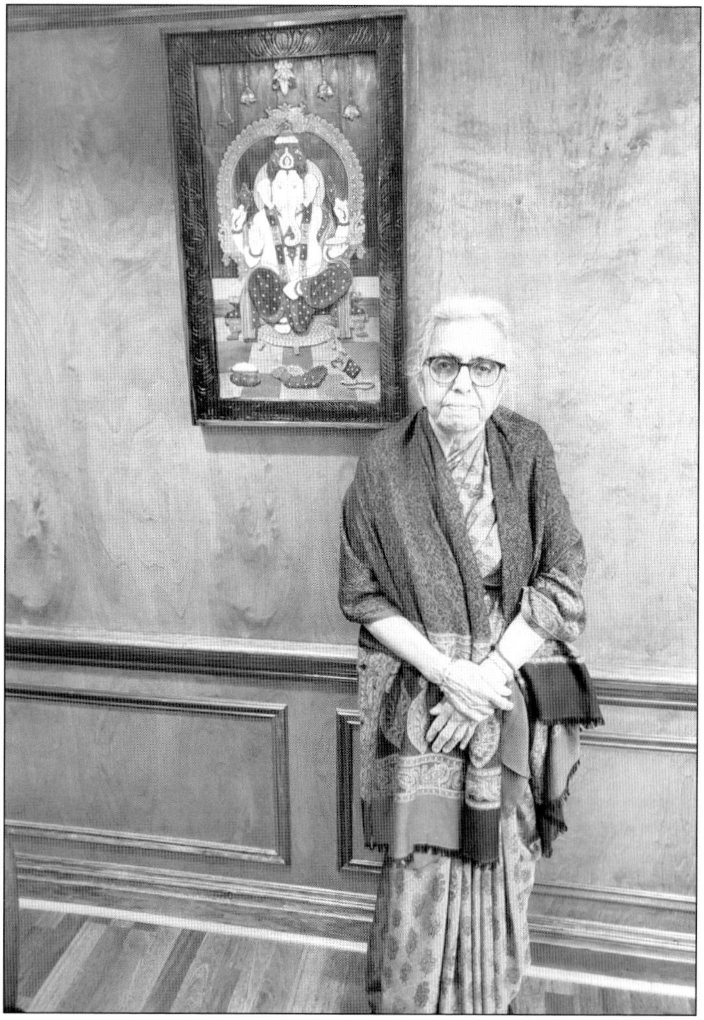

United Nations employee Alagappa Alagappan was one of the very few practicing Hindus in Queens in 1961, so he worshiped in his Jamaica Estates apartment's living room. The Immigration and Naturalization Act of 1965 opened the door for newcomers from South Asia, and OB-GYN Uma Mysorekar (left) arrived in 1976. With help from others, they opened Sri Maha Vallabha Ganapati Devasthanam, better known as the Ganesh Temple, at a converted Russian Orthodox church at 45–57 Bowne Street (below, opposite) in Flushing on July 4, 1977. It is the oldest traditional Hindu worship center in the entire United States. True to its nickname, the institution's main deity is Ganesh, an elephant-headed Hindu god of beginnings that is venerated as the remover of obstacles. He is also the patron of arts and science. (Above, Ganesh Temple; left, QTC.)

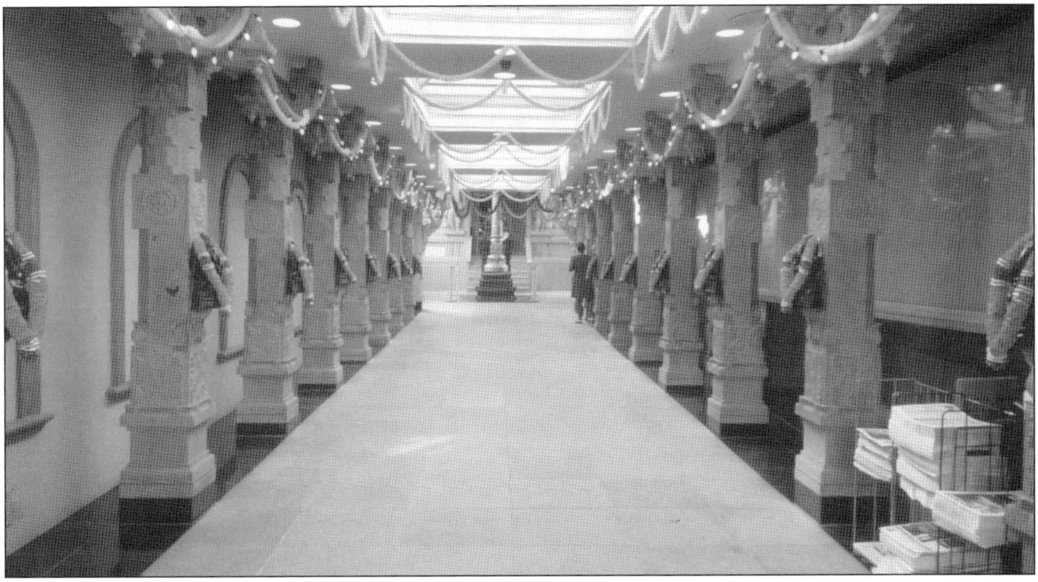

The facility features granite stones imported from India and arranged as per the Agama Sastras, which are ancient scriptures on temple buildings. The walls have tiered conical towers with intricate carved figures of eagles, monkeys, and peacocks. Inside, a large Ganesh statue greets visitors along with shrines to other divine beings in less prominent locations. The complex includes a *pathsala* (or school), cultural center, library, senior center, and yoga/meditation spaces. After various renovations, it is now twice as big as it was at first. On September 21, 1995, the site gained international recognition thanks to the Hindu milk miracle. Using a spoon, a devotee offered milk to the trunk of a Ganesh statue in India's New Delhi. The milk magically disappeared, according to reports, while the same phenomenon happened at the Ganesh Temple. (Both, Ganesh Temple.)

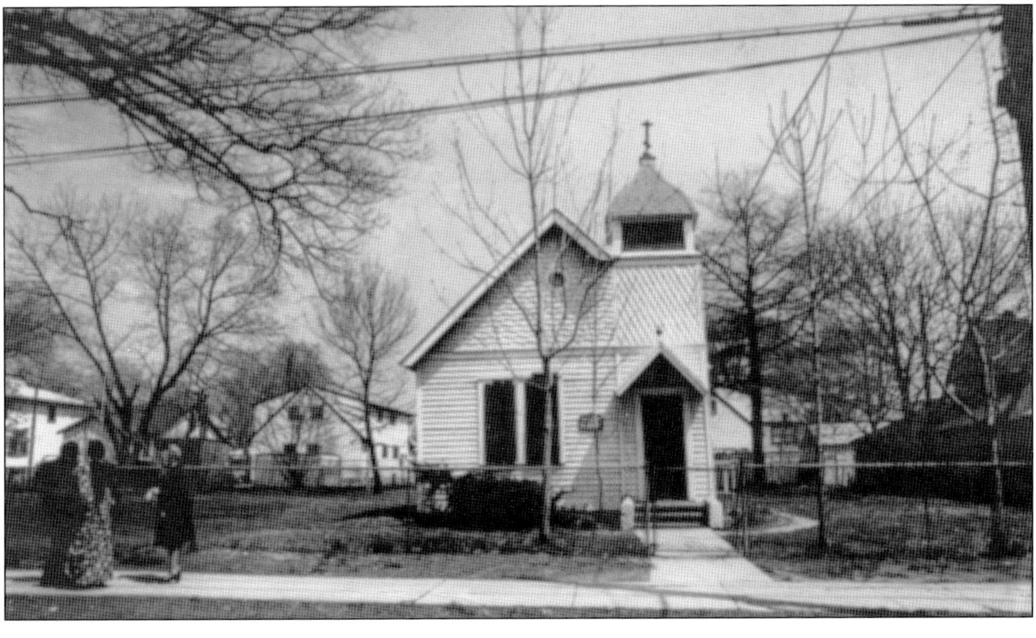

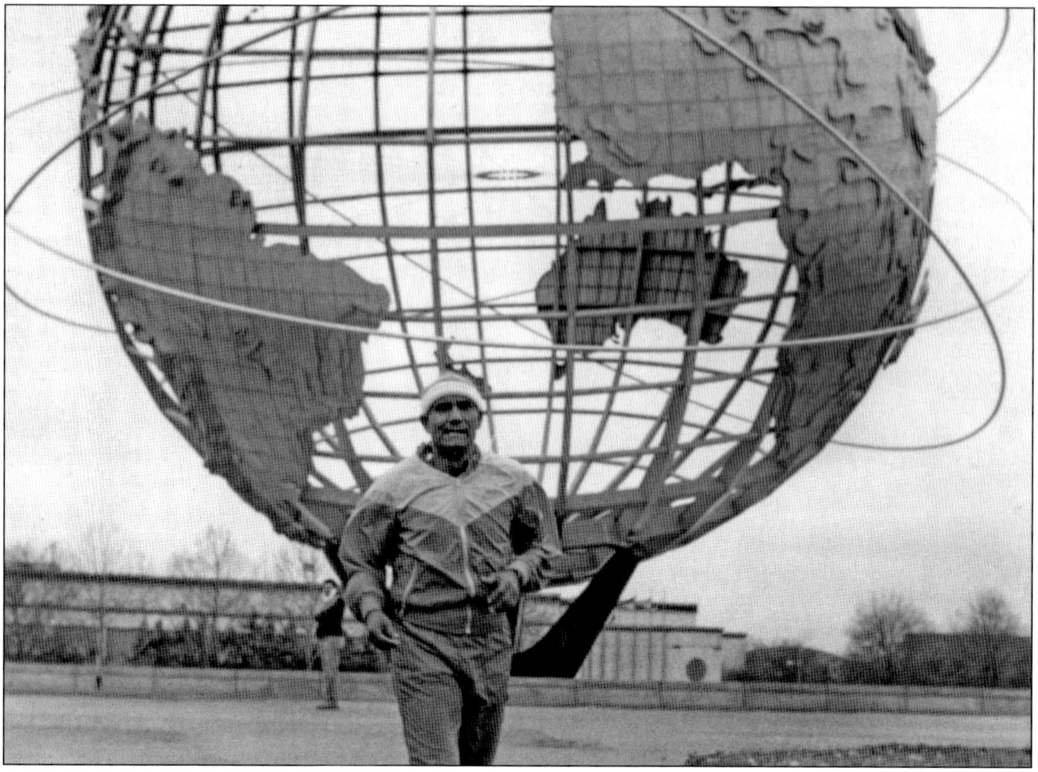

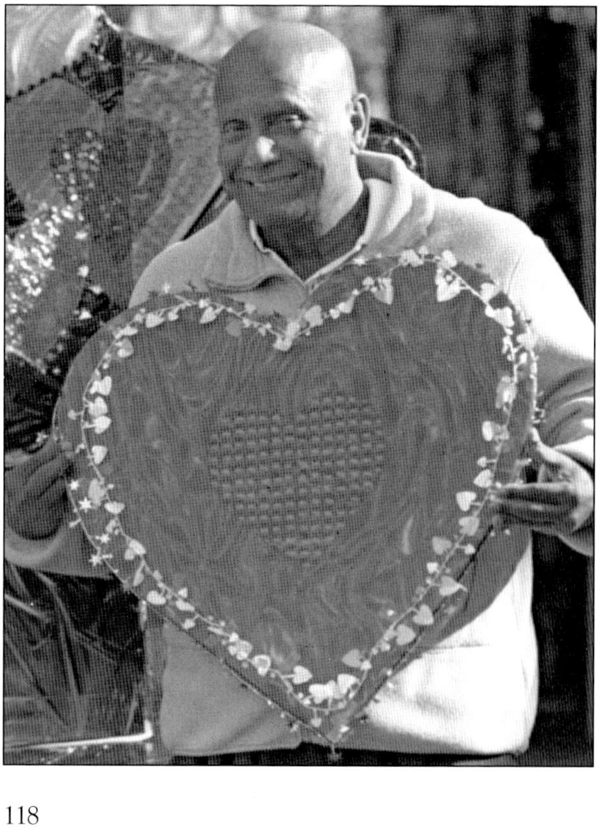

Pedestrians on Parsons Boulevard in Jamaica Hills have a good chance of seeing ponytailed European women dressed in Indian saris. The same strollers might dart into a vegetarian restaurant, mediation center, or store with a name like Guru Health Foods. Sri Chinmoy died in 2007, but the spiritual community he founded is still striving . . . and following his teachings. Sri Chinmoy entered an ashram (Hindu hermitage) in south India at the age of 12 in 1943. He spent 20 years there, meditating, exercising, writing poetry, playing dozens of instruments, and training. In the 1970s, he moved to Queens, where he preached peace, harmony, service, fitness, and tolerance to thousands of seekers in dozens of countries. He traveled the world to lecture, organize concerts, and hold public meditations. He also wrote more than 1,500 books and composed more than 20,000 songs. (Both, Sri Chinmoy Centre.)

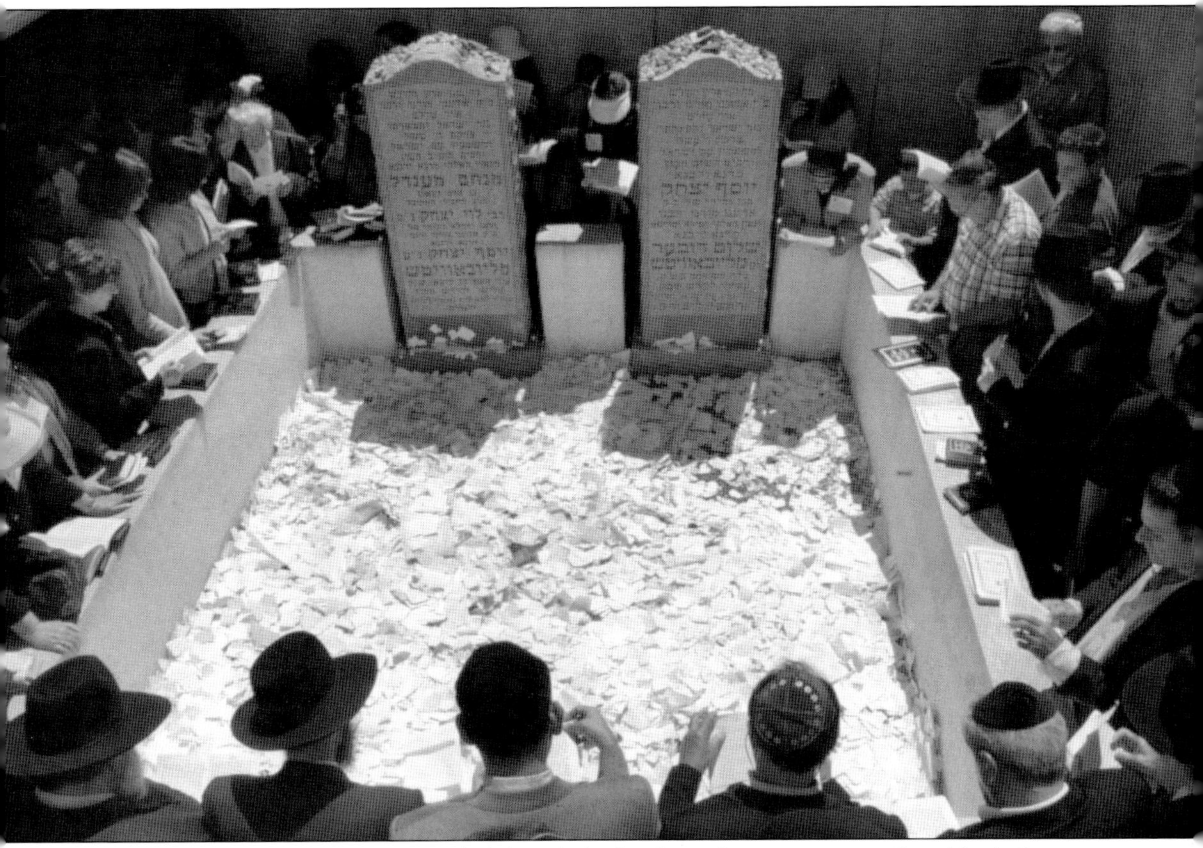

Rabbi Menachem Mendel Schneerson led the Chabad-Lubavitch community in Brooklyn's Crown Heights. Known simply as "The Rebbe," he was so respected that many ultraorthodox Jews thought he was the Messiah. After he died at 94 in 1994, he was buried in Montefiore Cemetery in Springfield Gardens in southeast Queens. Community leaders then built an *ohel*, a structure that is put over a righteous person's resting place. Ever since, several thousand Jews visit the ohel every year to pay respects, recite prayers, ask questions, seek blessings, and leave notes. Many report a spiritual feeling while there. Founded in 1908, the 114-acre Montefiore Cemetery is the final resting spot for many prominent Jews. The Shomrim Society, the fraternal society for Jewish New York Police Department officers, has a plot there too. (Alamy.)

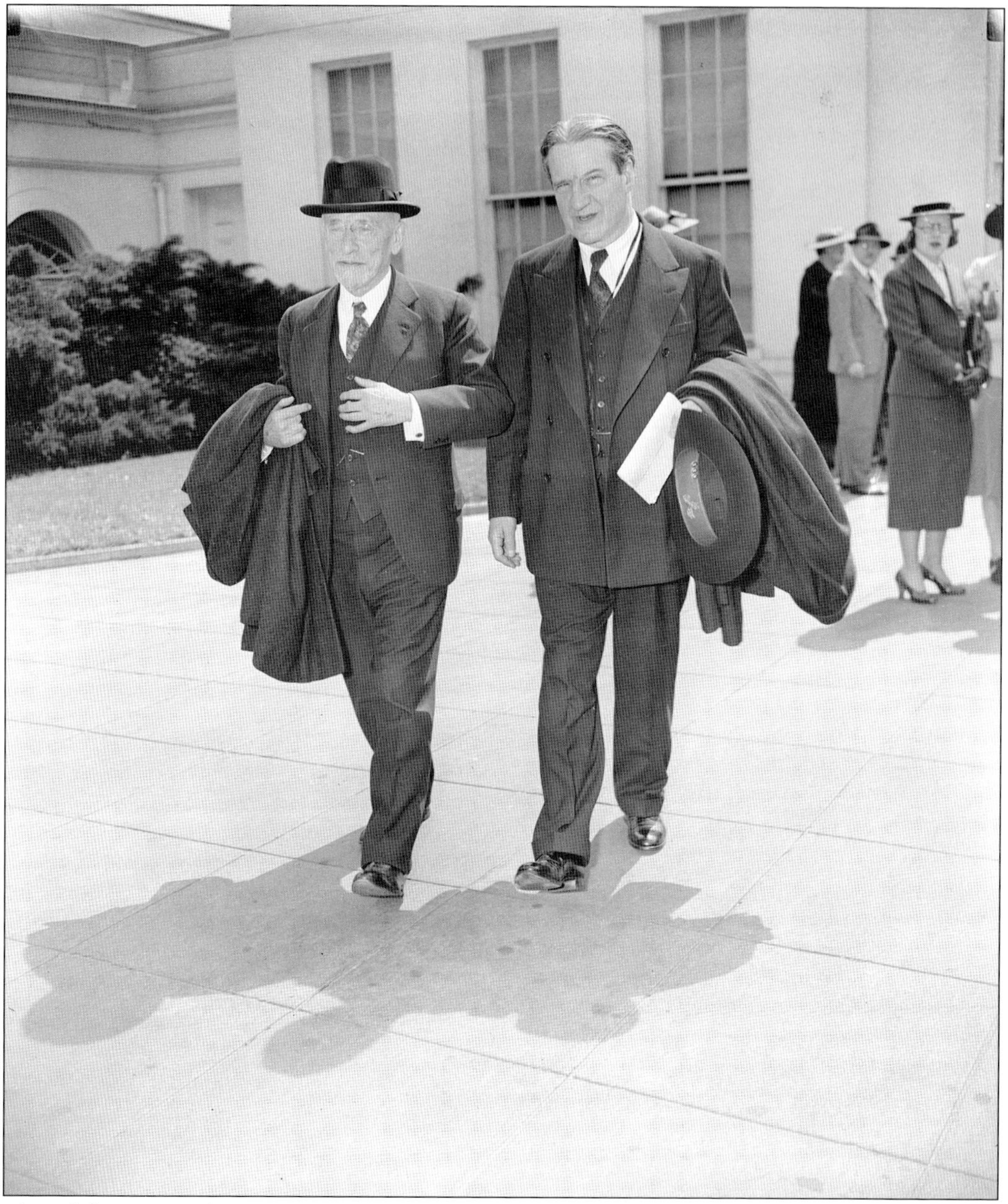

Though born in Budapest in 1874, Stephen Wise grew up in Manhattan, where his father was the rabbi of a conservative Jewish congregation. He followed in his footsteps but became disillusioned with his faith's religiosity. In 1907, he founded the Stephen Wise Free Synagogue in Manhattan, where he preached social justice, women's rights, and civil rights. Some Jews hated him, but he developed a loyal following. In 1917, his vision grew when his right-hand man, Rabbi Sidney E. Goldstein, and the Hebrew Women's Aid Society established the Free Synagogue of Flushing. It is the borough's oldest Reform temple, and the congregation is still involved in social justice issues today. Rabbi Wise (right) walks with Treasury secretary Henry Morgenthau (left) outside the White House in this 1938 photograph. They had just conferred with Pres. Franklin D. Roosevelt about helping Nazi refugees. (LOC.)

# Ten

# Queens Questions

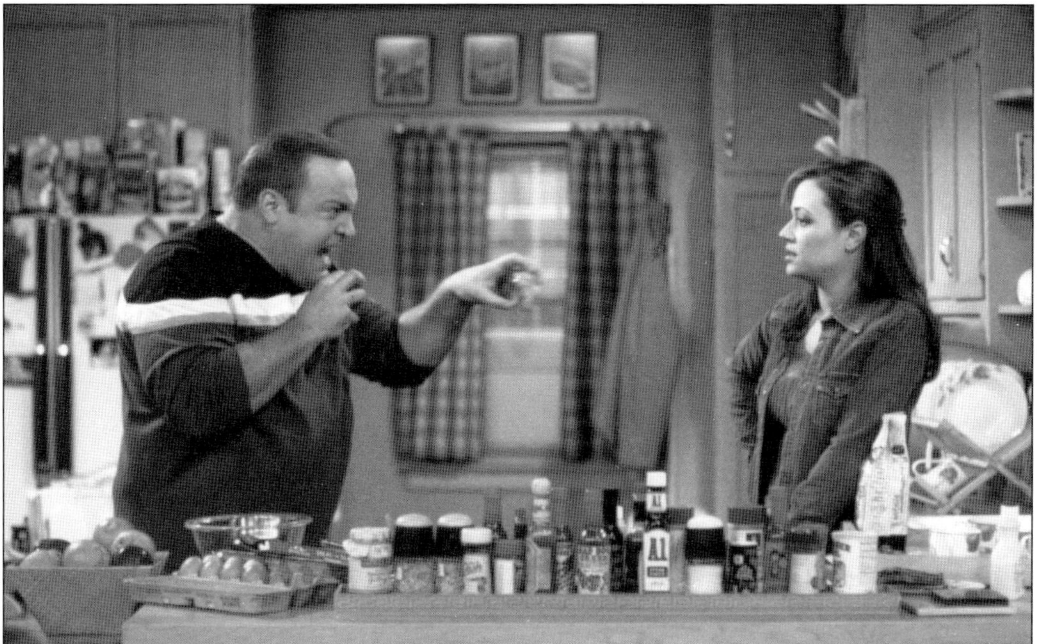

*The King of Queens* depicts a middle-class family who constantly trades insults in a loving way. Kevin James plays a happy-go-lucky delivery truck driver. Leah Remini is his sassy wife, Carrie, a legal secretary. The CBS sitcom, which ran from 1998 to 2007, was filmed at Sony Pictures Studios in California, but the couple, in the above still, purportedly live on Aberdeen Street in Rego Park. Almost, Hollywood. The neighborhood has an Aberdeen Road. (Alamy.)

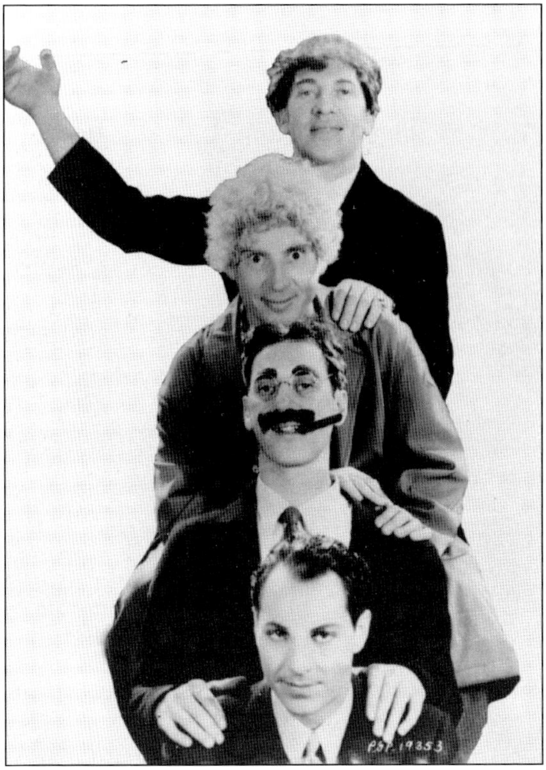

The Marx Brothers grew up in Manhattan, but they owe their success to Queens. Leonard, Adolph, Julius, Milton, and Herbert (also known as Chico, Harpo, Groucho, Gummo, and Zeppo) filmed their first movies in Astoria, and they lived on 134th Street in Richmond Hill in the early 1920s. Their German immigrant parents bought the home so the boys would have a crash pad between shows. (The parents are buried in nearby Mount Carmel Cemetery in Glendale.) Paramount relocated to California in 1932, and so did the Marx Brothers. They lived there for the rest of their lives but achieved immortality back in Astoria, where a seven-story, 33-unit residential complex on Thirty-Fifth Street is called The Marx. (Left, LOC; below, QTC.)

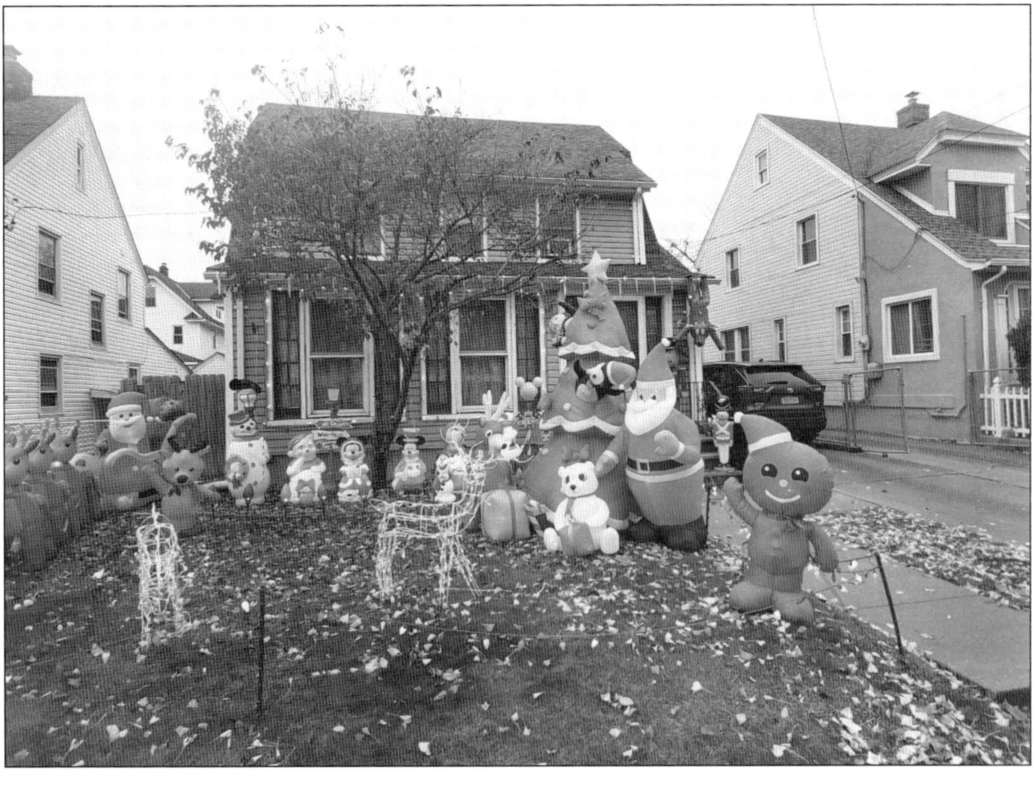

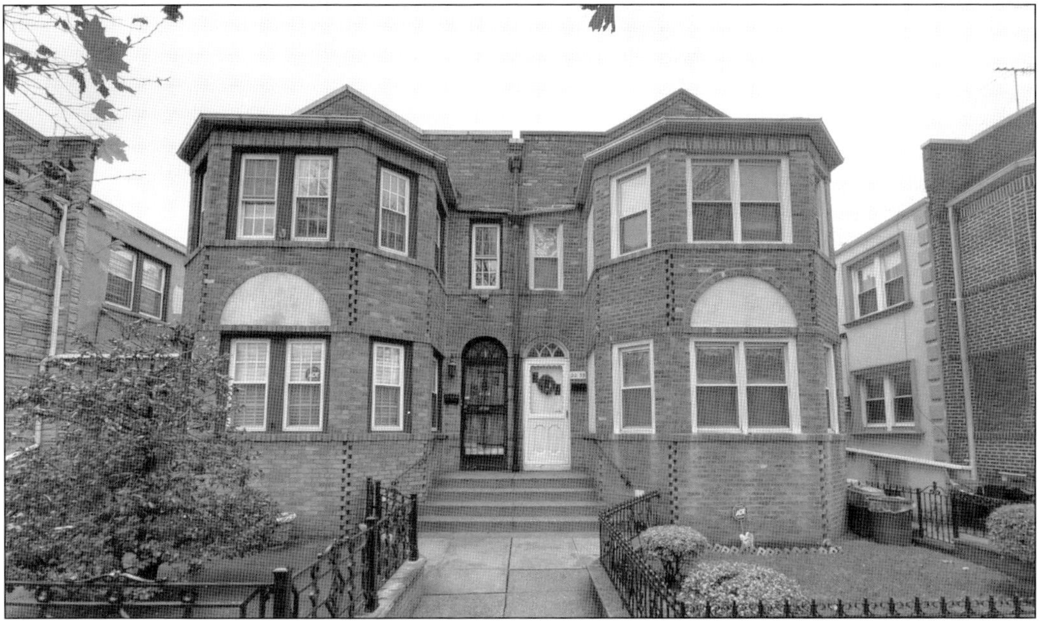

George Costanza (Jason Alexander), a main character on NBC's *Seinfeld*, had issues. Anxious, cheap, immoral, short, and bald, the 30-something was unlucky in love and could not hold a job. If that is not enough, he had an annoying Queens accent. At least he came by it honestly. His parents, Estelle (Estelle Harris) and Frank (Jerry Stiller), were just as neurotic. The three always screamed at each other, often in the parents' house where George sort of lived. It was quite amusing, but borough lovers have some bones to pick with the writers behind *Seinfeld*, which ran from 1989 to 1998. They put the house at 13–44 Queens Boulevard, where nothing exists. The humble abode in the scene changes is at 22 Thirty-Seventh Street in Astoria. (Above, Alamy; below, QTC.)

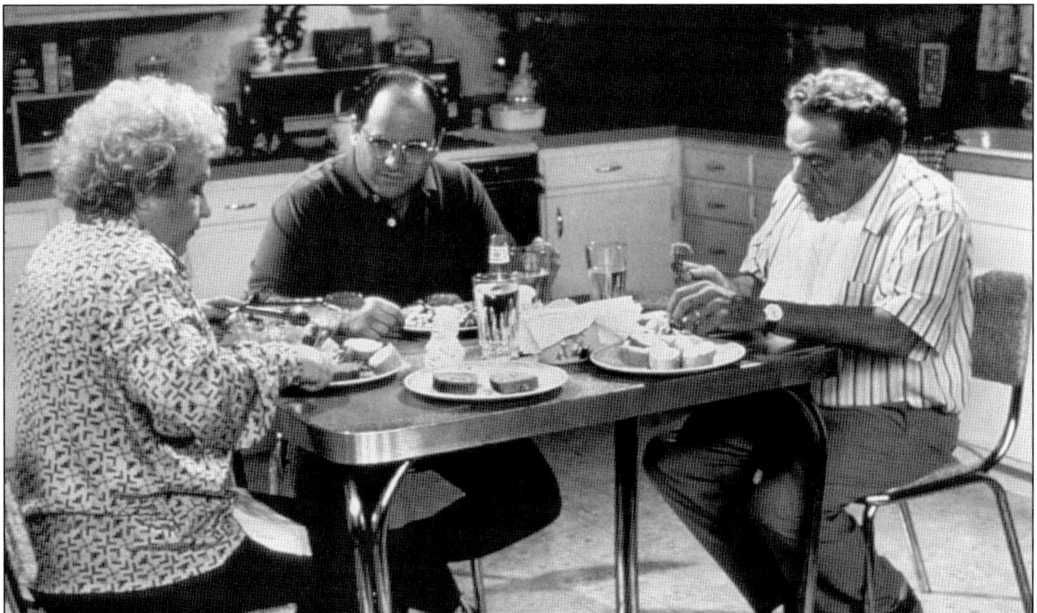

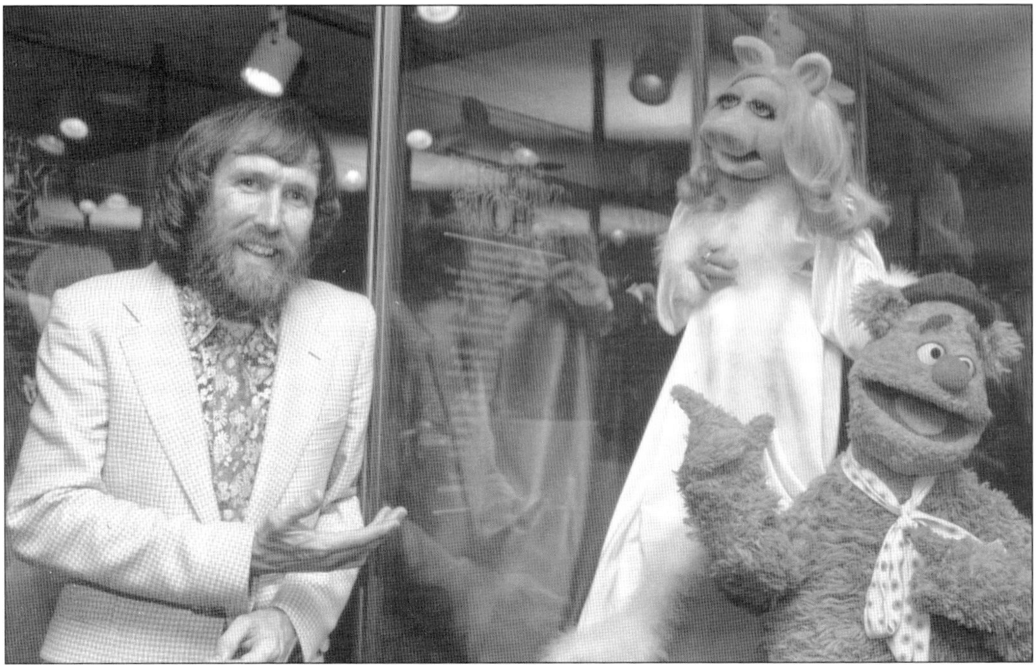

The Muppets live in Queens in real life. They work there, too. Since 1993, PBS's *Sesame Street* and the Muppet movies have been taped at Kaufman Astoria Studios (KAS)—to be exact, Stage G at first and Stage J since season 39. In fact, Elmo spoke at a ceremony announcing the facility's expansion. (He was KAS chairman George S. Kaufman's favorite Muppet.) As mentioned previously in the Marx Brothers caption, Paramount began in Astoria in the 1920s before moving to California in 1932. KAS took over the venue in 1977 to film *The Wiz* (1978). Since then, *The Cosby Show*, *Sex and the City*, and *Spin City* are among the shows that have filmed there. (Both, LOC.)

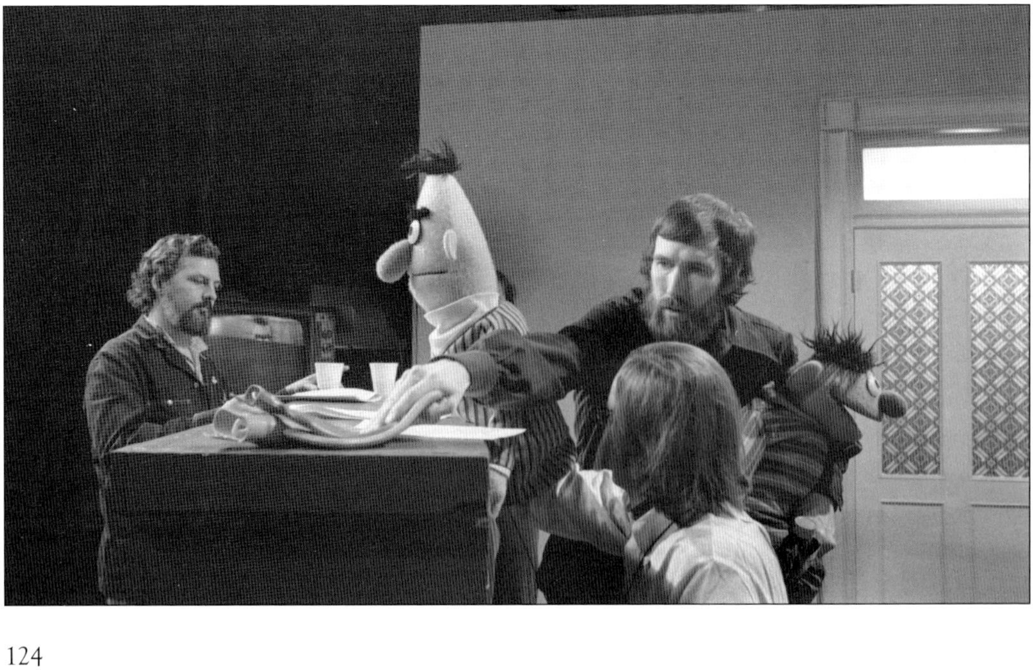

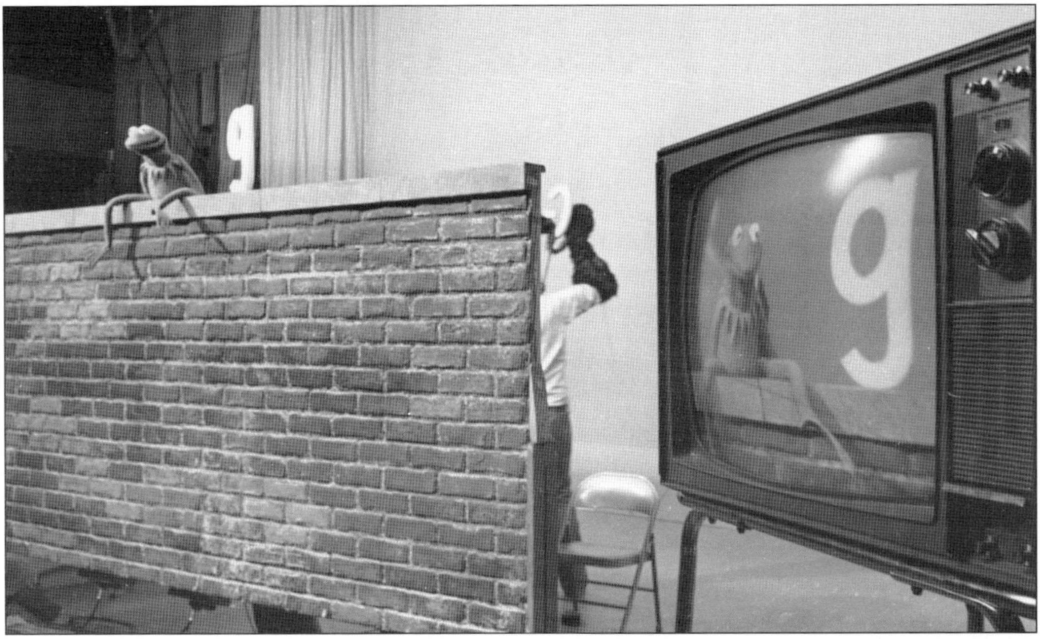

Due to security reasons, the exact location of the Muppets abode is a secret. However, the Museum of the Moving Image is located a block from Kaufman Astoria Studios at 36–01 Thirty-Fifth Avenue. On the second floor, the permanent Jim Henson Exhibition displays almost 300 objects from throughout the namesake's career. (Henson created the Muppets.) Retired versions of Kermit the Frog, Miss Piggy, the Swedish Chef, Big Bird, and Elmo are among 47 characters on display there along with character sketches, storyboards, scripts, photographs, and costumes from *The Muppet Show* and its related movies, *Sesame Street*, *Fraggle Rock*, *The Dark Crystal*, and *Labyrinth*. (Both, LOC.)

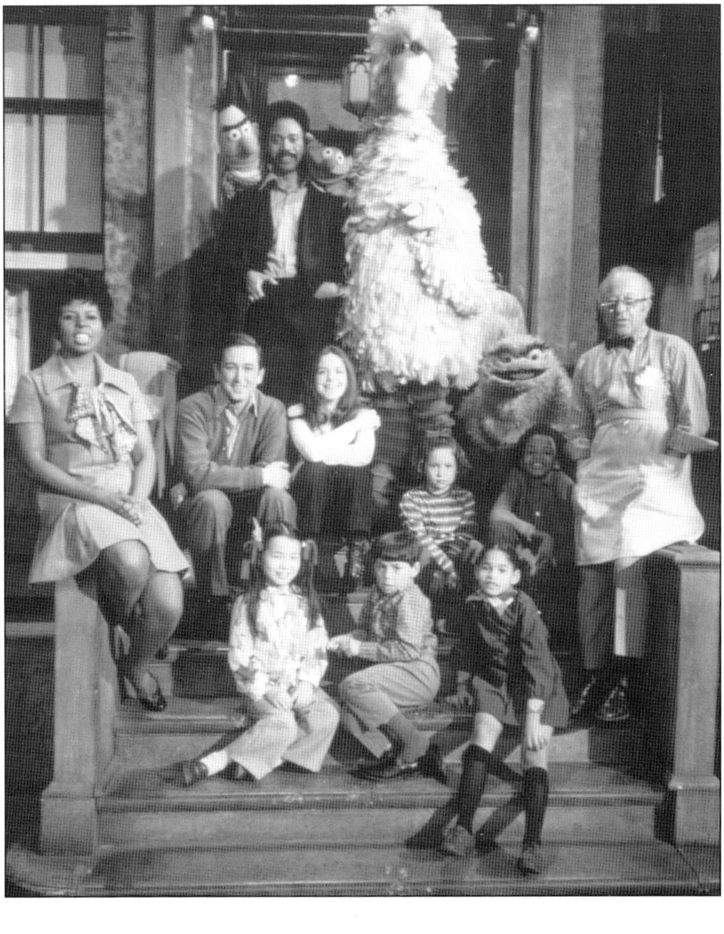

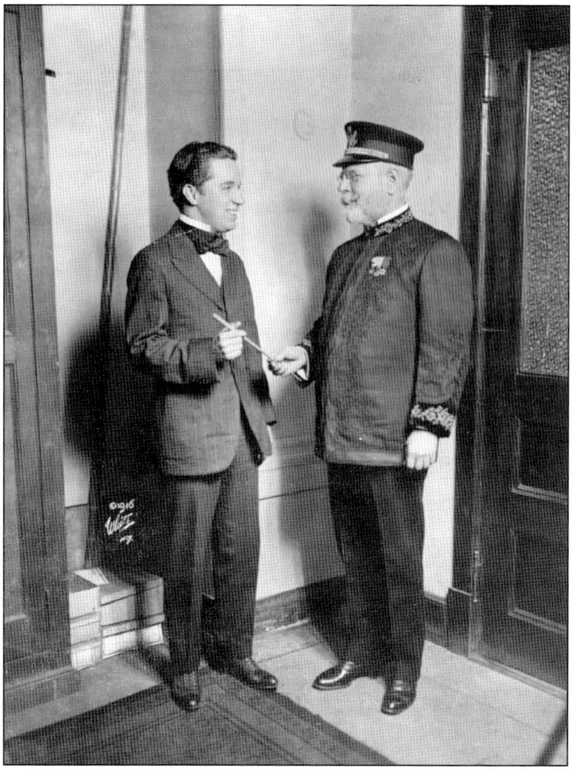

Because historians disagree that Charlie Chaplin ever lived in Queens, this segment is in the "Queens Questions" chapter. Some research informs that the comedic actor bought the house below at 18 Mowbray Drive in Kew Gardens in 1918 and lived there until 1922. Chaplin, who was undeniably born in London in 1889, first moved to the United States in the early 1900s to work the vaudeville circuit. Super talented, he was soon starring in silent movies that were being filmed at Paramount Studios in Astoria. But just like Paramount, he ended up in Hollywood, where he worked on talking pictures and even launched his own studio. In 1953, he moved to Switzerland, where he died at the age of 88 on Christmas Day 1977. Possibly due to his public support of Communism, he never won an Oscar, but his star joined the Hollywood Walk of Fame in 1972. He was also knighted in England. (Left, LOC; below, QTC.)

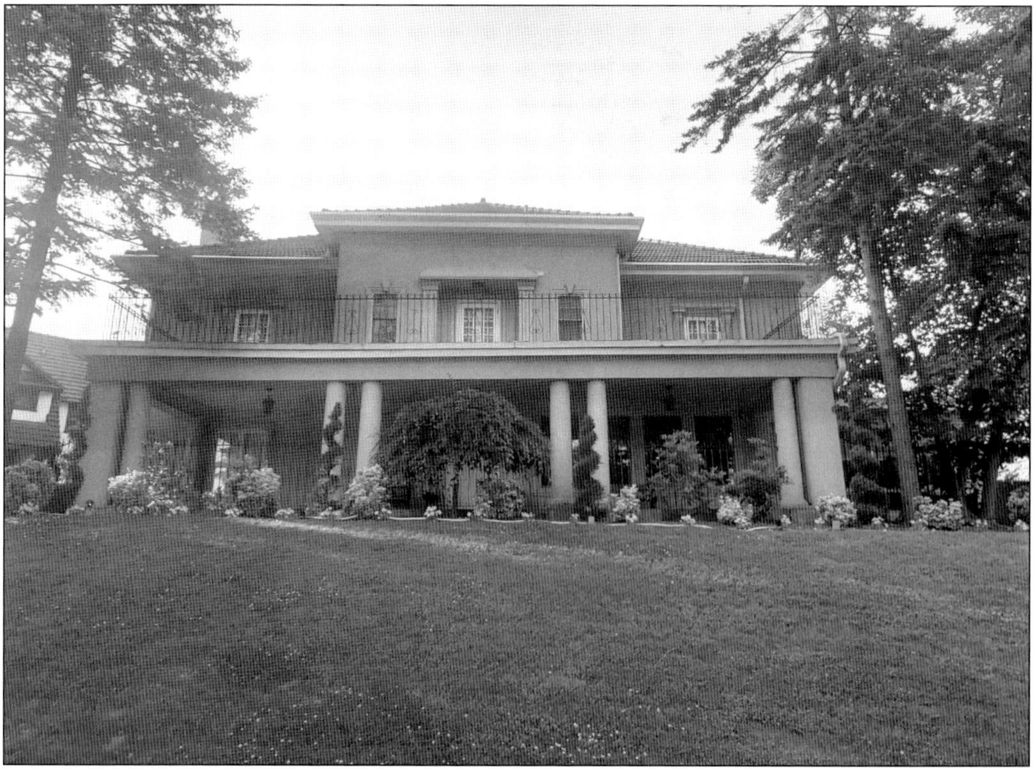

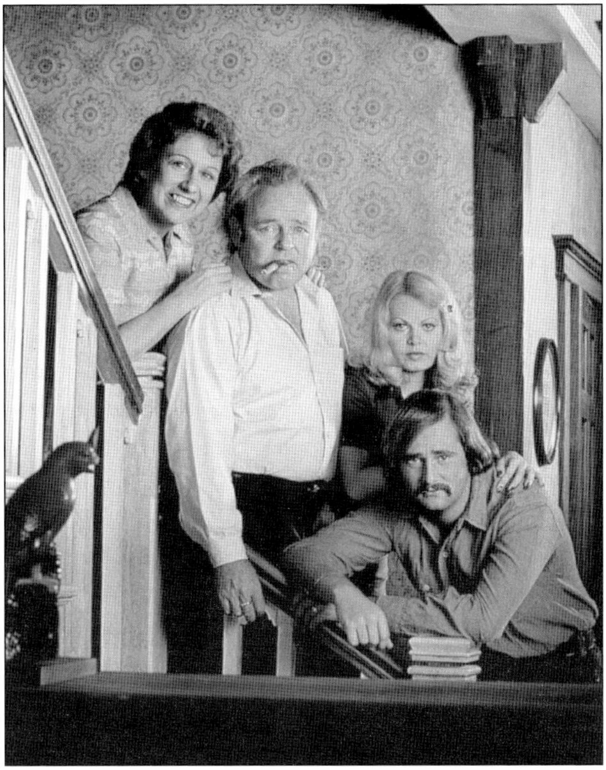

*All in the Family*, which CBS ran weekly from 1971 to 1979, is another example of Hollywood getting Queens wrong. The main family, the Bunkers, purportedly lived at 704 Hauser Street in Astoria, an address that does not exist. (The name comes from Hauser Boulevard in Los Angeles, where CBS was located.) During the opening credits, the camera takes viewers to the Bunker household at 89–70 Cooper Avenue in Glendale, which lies about 10 miles from Astoria. (Alamy.)

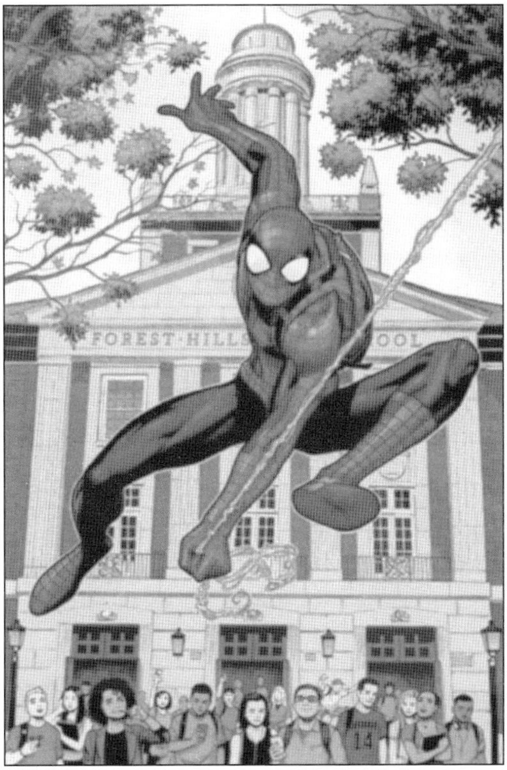

After moving to 20 Ingram Street in Forest Hills in 1974, Andrew and Suzane Parker were perplexed by all the mail addressed to "Peter Parker." Then one day in 2001, a reporter called to discuss the fact that Spider-Man's alter ego, Peter Parker, lives with Aunt May and Uncle Ben at the exact same address in the Marvel Comics series. Fact follows fiction. As this book went to press, a community project to install a Spider-Man statue in Forest Hills was advancing. (Michael Perlman.)